SPRINGDALE PUBLIC LIBRARY
405 S. Pleasant
Springdale, AR 72764

YOUR SONG CHANGED MY LIFE

YOUR
SONG
CHANGED
MY
LIFE

From Jimmy Page to St. Vincent, Smokey Robinson
to Hozier, Thirty-Five Beloved Artists on Their Journey
and the Music That Inspired It

BOB BOILEN

wm

WILLIAM MORROW

An Imprint of HarperCollins*Publishers*

SPRINGDALE PUBLIC LIBRARY
405 S. Pleasant
Springdale, AR 72764

YOUR SONG CHANGED MY LIFE. Copyright © 2016 by Bob Boilen. All rights reserved. Printed in the United States of America. No part of this book may be used or reproduced in any manner whatsoever without written permission except in the case of brief quotations embodied in critical articles and reviews. For information address HarperCollins Publishers, 195 Broadway, New York, NY 10007.

HarperCollins books may be purchased for educational, business, or sales promotional use. For information please e-mail the Special Markets Department at SPsales @harpercollins.com.

FIRST EDITION

Designed by Leah Carlson-Stanisic

Library of Congress Cataloging-in-Publication Data has been applied for.

ISBN: 978-0-06-234444-1

16 17 18 19 20   OV/RRD   10 9 8 7 6 5 4 3 2 1

For all the musicians inspiring life and imagination through this invisible art we call music. You spark ideas, shake the norm—and have completely changed my life. Thank you.

And with much love to **JULIAN, MAY,** and **BUZZY.**

CONTENTS

It's August 15, 1965, and a cool summer night as I look toward the glowing lights of Shea Stadium about ten miles north of me, imagining, no, *wishing* I was with The Beatles. I'm twelve years old and sitting on my stoop in Queens, New York, holding a Westinghouse transistor radio to my ear. The radio cost me five dollars and a label from a bottle of Listerine. It is tuned to WMCA, my favorite AM station (FM barely exists at this point). Less than two years ago, on the day after Christmas, WMCA played "I Want to Hold Your Hand," becoming the first New York station to play The Beatles. The night of the Shea Stadium show, I struggle to imagine what a concert there would be like. It is the first rock and roll concert to ever be held at a major stadium. Approximately fifty-six thousand

---

I've had this love for music a long time now. This is me and my record player in Brooklyn, New York, circa 1956. *Courtesy Roy Boilen*

people attend, including my next-door neighbor; the show sold out in seventeen minutes (mind you, there's no Internet).

I read the news the next day and see the black-and-white footage on TV the following night—the screams drown out the band, the meager sound system no competition for the level of noise produced by thousands of adoring fans, who faint with passion, their hormones raging as they shout the names of their favorites—John, Paul, George, and even Ringo. It's a monumental event, and one that will eventually pave the way for the sort of arena shows we'll take for granted fifty years later.

I loved, *loved*, The Beatles, and if I could turn back the clock to any one night and be someplace, it would be Shea Stadium on that night.

My love for The Beatles began alongside America's love for The Beatles, first with their songs on the radio and then with the newscast of their arrival at the newly renamed John F. Kennedy International Airport, a few miles from my house. President Kennedy was shot eleven weeks before they came to America, and I don't believe it's a stretch to say that our news media was happy to have something to celebrate after so much darkness. On February 9, 1964, two out of every five Americans turned on their black-and-white televisions to watch *The Ed Sullivan Show*. The Beatles' appearance had been booked three months earlier, at which point no one in America knew them and their songs had never played on American radio—in fact, you'd be hard-pressed to name *any* British act with a popular song on the U.S. charts then—but by the time they arrived in New York, "I Want to Hold Your Hand" had shot to number one. Credit their brilliant strategist and manager, Brian Epstein, and their sound, of course. I sat in front of the television with my mom, dad, and thirteen-year-old sister, May, and thought it was the most thrilling music my ten-year-old ears had ever heard. The Beatles were vibrant and young, none older than twenty-three, and on that night our screens filled with rock and roll, a departure for the normally tame variety show, which often featured Broadway singers, acrobats, comedians, and a magician doing a saltshaker trick.

Punk is often credited with shaking up the music world, while we tend to view the British Invasion the wave of British bands that followed in the foot-stomping steps of The Beatles—as cute and adorable. But everything about music changed after those Brits arrived. Sales of records and record players hit all-time highs, much of the teenage world bought guitars, and your next-door neighbor's garage was as likely to house a budding band as an Oldsmobile. In 1958, guitar sales in the U.S. totaled approximately three hundred thousand; by 1965, barely one year into the British Invasion, that number had exploded to one and a half million. The guitar replaced the piano as the main instrument in popular music. My sister and I took lessons—me with the intent to learn all The Beatles' songs. I struggled with the instrument, and my teacher later told my mom that I had no musical ability. I was crushed. Instead, I spun 45s endlessly in my bedroom, pretended to be a DJ, created secret make-believe pop charts, and fell deeply in love with music. When I wasn't in school, I always carried two items: my trusty transistor radio and a stickball bat. I lived for baseball and records. At night, I hid my radio under my pillow and listened to either New York Yankees games or rock and roll. My friends were The Zombies, The Kinks, The Rolling Stones, The Animals, The Beau Brummels, The Beach Boys, The Byrds, The Yardbirds, and so many others. I bought my first album, *Meet The Beatles,* at the radio and television repair shop at the local shopping center in Lindenwood, and often walked all the way to the Times Square department store to purchase my 45s.

I was raised in a middle-class family in a working-class neighborhood that consisted mostly of Italians and Jews. I was the latter. My dad, Roy Boilen, sold frozen meat and frozen food and the freezers to store them in. My mom, Buzzy, worked the phone, canvassing families and arranging appointments for my dad. He traveled a lot and wasn't home much during the week, but when he was, he listened to big band music. Benny Goodman, Artie Shaw, and Glenn Miller made him happy. I recall visiting his parents' house and listening to old 78s in the basement. It is a world of music I came to appreciate only much later. My mom loved show tunes and Barbra Streisand, music that I *never* came to appreciate: to this day it drives me up the wall, though my sister recently reminded me of my obsession as a six-year-old with the Broadway cast album for *Flower Drum Song.*

Some time around 1965, my dad bought a fancy stereo sound system, with a nice Scott FM tube receiver and some snazzy speakers, which I blew up about five years later listening to the deep synthesizer music of Emerson, Lake & Palmer at high volume. The year 1966 saw the evolution of FM radio, and that too changed everything. DJs like Alison Steele, Rosko, and Scott Muni, among others, started playing what they loved rather than music they were told to program. For a kid like me, the shift from AM, with its low quality and screaming commercials, to the low-key and high-quality sound of FM was mind-blowing. I think it's fair to assert that the development of FM was as revolutionary to the world of music as the one we've seen in the twenty-first century with the transition from CDs to digital downloads and now online streaming. With the advent of FM, music that catered to particular tastes rather than mass appeal had a home. It was the first time I heard The Velvet Underground, and it was the beginning of "underground" music, later called "alternative," later called "indie." The thread is long, but the aesthetic is the same—music as art, not commodity.

By 1966 technology made the recording process more expressive and the listening process more trippy (so did the drugs). Bob Dylan's "Like a Rolling Stone" (1965) and The Doors' "Light My Fire" (1967) were short songs on the AM dial, but twice as long and twice as interesting on FM. It was also a year of mind-altering albums, including The Beach Boys' *Pet Sounds,* The Beatles' *Revolver,* Bob

Dylan's double album, *Blonde on Blonde,* The Mothers of Invention's *Freak Out!,* and The 13th Floor Elevators' *The Psychedelic Sound of The 13th Floor Elevators.* Albums began to have concepts; no longer were they simply vehicles for hit songs. In fact, The Beatles released numerous hit singles that didn't even make it onto the UK editions of their albums, such as "We Can Work It Out," "Day Tripper," "Penny Lane," and "Strawberry Fields Forever."

In the summer of 1967, I went to my friend Alan's house. He'd just returned from the record store and played for me the most mind-boggling, beautiful album I'd ever heard: *Sgt. Pepper's Lonely Hearts Club Band.* If you're not as old as I am, it's important to note that music had never sounded like this before. Imagine growing up in a city and walking into a forest for the first time—that's what the experience of this album was like for me. We sat and listened to swirling, unidentifiable sounds from India, vaudeville, the circus, the farm, the classical concert hall, all otherworldly and newly created. We stared at the colorful cover art, a collage of people, some real, some fictional, known and unknown. The gatefold opened to a photograph of a band we recognized, but one that was also deeply changed, adorned by beards, mustaches, and bright red, green, pink, and blue, nearly Day-Glo military uniforms. Best of all, the lyrics were printed on the back cover, something I'd never seen before, so we could follow along word for word. It was an adventure, a journey, and—to steal a term from the day—a trip. For me, the album's closing track, "A Day in the Life," was the most startling of all. It's a song that changed my life forever. The lyrics are both straight storytelling and impressionism, pedestrian and poetic. It was two completely different songs sonically melded into one, opening with John Lennon's simple strumming of an acoustic guitar as he tells a tale inspired by two different newspaper articles, one about four thousand potholes to be repaired on the streets of Blackburn in Lancashire, the other about the death of Tara Browne, an heir to the Guinness brewery fortune, in a high-speed car crash.

He blew his mind out in a car
He didn't notice that the lights had changed
A crowd of people stood and stared
They'd seen his face before
Nobody was really sure
If he was from the House of Lords.

The lyrics were the result of the important and often disputed collaboration between John Lennon and Paul McCartney. Lennon admitted that Paul added the line "I'd love to turn you on" as a bit of a poke at the stiff-upper-lip British establishment. And Paul also had a bit of tune he was working on that didn't have much to it and that somehow found its way into the song, almost as a counterpoint to the poignant, impressionistic words sung by John. Paul sings:

Woke up, fell out of bed,
Dragged a comb across my head
Found my way downstairs and drank a cup,
And looking up I noticed I was late.
Found my coat and grabbed my hat
Made the bus in seconds flat
Found my way upstairs and had a smoke,
Somebody spoke and I went into a dream.

But it's the orchestral chaos that really takes this song to a whole new level. It's massive. It builds and builds, based on an idea producer George Martin claims Lennon gave him. In *All the Songs: The Story Behind Every Beatles Release,* Martin recounts the moment: "What I'd like to hear is a tremendous buildup, from nothing up to something absolutely like the end of the world." Martin hired an orchestra and recorded them multiple times, then mixed it all together, the equivalent of something like 160 musicians. That day, I left Alan's house floored, bought my own copy, and listened to it every day in whole or parts for years. To this day, I am astounded at the progression of this band from their first recordings in 1963 to what they accomplished by album number eight, *Sgt. Pepper*. There is a monumental difference between a simple song like "I Want to Hold Your Hand" and "A Day in the Life," just four years later. Because I witnessed that progression and understand how bands can change and music can morph, I've come to want all music to be like that. It's what keeps me searching for new songs and new artists, and what keeps me excited for an artist's second, third, even tenth album.

In 1968 my family moved from Queens, New York, to Bethesda, Maryland. It was a cultural shock, to say the least. I'd lived briefly in Poughkeepsie, but really knew only New York City. I was fifteen, a budding hippie with long, straight hair parted down the middle, but I still loved sports. Back in the late sixties, communication was much slower, so trends weren't as "national" as they are now. At the time, Bethesda was more a jock culture than a hippie one, and those two worlds didn't play nice. The baseball coach hated my long hair, often gave me a rough time, and never allowed me to pitch a game. I also found it hard to root for the Yankees while living in what felt like a southern town with its drawling accent. I was an oddball with bell-bottom pants, a common fashion back in Queens but not yet the norm in Maryland. And my accent—well, I never knew I had one till I hit Bethesda and the kids made fun of it. I receded to my room and my records, found a good local shop, Empire Music, which was within walking distance, and fell in love with Cream, Jimi Hendrix, The Doors, Neil Young, Jethro Tull, and later Pink Floyd, Led Zeppelin, Fairport Convention, David Bowie, Roxy Music, and Brian Eno. I turned off the AM radio for good around 1969 and never looked back.

In 1971, shortly after I graduated from high school, I started working full-time at a record store, the Rockville, Maryland,

I quit my job and bought this ARP Odyssey for nearly $2,000 in 1979, intent on joining a band and playing music. Within months we formed Tiny Desk Unit.
Courtesy Claudia Joseph

branch of a D.C.-area chain called Waxie Maxie's. The owner was Max Silverman, a cigar-smoking, completely hairless, old-school businessman, who received his music education alongside folks like Jerry Wexler of Atlantic Records fame. We sold albums for $3.99, 45s for 77 cents, and these newfangled eight-track tapes for about

$4.99. I worked forty-eight hours a week and made about $1.75 an hour. At the time, it was enough to pay my tuition at Montgomery Community College, which was about three hundred dollars a semester. I started out as a psychology major, couldn't stand it, and then transferred to the University of Maryland to study business. I attended school in the morning, then worked the 1 P.M. to 9 P.M. shift at the record store. I had Sundays to do my schoolwork. Over the years, I moved from simple record clerk to assistant manager and then, after I dropped out of college, manager at one of Waxie Maxie's stores. I think of those years as my musical education. I'd listen to records all day, talk about them with my workmates and the many geeky kids like me who came into the store to get turned on to something unknown, and who would sometimes turn me on to something unknown.

In 1975, I saw a photograph by Robert Mapplethorpe in the *New York Times* of a skinny young woman with a messy, boyish haircut wearing what looked like a man's suit and skinny tie. The woman's name was Patti Smith, and the photo accompanied an article about Smith's just-released album, *Horses*. The energy of this record reminded me of the burst of electricity I first felt in 1964 with The Beatles, only this was ballsier, more poetic, with Jim Morrison of The Doors and Lou Reed of The Velvet Underground as touchstones. It felt like things were about to change. The spacey sounds, the art and progressive rock I'd come to love, and the world of the bloated supergroup were about to be strip-searched and ransacked—and this was good. I loved the punk music coming from New York City and the UK.

In 1976, I was still working for Waxie Maxie's, now running their warehouse, filling orders from thirteen stores. I was also the import buyer for those weird records that might never make it in the U.S.—Nick Drake's *Pink Moon* and The Clash's self-titled debut are two memorable examples. But all the while I felt the tug, and groups like Talking Heads, Television, the Sex Pistols, Buzzcocks, and The Ramones called to me, forcing me to confront a secret wish I'd never admitted since those failed guitar lessons as a kid—I wanted to make music. A friend of mine, Jodi Bloom, took me downtown to an art space called the WPA, the Washington Project for the Arts. There I met painters, poets, musicians, writers, and photographers, a world of people with their heads buried in creation and expression. At twenty-five, my eyes were opened. I started attending shows at d.c. space, owned by my now longtime friend Bill Warrell. It was a bar and restaurant with a loft space for music often curated by Bill, who loved avant-garde jazz and new music in general. I saw John Cale of The Velvet Underground play a poorly tuned piano, saw Anthony Braxton and George Lewis play amazing jazz, and eventually began putting on my own shows there alongside my apartment-mate, David Howcroft; we would showcase musicians from New York, including James Chance's screeching, no-wave jazz band The Contortions.

As for making music, I still hadn't figured out a way to create my own sound. I didn't have the skill or the craft to pick up an instrument loaded with as much cultural expectation as the guitar. I tried twice and realized I'd never be as good as the folks I admired. Sometime around 1978, my friend David and I left the Maryland suburbs and moved to D.C. During our apartment search, we looked at a small building on Wisconsin Avenue and met with two young superintendents. I saw a *Talking Heads '77* album on the floor beside their record player, and knew it was home. We moved in a few weeks later.

Around 1978, the D.C. music scene was a strange mix of blues bands, rock and roll bar bands, and garage bands, some doing covers, some originals, along with a few arty-punky types and some progressive rock bands. The local radio station WGTB supported all these disparate strands of mostly guitar-based rock. On a Friday evening in the early days of 1978, at a restaurant turned nighttime hangout, the Atlantis Club, I saw a transformative show by the D.C.-based group the Urban Verbs. Their sound was brash, not punk, urgent, not angry, psychedelic, not retro, and arty without pretense. I loved Roddy Frantz's stuttered singing and poetry, and their drummer, Danny Frankel, was probably the first to ever make my feet move in a nightclub. I'm more an intense listener than a dancer. And the textures created by their two guitarists, Robert Goldstein and Robin Rose, distorted, delayed, sometimes melodic and somewhat dissonant, hit the pleasure center of my brain. The band's second guitarist eventually bought a synthesizer, adding to the group's mighty sound. I went to see this band a lot over the years—probably more than I'll ever see any other band— and I became friends with the members. One night after a show, as I was speaking with their guitarist-synthesist, Robin Rose, he asked if I'd like to borrow his ARP Odyssey for the weekend. It was a generous, thoughtful offer, and one that changed my life. I took the instrument and was soon enthralled by the soundscapes I could conjure. Unlike the guitar, it felt free of rules. I could create a variety of sounds by repositioning the sliders and switches, and the keyboard, though traditional with its black and white keys, didn't have to be played like a piano; each key's sound was determined by the position of the many sliders. The possibilities seemed endless.

A few months later, the superintendents of our building, the couple with the Talking Heads album, George and Elizabeth Brady, decided to move and help launch an "over the air" subscription TV service—this was before cable TV hit Washington. When they asked David and me if we'd like to run the apartment building, we said yes, even though we had no skills or experience—so now I had no rent to pay. I quit my job at Waxie Maxie's and spent the retirement benefits check they sent me on my very own ARP Odyssey. A few months later, I met a brilliant guitarist, Michael Barron, who was in search of a synthesizer player. He already had a singer in mind, Susan Mumford, and, along with my friends Joe Menacher and Chris Thompson, we formed Tiny Desk Unit. Before I knew it, we were onstage, my life was completely altered, and my secret dream—sparked by the punk attitude of the time and fueled by the creativity of my heroes, The Beatles in particular—was realized. Tiny Desk Unit was a psychedelic dance band. Our songs were long, meandering, and unexpected musical journeys. I developed my own sound on that ARP, often by listening to Michael's guitar harmonics and searching for tones that enriched and intertwined with his. Other times I was inspired by the voice or the drums, and produced sounds that were vocal or percussive. I could barely play a melody on the keyboard, and even all these years later, I'd be hard-pressed to play a simple C chord. I never mastered the basics, never really cared to. I took my limitations, my inabilities, and turned them into advantages, with no fear of doing something "wrong." There *was* no right or wrong, just choices that either satisfied my ears or didn't.

The Atlantis Club gave way to a more artist-friendly, dedicated venue in the same space—the 9:30 Club, at 930 F Street NW in Washington, D.C. On May 30, 1980, Tiny Desk Unit became the first band to play the 9:30 Club and soon became the "other" well-loved local art-rock band, next to the Urban Verbs, selling out most of our shows. We started a record label with newfound friends and released a live album, recorded at the 9:30 Club to capture the adrenaline of our live performances. We later made a studio EP, *Naples,* and then—with the aid of alcohol, heroin, and other street drugs—we self-destructed.

I became friends with Nick Koumoutseas, the engineer and owner of the studio where we recorded our EP. One day he handed me the studio keys and told me I could come in and learn the gear when no one was around. He didn't teach me about the equipment. Perhaps he thought it best for me to figure it out on my own. He had a digital synthesizer called the Synclavier II, and it wasn't long before I was deep into the mighty world of digital sound creation.

Shortly after the demise of Tiny Desk Unit, my friend Kirby Malone asked me to compose the music for his newly formed mul-

Tiny Desk Unit at its peak at the 9:30 Club in Washington, D.C., circa 1980. From left to right: Michael Barron, Terry Baker, Susan Mumford, Lorenzo "Pee Wee" Jones, and me with my newly built Serge Modular synthesizer connected to my ARP Odyssey. *Courtesy Mark Gulezian*

timedia theater collective, Impossible Theater. I had six weeks to compose songs for something like twenty-five scenes. I'd never actually written music on my own. I said yes—and to this day it's some of the best music I've ever created. A few years after that, I wrote another piece for one of their art installations. It imagined the history of sound from the beginning of time to the end. We called it "Whiz Bang: A History of Sound," and presented it at the Smithsonian Museum of American History. My music sampled everything from bees to sewing machines for rhythm, drones, and melody, and it was one of the earliest pieces to use the then new— now ubiquitous—technology called "sampling."

When NPR heard about the piece, they invited me on *All Things*

Considered. Ira Glass, a young show producer at the time, called me in to interview with host Susan Stamberg. I hadn't slept for thirty-six hours and had spent the past week in front of the new digital sampler, learning how it worked as I composed the music for our sound and slide installation. I had a deep love and respect for NPR even then. At first I said I couldn't do it. My thinking: I was exhausted and had spent the past six days with a manual on my lap and my hand pressed against my jaw like Rodin's *The Thinker,* and because of the constant pressure I could barely open my mouth. I later agreed. I didn't want to pass up a chance to be on NPR and to have this work heard by a larger audience. The interview went well, and for the first time I heard my voice on the radio.

Back then, in 1983, I was also working at a TV station, the same one my former superintendents had run off to start. It later became a regular UHF station with some nice production equipment, which I taught myself to use during nonwork hours. I then became a producer for their station, even though I didn't much care for TV. I had been in love with radio ever since I was that little kid with my transistor tucked under my pillow. Five years later, I quit my job, walked to NPR, and found that young producer Ira Glass. I told him I wanted to work there. He asked if I cut tape, and I said yes, though, honestly, I barely knew what he was talking about. I'd never cut an interview before. He gave me a reel, a razor blade, a grease pencil, and some splicing tape, told me to cut the interview down from twenty minutes to four, and said that it had to flow naturally, like a conversation. So that's what I did, and I guess I did it pretty well. After that, I showed up at *All Things Considered* every morning and asked if they needed help. They gave me temp work, and I began cutting tape regularly for the show. They'd hire me for a week, then two, and within the year, I was directing the show. To this day, I still find it hard to fathom.

▬

I believe that in life certain people see things in us that we don't see in ourselves. When Nick Koumoutseas gave me the keys to his studio, I believe he recognized my passion for music and technology and was confident I could figure out the equipment. When the producers of *All Things Considered* asked me to direct their evening news program, I believe they saw in me, a college dropout without a day's experience in journalism or radio, some sort of proclivity and talent, and I will be forever grateful to those who saw something special in me.

"A Day in the Life" tells two main stories, one of a man in his prime, whose life ends abruptly in tragedy, the other a tale of the mundane, the everyday, of waking up, running late, then falling into a dream. For me, these tales sum up life's preciousness and magic. The song inspired me to seize opportunities, to take chances, because we get only one shot at life. In this book you will hear thirty-five artists relate one basic story. It's the story of what motivates us, drives us toward this invisible and mysterious art we call music. It's the story of how a song can be a call to action, to pick up an instrument or a pen, to find your voice, to spill your soul and change your life—and, perhaps, someone else's.

YOUR SONG CHANGED MY LIFE

JIMMY PAGE

"I wanted to have my own approach to what I did. I didn't want to . . . do a carbon copy of, say, B.B. King, or whatever, but I really love the blues. The blues had so much effect on me that I just wanted to [make] my own contribution in my own way." Of all the musicians inspired by the blues during the sixties, Jimmy Page is the one who took the genre and reenvisioned it in ways most could never have imagined. As a young kid, growing up first in the West London suburb of Heston, then a few miles away in Epsom, Surrey, Page mined, appropriated, and appreciated the depths of American blues. The move with his family from Heston to Epsom turned out to be a life-changing one. In their new home he found a guitar that had been left there by its previous owner. At the time, the instrument didn't excite the eight-year-old James Patrick Page. It was 1952, rock and roll wasn't even on the radio yet, and no one in his family was a musician.

I often wonder about the nature of fate. I've heard so many stories about a song coming on the radio at a fragile moment in a musician's life, or in the case of St. Vincent, recounted later in this book, a box of records falling off a truck in front of her house. As a nonbeliever, I don't view these events as acts of God, or even as destiny, more as moments of opportunity. That guitar, found by a young Jimmy Page, could have been tossed or taken up by his mom or dad, but it wasn't. It remained in the house until, three years later, it became the medium that changed his life and, honestly, the lives of a million others.

Jimmy's story as a musician begins with the song that changed his life: Lonnie Donegan's "Rock Island Line," a big hit in England in 1955 as performed by the Scottish-born singer. It's an American blues tune about the Chicago, Rock Island and Pacific Railroad line. It was first recorded by John and Alan Lomax in an Arkansas prison, and later made famous by the Louisiana blues legend Lead Belly. Jimmy had heard Donegan's version many times on the radio, and even owned the record, but he wasn't inspired to pick up the guitar until the day he heard Rod Wyatt, a kid at school, play it on his. Jimmy told Rod about the guitar he had at home, and Rod promised that if Jimmy brought it in, he'd show him how to tune it and play a few chords. "It was a campfire guitar . . . but it did have all the strings on it, which is pretty useful because I wouldn't have known where to get guitar strings from. And then [Rod] showed me how to tune it up . . . and then I started strumming away like—not quite like Lonnie Donegan, but I was having a go."

Guitarists were few and far between in those days, and it's fair to say that Donegan was responsible for getting guitars into the hands of an awful lot of kids. John Lennon and Paul McCartney said that Lonnie Donegan and his brand of skiffle music inspired them as well. Donegan, though, was mostly inspired by jazz, particularly the New Orleans variety, including ragtime, swing, and

Dixieland; the blues and country and western were influences as well. Donegan played guitar and banjo with Chris Barber's band, a great traditional jazz band in England, and took his stage name, in part, from the Louisiana bluesman Lonnie Johnson, an artist Donegan met when his band opened for him in 1952 at the Royal Festival Hall in London. Even though Lonnie Donegan took another's name and played other people's music, he had a knack for making it his own. Listen to "Rock Island Line" by Lead Belly and you'll hear the tale of an engine driver evading the toll fee and lying about his freight (saying he has livestock when he really has pig iron). His 1937 recording chugs along, increasing its pace until it becomes a full gallop. The difference between Lead Belly's and Lonnie Donegan's versions, though, is like the difference between a horse-drawn locomotive and a steam engine. Donegan's rocked! His voice had vitality and a bit of a hiccup, and by the song's end, when the train is well past the tollgate and the engineer whoops and hollers out of earshot and reveals the real freight, you can hear the beginning of rock and roll.

And when she got up here to the tollgate
The-a depot, he shout down to the driver
He want to know what he got on board
So he say-a
What you got on board there, boy?
And the driver, he sing right on back
Down to the depot agent
Tell him what he got on board
He got a way of singing
I got sheep, I got cows
I got horses, I got pigs
I got all livestock
I got all livestock
I got all livestock

And the man say, well, he say
You're all right then, boy
You don't have to pay me nothin'

Donegan took the past, owned the present, and influenced a gen-eration of great rock musicians. "He really understood all that stuff, Lonnie Donegan," Page says. "But this is the way that he sort of, should we say, jazzed it up or skiffled it up. By the time you get to the end of this he's really spitting it out . . . he keeps singing, 'Rock Island Line, Rock Island'—[and] you really get this whole staccato aspect of it. It's fantastic stuff! So many guitarists from the six-ties will all say Lonnie Donegan was [their] influence."

For Jimmy Page, the impact of his discovery was almost im-mediate. One year after picking up the guitar, at only thirteen, he was already in a skiffle band and performed on BBC One as part of a talent show, where they played "Mama Don't Want to Skiffle Anymore." While still in his teens he became a session musician; at nineteen, he appeared on his first number-one record, "Diamonds" by Jet Harris and Tony Meehan, later playing guitar on records by The Who, The Kinks, The Rolling Stones, Marianne Faithfull, Van Morrison's band Them, and on the soundtrack for The Beatles' *A Hard Day's Night*. The list goes on. Sometimes he worked three sessions a day, more than a dozen a week—but by 1966 he tired of session work and quit. A week later, he heard about an opening for a bass player in The Yardbirds, a British band with a major-label contract that featured the electric guitar as a focal point. Eric Clap-ton had been in The Yardbirds, though when Page joined, Jeff Beck was the lead guitarist. Page eventually dropped the bass and joined Jeff Beck on guitar. In July 1968, The Yardbirds fell apart, and by October of that same year, in less than thirty hours, the first album by Jimmy Page's new project was recorded.

Three months later, in January 1969, I headed to the record store.

There were two main shops for me back then. When I wanted a good selection, suggestions, or merely a place for my sixteen-year-old self to hang, I'd go to Empire Music. It was a few blocks from where I lived in Bethesda, and I spent a great deal of my money and time there. When I was shopping for good prices, I'd hike up to the E. J. Korvette department store on Rockville Pike. Their selection was limited but their prices were great, so I'd often take a chance and buy unknown albums purely because I liked the cover art. On that day, in one of their standing bins, there was a black-and-white album cover with a flaming *Hindenburg* airship. It looked phallic and explosive, so I bought it. When I got home and heard those two opening crunchy guitar chords, then the ticking cowbell, then the blistering drums that fall in like a stumble through a lumberyard, I was hooked. Led Zeppelin was immediately my new favorite band. I liked British blues just fine back then, but this went beyond the blues, with a rock and roll thrust reminiscent of Donegan's steam locomotive—only this was fueled by electricity. There were old blues tunes from Willie Dixon and a few folk numbers, including a killer acoustic guitar version of the traditional "Black Water Side," renamed "Black Mountain Side" and played in a style similar to that of one of Jimmy's contemporaries, Bert Jansch. As a band, Led Zeppelin was only three months old, yet you could already hear them defining and honing *their* sound.

During my conversation with Jimmy Page in February 2015, he is out promoting two major projects: a brilliant photo book he lovingly created, a sort of autobiography in pictures, and a newly remastered version of Led Zeppelin's sixth album, *Physical Graffiti*—now forty years old. Page says, unabashedly, "It's like the mother of all double albums. . . . Isn't it? Really, let's be honest." From almost any other artist, I'd see this as bragging, but from Page it is simply the truth.

Physical Graffiti was another in a series of progressions for the band. It came six years after I first took a chance on their debut album. It was an eclectic compilation of influences, from the blues to the sounds of southern Morocco to progressive rock and flat-out, toughly played rock and roll. "We now had five albums. . . . And it was always a fascinating prospect to record, to be honest with you, because it was always going to be a sort of summing up of where we were at any given point in time. . . . And where we were was trying to push ourselves collectively. And in the process of that, because of the quality of these four musicians individually, let alone collectively, we were pushing the boundaries of music and [were] aware of that. And on this album—we should say the double album, *Physical Graffiti*—the whole thing is just full of character. And some [songs] are really, really groundbreaking, and you get things which are maybe very sensitive and caressing. You get other things which are really hard and coming at you."

For *Physical Graffiti* Led Zeppelin returned to the large residence, Headley Grange, where they had recorded their untitled fourth and most popular album. Once there, they set up their equipment in one big room, and ate and lived together in the house. Free of studio time constraints, they simply focused on creating the best music they knew how to make. "I just remember . . . the whole work ethic of this and that it was just so productive. It was on the fourth album, and lo and behold, here it was again. But the whole revisiting of Headley Grange . . . I sorta knew what could be done there as far as a huge drum sound . . . and the coziness of this sort of room, where we could just run through things."

There's a lasting notion about rock and roll that it's easy, that it's fun, just a bunch of friends getting together to play music, and a lot of bands fit that bill. Led Zeppelin is not one of those bands. Jimmy Page, Robert Plant, John Paul Jones, and John Bonham worked diligently on their sound. There was something almost mystical about their energy. They seemed bound together for a reason: to change the direction of music for generations to come. "Well, the whole thing about it is, you could already see what we were doing. We were really exploring music. We weren't doing singles. We didn't have a ball and chain on the group. We were able to just really push. . . . And that's what it was about. It was important that we did that."

In 1975, the famed Beat Generation novelist, essayist, and innovator William S. Burroughs interviewed Page for a feature in *Crawdaddy*, the first American rock music magazine. "I was contacted and asked if I'd like to do an interview with William Burroughs, and I went, 'Absolutely, 100 percent, 1,000 percent.' . . . He'd actually been to see Led Zeppelin at Madison Square Garden because he was in New York, on not just one occasion but numerous occasions. . . . He was connecting the essence of trance music, with riffs that repeat over and over and over, with what he had experienced when he was in Tangier in Morocco, and the—like the Joujouka musicians, et cetera, et cetera—and he wanted to do an interview connecting this whole aspect of things with . . . what we were doing." Page goes on to describe a discussion with Burroughs about pyramid energy, the belief that pyramids hold paranormal powers (one of these being that a dull razor blade would be sharpened if placed in a model pyramid). The popular belief that these "pyramid cones" transmitted energy fascinated Burroughs and he believed rock and roll music had a similar effect—it was all about the transmission of energy. In that *Crawdaddy* article Burroughs writes, "The essential ingredient for any successful rock group is energy—the ability to give out energy, to receive energy from the audience and to give it back to the audience. A rock concert is in fact a rite involving the evocation and transmutation of energy." What a perfect way to describe rock and roll.

Lonnie Donegan began his career with rehashed music from a bygone era, music I'd characterize as a formerly sharp blade that had dulled over time, and—if I may continue with this metaphor (perhaps I've been reading too much Burroughs)—he sharpened that blade with energy culled from the post–World War II culture of optimism, and then layered it with his own natural talent. Like Donegan before him, Page, along with his bandmates, took songs that weren't his and made them his own. He took the well-worn blues traditions and created a wholly new brand of music. Page plays the guitar like no one else, with a rhythmic stutter and power inspired by John Bonham, and melody inspired by Robert Plant and John Paul Jones. Page's guitar has a reverb surf sound, lonely and hollow, and every note counts. Then there is the texture that cements all the parts in place—and what a texture, with sometimes ten or more layers of guitars, the strings of which are bowed, plucked, pounded, pumped through mighty amps and circuits that distort, double, delay, and more. As Page asserts, "All the guitarists that you like—you can recognize them straightaway. And that's quite something, isn't it, from six strings." The sound of Led Zeppelin, a sound completely their own, can trace its roots to a random guitar in a random house and a chance encounter with a young kid and a classic song by an American blues musician. First transformed and made newly relevant by Lonnie Donegan, and then by one of the greatest guitarists and one of the greatest rock bands of all time.

CARRIE BROWNSTEIN

"I didn't just want to watch. I saw it as a conduit for expressing myself. I always wanted to be a performer." Even at sixteen Carrie Brownstein knew she wanted to be in a band. It was the early nineties at Lake Washington High School and a lot of her friends were doing it. "I went to high school with Jeremy Enigk, who would then go on to be in Sunny Day Real Estate, and [he] was hanging out with this guy named William Goldsmith, who ended up as a drummer in Foo Fighters and Sunny Day. All these people . . . play[ed] in punk bands in high school. And we would go to their shows."

These days, on any given night, you can see Carrie Brownstein in the IFC show *Portlandia,* a funny spoof on life in Portland, Oregon.

Carrie Brownstein, along with Sleater–Kinney, at their reunion concert in Washington, D.C.

She cowrites and stars with her best buddy, musician and comedian Fred Armisen. You can also see her as a recurring character in the Amazon TV series *Transparent*—and a few nights ago I saw her twice with her band Sleater-Kinney. After nearly a decade apart, they're back together. Carrie Brownstein is a kick-ass guitar player, a jubilant performer, a former NPR Music blogger, and a brilliant, thoughtful writer of music and comedy. She has, undeniably, fulfilled her dream of not just wanting to watch.

Carrie was a batcaver in 1990, and so were her friends. "There was a group of kids at my school who collectively were deemed and called the batcavers. And the year is actually important because pre-Nirvana, the term 'alternative' did not exist as a music genre, as far as I knew, officially. Nor did that term exist in terms of describing how people looked. There were a lot of other words. Instead of this big umbrella of alternatives, there were rockers and heshers, punks and SHARPs, which was the nonracist skinheads—Skinheads Against Racial Prejudice. There were all these microcategories, but you had to find your own umbrella term for them. That was batcavers at my high school. That was the goth. It was everyone that wasn't *normal*. I was very drawn to them because, first of all, it seemed like an interesting group of people. They outwardly embodied the kind of outsider feeling that I had on the inside. I really started talking to them and asking them questions about music. I had a student teacher in my chemistry class that brought me the vinyl of The Jam's *All Mod Cons*. . . . He had noticed that I was sort of transitioning from this sort of preppy kid to, I guess, what you'd call a punk, although I did it very awkwardly. . . . I never was quite able to look as much a freak on the outside as I felt on the inside. But he definitely noticed my interest in music. And he brought me that album. So, yeah, I sort of started down the path of being schooled on music." Carrie can't remember the teacher's name, only that he had a mullet, "a strange, strange mullet, not a rocker mullet, just a mullet."

Back then, for an outsider like Carrie, seeing her friends in bands was a revelation. "It just seemed like it was going to be a nexus of everything I'd wanted. . . . All of a sudden there was a medium that could hold all of the anger and frustration that I felt. I think it was more friends that made me want to actually play, but certainly in terms of *what* I wanted to play, [that] came from the records. That came from The Ramones, The Jam, The B-52's, The Replacements."

She shopped at record stores around Redmond, Washington. There were two at the time, Cellophane Square in the Bellevue Square Mall and Rubato Records, located in the bottom of a strip mall and run by a couple who were former band members from Seattle. "I think [their band] was called The Nurses. And they were great to me. I would be picking up Nirvana stuff and trying to get contemporary Seattle music. I remember they had Television's *Marquee Moon* and *Adventure,* the next album. They said, 'You should get these records. They're really good.' Or they had the Shocking Blue album, and they said, 'You like Nirvana? "Love Buzz" is the cover of the Shocking Blue song. You should get this album.' These people were invaluable to me . . . they had the generosity and the time to really kind of walk me down certain paths, and that was really exciting. I was very completist about it. I wanted to start at the beginning of punk. I wanted to know about The Ramones and the Sex Pistols and Buzzcocks and Slits and Delta 5. In the pre-Internet era, you kinda figured out different paths to go down because you couldn't just type something in or look [it] up on Wikipedia."

Sometimes Carrie would research bands based on their geography and search out music from different cities. Other times she'd look for groups with similar names. "I remember there was a woman [at school] named Courtney Reimer. I remember literally asking what is the difference between Ministry and The Church. Or I would ask [Courtney] about Replacements lyrics. Everybody became a teacher to me and a mentor. Everyone had their different shades of what they listened to. There was [another schoolmate] who really just listened to metal. I kind of got a little bit more of an education in Iron Maiden or early Metallica. There were the guys who were listening to hardcore music. I could go down that path."

Carrie would sit in her bedroom and play music on a cheap combination hi-fi with a record player on top. Eventually she inherited her dad's older components, and they sounded a lot better. "I would just sit in my room and listen to records and 7-inchers and CDs, which were, of course, really popular in the early nineties." She tells me, "I was mostly raised by my dad. . . . He was very respectful of the . . . interior landscape of a teenager. I think he gave me a lot of space and room to hide out and kind of inflate or just be with my friends. I probably had the door closed a lot, more for privacy and being a teenager [than] in terms of volume and whatnot." Carrie had her electric guitar, an Epiphone copy of a Fender Stratocaster. It was cheap and cherry red, and she played it through an off-brand Canadian amp. Most guitarists like to practice riffs and learn from the greats—Led Zeppelin, Pearl Jam, or Pink Floyd—but Carrie quickly dove into writing her own music. "I think part of that was starting to listen to bands from Olympia, where you'd hear Beat Happening, and you'd just think, 'I can do this. I can do this right away.'" Well, almost right away. Carrie could never play guitar or sing while anyone was in the house. "That's too vulnerable."

I totally get that. Every year during the month of February I make an album in my apartment, and I'm always far too self-conscious about my work if anyone's around. For Carrie, though, there was always a moment of confidence once she'd worked it out. "The part of me that was such a ham, the minute I had something that was worth sharing, I immediately dragged my sister into the room and played [the] song. I couldn't wait to have something that was presentable." While writing, she used to sing out loud to find the melody. "I still do this now, where I'll find the melody first and maybe some words that kind of anchor the song or anchor the theme. Then I'll go back and refine." She'd scribble the words on paper. I ask if she still has any of the songs she wrote as a teen. "Yeah, I have the song 'You Annoy Me,' which I feel like, in the course of my music career, I've basically [re]written . . . twenty times, with, hopefully, more gradual levels of sophistication. It's really funny how sometimes it boils down to that. I think before 'You Annoy Me,' I had a song about our dog that was just called 'Buffy Is Fluffy.' And that's the kinda thing that was easy to share with my sister because there was no vulnerability . . . it was just a joke song. Maybe I technically was actually doing something more *Portlandia*-esque before I was doing Sleater-Kinney."

All these songs, all this listening, shifted her attitude and outlook. Music became both confessional and confrontational. Olympia bands like Bikini Kill, Kicking Giant, Slant 6, and Heavens to Betsy were some of the locals that mattered to Carrie. As far as guitar playing, her influences came mostly from an earlier generation. "I think Ricky Wilson from The B-52's was someone I was drawn to immediately because of the economy of it. It was catchy. It didn't really sound like anyone else. It was inflected with a little bit of a surf sound but with a kind of yearning and angularity that isn't [found] in surf music. He was someone that I really liked. I also liked how his phrasing was part of the melody. You needed his sort of call-and-response with a guitar to make the songs unique. Tom Verlaine—I love Television—and I think Gang of Four was a huge influence on my guitar playing. In terms of actual songs that just really made me want to play and figure out how to express myself through song, it was probably The Replacements."

The Replacements were a band from Minneapolis led by guitarist and songwriter Paul Westerberg. Westerberg was born on the last day of the 1950s, and his music was steeped in the sounds of the early sixties. When I saw his band at the 9:30 Club in the early eighties, I could hear his love for The Beatles and The Rolling Stones, but they packed a punch to the belly those bands didn't always deliver. I didn't think of The Replacements as punk, but they'd been revolutionized by a new generation of Brits with band names like The Jam, The Damned, and Buzzcocks. Carrie felt a strong sense of belonging with The Replacements, though, that these other bands couldn't match. "I don't know how Paul Westerberg did it. But he somehow summoned the fear of obsolescence that an adult has with the angst and yearning of a young person. He was neither young nor old when I was listening to The Replacements. I loved all of the experience and [the] sense of possibility that he could kind of pour into a single song or a single lyric. Especially on something like 'Bastards of Young' that I heard in high school, I just would write those lyrics down all the time. They just felt so crucial and like something I knew, but something that was still very *unknown*. I liked that feeling a lot—that after a certain point I would understand the song better. Like, when I get a little older, this will make more sense to me, but right now, it's something I can hold on to. I love that combination."

"Bastards of Young" was the first song on side two of *Tim,* The Replacements' fourth album and their first major-label release. It received much praise but didn't make a big splash beyond those whose love for discovering new music was more passionate than passive, more identity than background. Carrie and her batcavers fit that description, while those listening to Wham!, Huey Lewis and the News, and other mid-eighties hit makers did not.

Music can act as an invisible uniting force that claims the unclaimed and defines the outcasts of a culture, and this song, the one that most changed Carrie Brownstein's life, is all about defining an undefined generation—one unlike the World War I or World War II generation or the Vietnam generation, fortunate enough to not be named for a war, but one that also lacked a clear identity. The words to "Bastards of Young" spoke to her and to others willing to toss off the past and grab on to the present.

Clean your baby womb, trash that baby boom
Elvis in the ground, no waitin' on beer tonight
Income tax deduction, what a hell of a function
It beats pickin' cotton and waitin' to be forgotten
We are the sons of no one, bastards of young

"[It] was that sort of endless struggle to be understood and have the people that you wanna love you, love you. That made so much sense to me in high school. And just 'We are the sons of no one, bastards of young' . . . It was so important to me at the time. It seemed an anthem of wanting to be claimed. I wrote a lot in my book [*Hunger Makes Me a Modern Girl*] about just feeling unclaimed and all the kind of journeys you go on to try to feel claimed by something. I think that song really summed that up for me."

A few years earlier, before The Replacements formed in the late seventies, music-making punks defined and then established an overt cultural attitude—they didn't care if anyone loved them. In many ways, punk music was a big middle finger to the world. "Bastards of Young" is the opposite, a song for those seeking acceptance and a like-minded group. It was released in the mid-eighties. By the end of that decade small music communities had formed everywhere, friends making music for friends: less a middle finger and more an outstretched hand. The Olympia riot grrrl scene is one example. "There was . . . a collective kind of reaching out. It was almost like people that felt alienated . . . were coming together to be collectively understood, and then were immediately misunderstood by a lot of the mainstream."

Sleater-Kinney formed in 1994 from two different Olympia bands. Carrie was in Excuse 17 and Corin Tucker was in the riot grrrl band Heavens to Betsy. Their music was inspired, in part, by all the listening Carrie had done, especially Television and Gang of Four, and like those bands, Sleater-Kinney's guitarists formed a musical conversation, with Carrie doing much of the talking as lead, and Corin Tucker responding on rhythm. Politics and feminism distinguished their lyrics and attitude, and earned them a fan base. And that's the connection, I think, between Carrie's passionate response to "Bastards of Young" and the music she'd later make. It's about belonging, belief, and community. There's a sense of standard-bearer about Sleater-Kinney that their fans can attest to, a sound that helps define and reaffirm a specific life attitude, even if that attitude is, as Carrie claims, just another version of "You Annoy Me."

SMOKEY ROBINSON

There's something wonderful about being told, "You're wrong!" by Smokey Robinson. In the world of radio, we consider a thousand-mile separation and two voices connecting via fiber and wire a "meeting," and that's how I meet Smokey. I'm at NPR in Washington, D.C., and he is at NPR West in Culver City, California. He is about to release an album of duets, *Smokey & Friends,* and I'm thrilled to spend time with an artist whose songs and voice helped form the very fabric of American pop culture. I've invited him to guest-DJ *All Songs Considered* and play the songs he loves by other artists. Then I'll play music—some of it his—and a conversation will unfold.

For this particular show, I decide to break my usual rule and begin with a song by another artist, Jackie Wilson, a great one called "Lonely Teardrops." I apologize to Smokey for not starting with "his music," and he politely but emphatically corrects me:

"You're wrong about that, Bob," he says in his warm but firm demeanor. "That *is* my music, man, because it's the music that I grew up with. Jackie Wilson was my number one singing idol as a kid. . . . When I first met Berry Gordy—Berry Gordy, of course, everyone knows was the guy who started Motown . . . [he] is my best friend. I first met him at an audition for Jackie Wilson's managers, in Detroit, with my group. Berry was there to turn in some new songs. You just played 'Lonely Teardrops,' and 'Lonely Teardrops' was one of the songs that he had with him that day." This is 1957 Detroit, the Motor City. Berry Gordy hadn't yet started what would become one of the most important labels of all time, Motown Records. "When Berry wrote 'Lonely Teardrops' it was like country and western; it was slow." Smokey sings a slow rendition of the tune. "'My heart is crying, crying lonely teardrops.' It was like that, one of those bluesy, kind of slow [songs]. He gave it to Jackie that day. When he heard it, at first he was disappointed because of the treatment that Jackie had done on it, but then it was a huge hit, so everybody was very happy.

"Yeah, I was about seventeen years old, but I'd been listening to Jackie Wilson, man. Jackie Wilson, people don't know—some people probably know, but anyway, there was a group called Billy Ward and the Dominoes. Billy Ward and the Dominoes were a huge group in the black areas, in the black neighborhoods and stuff like that, as a kid, when I was growing up. They had a guy named Clyde McPhatter, who turned out to be a really great artist on his own, too, after he left them. Clyde McPhatter was singing lead for Billy Ward and the Dominoes and Clyde left to form The Drifters. You see? People don't know this stuff, but I know. I'm a historian, man. Billy Ward hired Jackie Wilson to take Clyde McPhatter's place. Jackie Wilson took his place, and there's a theater in Detroit, or there was one, called the Broadway Capitol, where all the stage shows came into town and played. I went to the Broadway Capitol—I was about ten—to see Jackie Wilson with Billy Ward and the Dominoes. That was when I first became aware of him."

There are a few important things to note here. In the 1950s, radio listenership waned with the rise of television, and stations were desperate to capture a larger audience. One development was "Negro stations" that appealed to the black population; by the late 1950s there were about four hundred of them. Top 40 radio, another growing format, played hit songs, a mix of rock and roll, rhythm and blues, and other popular but mostly "safe" music. At its best, Top 40 brought black music to white listeners. At its worst, it replaced the outrageous Little Richard's "Tutti Frutti" with a vanilla counterfeit by Pat Boone, who decimated the frenetic energy to create a sanitized Top 40 version. Needless to say, a lot of black music was never heard by white audiences.

Smokey Robinson grew up poor in Detroit's North End. His mom had a love for music and an extensive music library. She died from a brain hemorrhage when he was only ten years old. "There was a huge record collection at my house, because [of] my mom—and I had two older sisters—[and] I had every kind of music you can think of. Everything from gutbucket blues to gospel to jazz to classical was being played in our house. . . . I grew up loving music from the time I could hear it, and there was always music in the house. I was very influenced by the people that I was hearing at that time. Sarah Vaughan is the first voice that I ever remember hearing, as a baby, growing up in Detroit. I must have been two years old or so. Sarah Vaughan, singers like her and Ella Fitzgerald and those, they were instruments, they had those voices that were unmatchable. . . . I started to buy music for myself when I was about eleven or twelve years old, and the first record that I purchased was a record by a group called The Spaniels, called 'Baby, It's You.'"

As I listen to Smokey talk about the music he loved, I can see a clear connection between the songs he grew up with and those he'd later write. His songs weren't written with the intention to write hits—they were songs for the ages. "When I write a song, man . . . I want to write a song because I know that . . . it has a chance to live on and on and on and on and on. My first goal is not to write a hit record. Of course I'd like it to be a hit, but I want to start with a song, something that if I had written it fifty years before now, it would've meant something, and today it's going to mean something, and fifty years from now it's going to mean something, it's going to have the content that allows it to mean something to people forever. So that's my first goal as a songwriter, and that's what I try to do every time."

Over the course of Smokey's career, the sheer number of great songs he's written—some performed with his group The Miracles, others solo, and many by other artists—is mind-boggling. It's hard to imagine pop music without "Shop Around," "You've Really Got a Hold on Me," "My Girl," "Going to a Go-Go," "The Tears of a Clown," "Get Ready," "The Tracks of My Tears," "The Way You Do the Things You Do" . . . the list goes on and on. After fifty years, you'd think he'd be tired of these tunes, but you'd be wrong. "I mean this from the bottom of my heart, I've been doing concerts now for over fifty years and those songs that you're playing and that I sing every night, every night they are new to me. They are new to me because I love my job, I love my work. I am living my wildest, most impossible, childhood dream. You see? So I'm very blessed. I get a chance to live a life, earn a living doing what I absolutely love. Every night those songs are new to me."

Smokey Robinson's first tune with The Miracles was an "answer" song called "Got a Job." He wrote it with Berry Gordy, in response to a doo-wop hit by The Silhouettes called "Get a Job." Theirs was about an unemployed man and his girlfriend, who won't stop bugging him to get a job. Smokey's "Got a Job" was about that same guy, this time employed but bemoaning his menial grocery store work:

You've been houndin' me to get a job
Well I finally did and my boss is a slob

He's on my back really all day long
It seems like everything I do is wrong
Well, I fin'lly fin'lly fin'lly fin'lly fin'lly (got a job)

It's not exactly genius writing, and it didn't last the ages, but soon after his initial attempt Smokey changed the art of songwriting for the better, forever. End Records out of New York released "Got a Job," and it inspired Berry Gordy to launch a label focusing on Detroit music. Then Smokey's band, The Miracles, turned that dream into a possibility. The song that changed Smokey Robinson's life is actually his own: "Shop Around."

"I had written it for a guy named Barrett Strong, who had a record called 'Money (That's What I Want).' He was one of our artists, and Berry had me do an album on him. 'Shop Around' was the first song that I wrote for that album. I played it for Berry and I sang it for him and he loved it so much with my voice on it, he had me record it with The Miracles." Barrett Strong's bluesy version of "Shop Around" had already been released in the Detroit area, but that didn't stop Berry. "[He] called me at three o'clock in the morning and said, 'Hey, man.' He said, '"Shop Around" won't let me sleep, so I want you to get the group right now, come to the studio. I'm changing the sound, I'm changing the beat, I'm changing the rhythm, and it's going to go to number one.' We went to the studio at three o'clock in the morning and did that, and the rest is history. 'Shop Around' was the first million-seller for Motown, the first million-seller for The Miracles and me. It was a huge boost in our lives and in our careers. It started the ball rolling for many, many people and many things, Motown, us. So 'Shop Around' will always be special in my heart."

The ball Smokey refers to was more like an avalanche: 110 Top 10 songs over the next decade, to be exact. The Motor City sound was an American phenomenon, and its pop backbeat and melodic call-and-response was soon loved worldwide. Motown had as significant an effect on music as the British Invasion would in the mid-sixties. The soulful, happy sound, shaped by Smokey Robinson, Berry Gordy, and the other great musicians and songwriters of Motown, was timeless and continues to influence modern music. Remember what Smokey said: "something that if I had written it fifty years before now, it would've meant something, and today it's going to mean something, and fifty years from now it's going to mean something."

That is why generations of musicians from then to now clamor to make records with William "Smokey" Robinson—timelessness.

DAVID BYRNE

David Byrne is a man of many colors. Just in the past few years, a theater piece he wrote with Fatboy Slim called *Here Lies Love*, based on the life of Imelda Marcos, the flamboyant first lady of the Philippines, had successful runs in New York and London; he recently toured with St. Vincent; the latest of his nine books, *How Music Works*, is part music theory, part autobiography. Before that he wrote *Bicycle Diaries*, which consists of urban observations from a longtime passionate cyclist. He's composed for other musicians, film, dance, and theater—and has recorded more music as a solo artist or collaborator, including with Brian Eno, than with the band we all know him best for, Talking Heads. I came to know David back when I was running a record warehouse, in 1977. Among the plethora of new bands I discovered in the late seventies, Talking Heads had the freshest sound. In their early days, Tina Weymouth, David Byrne, Chris Frantz, and Jerry Harrison made relatively spare music with a can-do spirit. Their attitude of spunk over musical craft inspired and spawned yet another new wave. And while many of the punk bands of the day were angry or pugnacious, Talking Heads were whimsical. Their songs dealt with pedestrian life and matters of the heart. Tina, Chris, and David met at the Rhode Island School of Design. David and Chris formed a band called The Artistics; Tina was just a fan and friend back then and didn't pick up the bass until the group first performed as Talking Heads in 1975. Jerry Harrison joined later, prior to their first album. Before that he was in a band known as The Modern Lovers, with Jonathan Richman. Their sound was closer to Talking Heads than any other band I know. Both Jonathan Richman and David Byrne were quirky, wide-eyed, insightful innocents, though David leaned more toward scary and Jonathan toward adorable.

I first met David under unusual and somewhat uncomfortable circumstances during the band's early days. He grew up in a suburb of Baltimore known as Arbutus. I lived somewhat nearby in Silver Spring. His parents are Scottish—he was born there—and though he recently applied for American citizenship, he's actually legally a Brit. David's mom worked in mental health, and I knew a woman she worked with. It was a time when Talking Heads still wasn't a big deal for most, but I was a huge fan. So when my friend told me the Byrnes were throwing a party to welcome David home from tour and invited me to come, I hesitated, imagining him returning to a houseful of strangers—it felt uncomfortable to me. I was persuaded, though, when my friend told me he'd love to meet a fan. In many ways, that party was just as awkward as I'd imagined—I trust for both of us—and also absolutely memorable for me. I tasted my first Scottish meat pie, baked by David's mom, and clearly recall how the music wafted from his room upstairs to the small downstairs living room where we gathered. David would run upstairs every seventeen minutes to flip the record, Bob Dylan's *Blonde on Blonde*.

Back then, part of what I loved about Talking Heads was how

unexpected they were, and I asked David what the band planned to do next. He told me their next adventure was with Brian Eno, my musical hero, and I was thrilled to hear it. Some time after that party, they traveled to Compass Point Studios in the Bahamas to record what became my favorite Talking Heads album, *More Songs About Buildings and Food*. I didn't meet David again for more than thirty years. The next time, I was an NPR journalist attending the White House Correspondents Dinner with Annie Clark (St. Vincent), and the time after that was at the tour rehearsals for Byrne and Clark's collaboration *Love This Giant*. Byrne was always friendly, albeit reserved and focused.

When I meet him at his work space in SoHo, in the summer of 2014, to talk about the music that inspired him, he drops the reserve and is simply a delight. Our conversation lasts well over an hour, as I try (and fail) to pin down one song that changed him. Our exchange begins with kiddie records and ends with Sun Ra, sort of summing up his lovable creative eccentricity. I learn that his parents used to play traditional Scottish folk music, like Jean Redpath, around their house outside Baltimore. "And they probably had some Gilbert and Sullivan records, probably some Woody Guthrie or Pete Seeger. Definitely Pete Seeger records, like the Pete Seeger children's records. And then there was probably like a *Sound of Music* LP. It's kind of hard to believe now, but yeah, those were the big pop hits then." Around then is 1965, and one song David remembers hearing on his transistor radio was "Mr. Tambourine Man" by The Byrds. "The sound itself sounded like nothing else. This is definitely not in the world of *My Fair Lady*. And sonically it sounded miles and miles away from Pete Seeger and everything else, although I probably didn't realize it at the time, but there was a big connection. But, sonically, it sounded like something completely else, which immediately told me there's another world out there. There's a world that's really different than what's represented in my living room and in my parents' house, as open-minded as they are. I thought, There's something else going on somewhere out there—that's where it's at. That's where things are really happening and really exciting."

In those days David bought most of his music at the E. J. Korvette department store. It had a decent record section and the best bargains, around $2.99 an album. I know because I used to walk along the Cross Island Expressway from my home in Queens to my local Korvette's. It might not have been "Mr. Tambourine Man" that inspired David to buy a guitar, but he did so around that time, and it may have been from Korvette's. "Everybody was learning the same things. Everybody was learning just the nah, nah, nah nah nah, nah nah nah thing from 'Satisfaction,' or they were learning the riff from 'Day Tripper,' or they were learning the kind of bom, bom bom bom bom, and bom thing from 'My Girl.' All these kinds of really basic guitar things. [I] tried to put a band together. I was not the singer. Another guy was the singer. I remember they would have Battle of the Bands in the junior high school or some auditorium. I think one of the competitor bands went and pulled out our plug during our [set], which pretty much ruined it. Pretty much destroyed our chances." His band was called Revelation, and soon after that show Byrne went solo. "During high school I had an acoustic guitar. I had a ukulele. I had a hand-me-down violin and stuff like that. Worked up a little kind of set that I could do in local coffeehouses, [that] kind of thing. I would do Chuck Berry, and I remember doing that and 'Summertime Blues' on the ukulele. . . . I tried to . . . shift the context of everything. Like do the hard rock stuff, but do that on the ukulele. And then the rock stuff I would do on the acoustic guitar and the context was in a folk club. . . . People who [have] seen the Coen brothers' movie [*Inside Llewyn Davis*] will maybe get a little idea of that . . . it was a very prescribed world. So the folkies didn't know rock and roll music. They didn't know what anybody was writing. They didn't know the songs of The Kinks or anybody. And I thought, Wait a minute, there's all this incredibly literate, really inventive songwriting going on, but they are refusing to listen to it because it's got electric [instruments] and it's on pop radio and they feel like it's a sellout. It's all commercial. I'd do a Who song or a Kinks song or something like that on acoustic guitar and it was kind of like, 'That's [a] really nice song. Where did that come from?' "

David particularly loved The Kinks' "Sunny Afternoon," which later helped inform his style when he started writing his own songs. "With early Talking Heads stuff, I got either accused or pointed at or whatever, it seemed like this guy writes a lot of ironic material. And I thought, well, maybe I picked that up from some of these earlier things like that song 'Sunny Afternoon,' where it's a criticism of a kind of upper-class guy who has no income but has his mansion and his big car and a swimming pool and everything, but he's basically having to sell everything off because he has no viable income and he's all inherited wealth—so Ray Davies is singing from his point of view."

When Byrne tried to write original material back then, though, he usually failed. "Bald-Headed Woman" is one title he recalls. In the early seventies, he tried again. "I was an art school dropout hanging out with other art school kids and at some point I thought, I'm going to try my hand at writing a song again. And I wrote 'Psycho Killer' and had my friends Chris and Tina help. . . . It was not written as a serious musical statement . . . it was more like, Can I write a song? Can I figure out the, whatever, verse and the chorus and all that kind of thing? And I thought, Oh yeah, I did it." His inspiration isn't obvious, but like so many young songwriters, he drew from his contemporaries. "I was probably thinking along the lines of imagine Alice Cooper but done by Randy Newman, which—it's not that big of a leap, really. I mean, he would probably do that." Randy Newman's songs are "incredibly catchy and the arrangements and the melodies . . . immediately, emotionally you just get sucked right into it. And then you realize this is a song about a pervert. And it's from the pervert's point of view!" Regarding Alice Cooper's influence, David says, "Alice Cooper songs don't kind of suck you in the same, but they're equal—I thought equally just super well done, catchy, and really kind of anthemic and clever."

As David speaks, my eyes drift around his office space and notice the walls covered with art, a poster for the Tokyo subway, and paintings of Talking Heads album covers. The shelves are stacked with film, audiotape, videos, vinyl, cassettes, scripts, posters. It's a well-kept and seemingly organized archive of mixed media. And our conversation bounces around an equally mixed world of music—from his love for Brazilian music, inspired by his trumpeter friend and collaborator Jon Hassell, to the time he was turned on to Richard Thompson through his friendship with Brian Eno, and in particular to one of my favorite tunes, a fourteen-minute live rendition of "Calvary Cross." We talk about Duke Ellington's "Creole Love Call" and the way something old can feel new if you've never experienced it—and how wonderful that is. He mentions seeing the English folk group the Incredible String Band in college, and how people used to approach him during his prime Talking Heads days to turn him on to Miles Davis records he didn't know.

From our conversation and as a lover of his work, I can tell David is an ecumenical listener. I think that's what makes it so hard for him to pin down one moment, one song that shook and changed him. Frankly, there are too many *him*s. However, one artist and one song do seem to have influenced him more than the others: "Cold Sweat," by James Brown. During David's early days, when he was learning to play The Temptations, The Rolling Stones, The Who, and so on, he heard James Brown for the first time and experienced a revelation. "Oh, the guitar can be like a percussion instrument! And it's something I didn't think of. You always think, Oh, it's chordal accompaniment, and then you hear that and you go, Oh, it can be a percussion instrument that plays a repetitive part [and] kind of interlocks with the rhythm in these other parts . . . it's a really radically different approach to how the music is put together. You realize that there's all different ways that the instrumental parts could be used to build a song. And one thing about those songs, like a James Brown song, was that each part—each instrument—the part that each instrument was playing had in a sense more integrity . . . In the sense that parts were more autonomous. . . . It wasn't like the guitar just played the chords and the piano played the same chords and the bass played the root note of those chords. This was more like a puzzle, where you had all these different interlocking parts and no one instrument played the whole—the chords." For David, hearing Brown's music was like seeing a machine in action. He saw how each gear could serve the greater goal. "And only by putting them all together do you get the thing. So that it only exists when all the parts are there. If you take one part out, there's a hole . . . it's like if you go to a guitar player and go, play the guitar from 'Cold Sweat' or whatever, it sounds ridiculous. You wouldn't know what it was. And that was a huge thing, and . . . I definitely applied or tried to apply some of that to some of the Talking Heads stuff, not all of it, but just some of it. . . . [I'd think,] Let me see if we can do a song that way, where the different parts are each doing something very different, and then when you put them together, it kind of clicks into place and makes the thing, but . . . the thing doesn't exist in any part alone." You can hear this kind of experimentation in "I Zimbra," from *Fear of Music,* and in "Born Under Punches (The Heat Goes On)," from *Remain in Light.*

As a longtime fan and observer of his art, I would say David is best at injecting his many personality traits—whimsical, serious, quirky, and visionary—into his hundreds of collaborations. There's a bit of rock and roll to what he does, but there is also disco, jazz, classical, folk, pop, and rhythms inspired by his travels, keen listening, and idiosyncratic interpretations. There's no one thing that changed him, rather a series of singular standout sounds that continue to keep him fresh and vibrant. In many ways David Byrne is a mirror of our times. Throughout his career, he has been able to cast his reflection on every sound he hears; his art is the result, a kaleidoscope of cultures, American, African, Asian, and South American. His music isn't derivative, it's distinct, and this unusual talent makes him simultaneously amorphous and singular. It reminds me of the dichotomy from the lyrics of "The Great Curve," on the 1980 Talking Heads album *Remain in Light:*

Sometimes the world has a load of questions
Seems like the world knows nothing at all
The world is near but it's out of reach
Some people touch it . . . but they can't hold on.

It also reminds me of James Brown's band. Like them, you can't understand the whole of David Byrne by viewing his career in parts, and you can't understand his music by hearing one song, just as he can't point to merely one as inspiration. Perhaps, as in "The Great Curve," these contrasts must coexist, the light and the dark, in order to "move the world" as he has done.

ST. VINCENT

Annie Clark (aka St. Vincent) had a dream "when I was ten [or] eleven years old. I thought I would go to a Pearl Jam concert, [and Eddie Vedder] would see me, he would see that I was special, and he would pull me up onstage and have me sing 'Rockin' in the Free World.' And he [would ask] me to sing the one verse that I actually really, really know. Like know like the back of my hand, and I wouldn't fuck up." Annie's dream stuck with her for a long time. One day it came true.

Annie Clark is a remarkably creative guitarist, songwriter, and singer. Her music is built on the backs of the great guitar rock heroes of the past. She then strips it of ego and reinvents the sound.

Annie Clark (aka St. Vincent) performing one of my favorite shows of 2014 at the 9:30 Club in Washington, D.C.

It becomes less about long solos, more about succinct statements and poppy, twisted tales. Born in Tulsa, Oklahoma, in 1982, Annie grew up in Dallas, Texas. As a kid, she enjoyed sports, wasn't terribly into listening to the radio, but liked her older sister Amy's records. Then one day in the early nineties, an almost divine act occurred: a box of CDs bounced off a truck right in front of her house. "They had weirdly good taste. I mean, it was like Pet Shop Boys and Cypress Hill and I wanna say Metallica, *The Black Album,* Nine Inch Nails, *The Downward Spiral.* . . . I just remember this shoebox full of records kind of fell on our doorstep, literally. I remember scanning through all of those records and just devouring them all."

One of the CDs was *Bill,* the first album by local psychedelic pop band Tripping Daisy. Soon afterward, Tripping Daisy moved beyond regional success and, in 1995, released *I Am an Elastic Firecracker* on a major label, the first album Annie ever bought with her own money. Tim DeLaughter headed the band. Around that same time, at twelve years old, Annie picked up the guitar. A few years later, DeLaughter started a new Dallas band, the sprawling, twenty-plus-member group known as The Polyphonic Spree. In the odd way the music world works, that box of CDs set Annie on a course that later led to her becoming a touring member of DeLaughter's new band.

Annie has a famous uncle, Tuck Andress, the guitar-playing half of the married jazz duo Tuck & Patti. As a teenager, she worked as their roadie, tour manager, and, later, opening act. "My mom saw that it wasn't like, Oh, Annie wants to be a musician. Oh no, she's going to be homeless. It was like, Okay, that's a career."

When she was fifteen, Annie went to visit her aunt and uncle in California. Palo Alto seemed exotic to a young girl who'd seen only Tulsa and Dallas. It was also a life-changing and life-affirming trip. "I think they were kind of priming me for the idea of taking me on the road. So this was like a little test run. I was with them for a couple of gigs that they played locally and then their gig in, I think, in Lake Tahoe. And then the night before I was supposed to leave, it was very sweet, they had this sort of ceremony for me. They lit these candles, and they put on Oliver Nelson's *The Blues and the Abstract Truth,* and we listened to it in the dark. 'Stolen Moments,' that was the track that killed me."

Annie and I are on her tour bus in front of the 9:30 Club in Washington, D.C., where she's about to play two sold-out nights. Her eyes brighten and grow wide as she speaks. It's easy to see the remarkable impact that moment had on her, half a lifetime ago "They were like, 'Here, here is the secret universe. Welcome. Welcome to it.' It was really, really, really, really intense. And I remember crying a little bit and just feeling so overwhelmed by the spirit of it—it was [a] pagan ceremony kind of thing."

So far Annie has told me about the random box of CDs and the self-described pagan ritual with her relatives, but there's another moment that was key to her becoming a musician. When she was around ten years old, her dad gave her a cassette for Christmas, the debut album, *Ten,* by the Seattle band Pearl Jam. "My stepmother at the time thumbed through the lyrics and saw that it said 'fuck,' and threatened to take it away because it was obscene for children. But luckily, idiotic and puritanical though she was, she was also forgetful. So I found it and got it back."

Annie discovered Pearl Jam while watching MTV at her friend's house. "It was a girl on my soccer team. I remember her parents had very bad boundaries, like would walk around in states of undress that even as a ten-year-old I was like, That's inappropriate. She was one of the kids who had MTV. You know, like, no boundaries. I saw the video for 'Jeremy' and I heard the song for the first time. And then I was just off to the races, I was obsessed, completely obsessed with Pearl Jam . . . and I just remember it being . . . like, Okay, I know what I want to do."

Annie was captivated by Eddie Vedder's fiery voice. The song

"Jeremy" was based on the true story of Jeremy Wade Delle, a sophomore at Richardson High School in Texas who shot and killed himself in front of thirty classmates. The video that Annie, her friend—and much of the country—saw on MTV was intense, to say the least. It featured close-ups of Vedder's demonic-looking eyes as he sang:

Clearly I remember
Pickin' on the boy
Seemed a harmless little fuck
But we unleashed a lion

The video was interspersed with images of a young, handsome, sometimes shirtless, frantic, and troubled child. The word "fuck" and the original ending, which featured Jeremy putting a gun to his mouth, were cut from the MTV version. However, there was still a brief shot of him lifting the weapon and the final image showed the classmates, white shirts covered in blood, as Vedder sang the infamous line "Jeremy spoke in class today."

The album containing that song is Pearl Jam's biggest commercial success. Thirteen times platinum, it touched many, Annie in particular. "It's like when you're a kid and you finally have something that expresses that which you don't know how to express. And you have this way to construct your identity . . . it was interesting because everybody liked Pearl Jam at that time. Everybody liked Nirvana, everybody even liked . . . Red Hot Chili Peppers and Soundgarden and that was the wave. You know? But I always felt like, Oh no, you don't love Pearl Jam as much as I love Pearl Jam. You couldn't possibly understand the depths. Oh, you like Pearl Jam? Oh, well, did you know this B side? Do you know this rarity? 'Cause I do, I have all those tapes and all those bootlegs. And you know, God bless my parents for letting me." Annie had a five-CD-changer boom box with a microphone and karaoke mode, which she'd use to sing along with Eddie Vedder. "When I was first playing guitar, when I was twelve and learning songs and writing my own songs, I was doing an Eddie Vedder impression. That's how I was learning to sing."

Even though "Jeremy" was the song that turned her on to the band, it was one of the deeper cuts that she says changed her life. "Oceans," on the same album, was different from everything else on *Ten*, and that was part of its appeal for an über-fan like Annie. It was a single in much of the world but not in the U.S., with a sound more reminiscent of Led Zeppelin's acoustic side than Pearl Jam's popular rocking side. The lyrics play on Vedder's love for surfing and waves, though it seems more about love for a girl than the ocean:

Hold on to the thread
The currents will shift
Glide me towards you
Know something's left
And we're all allowed to dream
Of the next time we touch . . .

Guitarist Stone Gossard and bassist Jeff Ament cowrote the song along with Vedder. In a 2009 article in *Seattle Sound Magazine*, Vedder spoke about its inception: "I remember for 'Oceans,' someone asked me to put change in the parking meter for them. I went and did that and then I came back and was locked out. It was drizzling and I wasn't dressed for an outing in the rain. I had a scrap of paper and a pen in my pocket, and they were playing this song [inside]. All I could hear was the bass coming through the wall, this window that was boarded up. So I wrote the song to the bass. I wasn't even listening to hear the song at first. When I heard a break, I'd start pounding on the door . . . trying to get out of the rain. So as I was doing that, I thought, Fuck it, I might as well write something."

The band performed "Oceans" on their *MTV Unplugged* session, but until 2009, that version could only be found by fans (like Annie) on bootlegs. Another song left unavailable until a later DVD reissue was their cover of Neil Young's "Rockin' in the Free World." Annie knows this history well. Her obsession with Pearl Jam may have cooled in her later teens, but her love for the band never went away. Remember that dream, the one where Eddie Vedder pulls Annie Clark from the audience and they sing Neil Young's anthemic tune together?

On Friday night, November 15, 2013, for Pearl Jam's second encore at the American Airlines Center in Dallas, and with the help of her friend guitarist Carrie Brownstein, Annie Clark's dream came true. A review by Preston Jones on DFW.com says it simply: "And for the second encore, Pearl Jam blew the roof off the place by bringing out Carrie Brownstein and Annie Clark (better known as St. Vincent) to help out on Neil Young's 'Rockin' in the Free World.'" On her bus, in front of my favorite nightclub, Annie puts it this way, "We did a little jam sesh. You know, in front of thirty thousand people."

This evening, with her guitar in hand and a set of mostly new songs, the modest yet stunning St. Vincent mesmerizes a crowd of twelve hundred in one of the most perfectly choreographed and greatest performances I have ever seen on a stage. I'm certain that somewhere in the young audience a fan dreams of being plucked from the throng by their idol St. Vincent to sing a verse of "Digital Witness" or "Cheerleader." Life has a strange way of making the extraordinary a reality, and—in the words of Eddie Vedder, from Annie's life-changing song—"we're all allowed to dream."

JEFF TWEEDY

Jeff Tweedy is a great American songwriter. He's from the heartland, raised in Belleville, Illinois, east of St. Louis, a town of about forty thousand. Tweedy, born in 1967, describes Belleville as "pretty isolated" and "not really a suburb of St. Louis, more of a working-class town, when they used to have breweries and stove factories and stuff like that." His music echoes the sounds of other great American singers and songwriters like Hank Williams, Woody Guthrie, and The Carter Family. His influences were clear back when he and fellow Belleville buddies Jay Farrar and Mike Heidorn played together, first as the cover band The Primitives, then as Uncle Tupelo, whose first album, *No Depression,* was named for the Carter Family

Jeff Tweedy performing with his son Spencer as Tweedy at the Lincoln Theatre in Washington, D.C.

song they covered on it. Uncle Tupelo made four fairly influential albums between 1990 and 1993. Their songs dealt with life in working-class Belleville and mingled country flavor with a love for punk, a musical mix that around that time became known as "alternative country," even though the sound has long been present in rock music, going back to The Byrds, The Flying Burrito Brothers, Gram Parsons, and certainly Neil Young. Jeff Tweedy and Jay Farrar, the two principals in Uncle Tupelo, famously didn't get along, which led to their breakup in early 1994. Farrar went on to form Son Volt and Tweedy formed Wilco. More than twenty years later, both bands are still recording, though in my opinion Tweedy's has clearly been the more musically innovative of the two. Wilco stretches the boundaries of "alternative country" and mixes a measured dose of electronics, noise, and free-form jazz with its traditional roots.

Tweedy owes much of his musical taste to his family, particularly to his older sister, Debbie. His siblings were all children of the 1950s, so their musical passion was primarily based in the '60s and '70s. When Tweedy's two older brothers, Greg and Steve, and his sister headed off to college, they left their record collections behind. Jeff became the beneficiary. "I think I had mostly my sister's records and maybe a few of my brothers'. . . . My sister had mostly 45s, like 'Bang Bang' by Cher." Two songs in that old collection of 45s are, today, vying for the song that changed his life: "Turn! Turn! Turn!," by The Byrds, and "Daydream Believer," by The Monkees. Oddly, or maybe not so oddly, the songs he finds most attractive are rooted in the American folk revival of the 1950s and '60s. Singer John Stewart, a member of The Kingston Trio, wrote "Daydream Believer," and The Byrds took their version of "Turn! Turn! Turn!" from Pete Seeger. Seeger's side of folk was more activist, words to inspire, not the simple sing-along you'd hear from a group like The Kingston Trio.

For Tweedy it's a tough choice. "It's hard to pick one, because they were all pretty instrumental, because those were good periods of music." He then rattles off bands from his childhood collection, and my mind reels—those were my records, too. I had "Turn! Turn! Turn!" on a 45, and distinctly recall the red Columbia Records label spinning on my player in Queens. It was an astonishing sound. The term "jangly" gets tossed around a lot the moment someone mentions The Byrds, and it really is a perfect description of their sound. When he first heard them, Tweedy thought they were The Beatles: "It was somewhere between The Beatles and Bob Dylan, which I liked a lot, both of them already. Those are really magical recordings, those early Byrds sides. I'm still really interested in shapes of songs, and that's a really interesting shape of a song. It's not a traditional verse-chorus, verse chorus, verse-chorus pop song. It's a cyclical-like melody—it's like a psalm or something."

As for his other possible choice: "'Daydream Believer' probably has more to do with [my] thinking those guys get lots of girls." I agree, and wasn't a fan of The Monkees' music—not much innovation there—but I was a fan, as was Tweedy, of their silly television show. It was a clear rip-off of The Beatles' 1964 film *A Hard Day's Night* that was then digested into a cute sitcom format. Tweedy says, "The Monkees were in syndication . . . and I think that's an early formative memory for me that I've chased my whole life, thinking that a band's supposed to live together and have madcap adventures together. I always really looked for that intimate relationship with a group of guys who just are all cool."

It took Tweedy the better part of his life to find and develop that sort of relationship between his band members. I already mentioned Uncle Tupelo and Jay Farrar—hardly a rollicking romp through a grassy field—but the relationships among Wilco's members have been difficult to maintain as well. Some of the issues were Tweedy's: an addiction to painkillers and his struggles with migraines, depression, and panic attacks. Others were simply creative conflicts, which culminated with the firing of bandmate Jay

Bennett before the release of *Yankee Hotel Foxtrot* in 2001, a record that has more in common with The Beatles' "Strawberry Fields For- ever" than Neil Young's style of singer-songwriter storytelling. To this day, *Yankee Hotel Foxtrot* is my hook to Jeff Tweedy. Oh, I liked Wilco before, but the adventurous spirit of that album epitomizes the qualities I crave in music, an element of surprise mixed with memorable hooks—like I said, more "Strawberry Fields" than "Sugar Mountain." There were other Wilco personnel changes, including the addition of genius drummer Glenn Kotche, who first appeared on *Yankee Hotel Foxtrot*, and, a few years later, guitarist Nels Cline, a brilliant, frenetic talent.

These days they may not share the boisterous banter of The Monkees, but in Tweedy's eyes Wilco is a chemically compatible, cohesive group. And the changes in their sound—the odd noises, experimentation, increased introspection, and poetic songwriting— are all traceable to his sister's record collection and his family's taste in music. "It's amazing how formative all the records were in the house, how I can draw a direct line to something I'm still inter- ested in listening to. My dad had a record of steam engines, just the sounds of trains, recordings of dust storms in the thirties, and stuff like that. I love anything like that. And it's [probably] been instilled from all those records."

His mom, Jo Ann, bought Tweedy his first guitar when he was six years old. She, too, loved music, and wanted to be a singer. "They were both very supportive of me playing music but maybe less understanding about the concept of [being in a band]. . . . I re- member we made a fair amount of money as The Primitives before Uncle Tupelo because we would play dances and . . . play all sixties garage songs, and that was palatable enough for teenagers to come and we would make money doing that. And when we switched to just playing our own songs, my mother really didn't grasp that." It's clear the experience of playing those garage rock songs by The Pretty Things and The Kingsmen served him well. "I think [it's] really good to learn a lot of other people's songs as a formative part of your musical education. I think that doesn't happen quite as much these days . . . a lot of young bands don't come at it having learned a whole lot of other people's songs."

Tweedy's roots are working-class. His mom and dad both dropped out of high school in the early 1950s when she became pregnant, and Robert Tweedy found a job working "underneath the trains in the pits." East St. Louis was home to Alton & Southern Railway switching yard, where his father worked for forty-six years. "At some point somebody realized that my father was very smart, even though he didn't have a diploma. And they sent him to Arizona in 1960 to take a course. . . . Somebody taught him how to program computers with punch cards, so then he got promoted to the tower and eventually he was the superintendent of the switching yard."

For Tweedy "music has represented a liberating pathway to not being ashamed of being philosophical and intense and smart." During our conversation, he talks a lot about the sort of anti-intellectual attitude that pervades small towns. To him, Belleville had that outlook. "I think that I grew up in a place where [we were] maybe on the early edges of anti-intellectualism, or maybe it's just a small-town thing that's eternal. I'm not saying that there aren't smart people that grew up or lived [there], but it's frowned upon to allow that to be a part of who you are. [As if] you're not supposed [to] make other people feel bad about themselves by being good at something or outstanding unless it's something that's agreed upon: you know, you can be good at baseball or something. I don't know what exactly happened to me to make me feel so alienated and hurt. But I really have always kind of [been] drawn back to being a smart young boy, and somehow intuiting or feeling like that's not okay." As he continues, it's clear to me that despite his love for "Daydream Believer," Tweedy's belief that a song should be thought provoking and poetic brings him back to The Byrds.

Songwriter Pete Seeger took the lyrics for "Turn! Turn! Turn!"

straight from the biblical book of Ecclesiastes. Purportedly written by King Solomon, it focuses on the vanity of human life. This is the song that changed Jeff Tweedy, one that sticks with him still. "I think I've always been a fairly introspective lad and philosophical in some ways. And I'm sure that appealed to me a lot, like Dylan . . . [it's] just mysterious, ethereal, and earnest, and somehow light and serious at the same time." Tweedy is describing one of the biggest changes to pop music in the mid-sixties, when rock and roll became a rebellious teenager and lost its childlike innocence. His word choice—ethereal and earnest—is also the perfect description of the music he creates with Wilco. He tells me, "I think the actual learning how to disappear into the act of creativity is a tremendous gift. I would be completely lost without it."

When you're back in your old neighborhood
The cigarettes taste so good
But you're so misunderstood

—FROM "MISUNDERSTOOD," ON THE WILCO ALBUM *BEING THERE*

(1996)

JAMES BLAKE

It speaks to the power of music that a twenty-five-year-old electronic musician from England could be so inspired by a long-dead R&B singer from Clarksdale, Mississippi. The London-born James Blake loves the music of Sam Cooke. It wasn't the hit singles his musical father played for him as a child, though. Yes, he liked the brilliant "You Send Me," a hit in 1957, and was familiar with the posthumous civil rights anthem, "A Change Is Gonna Come," but he wasn't inspired to evolve from a producer of instrumental music into a vibrant, soulful singer until he heard *Night Beat* (1963), the one and only blues album Cooke ever recorded, specifically his version of Charles Brown's "Trouble Blues."

A stark and stunning concert from James Blake at the Music Hall of Williamsburg in Brooklyn, New York.

I must admit that as a fan of both Sam Cooke and James Blake, the connection between these seemingly disparate artists has escaped me until I hook up with Blake one night in early November 2013. I walk into the well-lit upstairs dressing room at the 9:30 Club and am greeted with the club's now famous chocolate cupcakes. Blake is set to perform his second of two sold-out nights supporting his album *Overgrown*. His live shows are sonically mind-blowing, and I see him every chance I get. This is my fifth time, and I was here the previous night, too.

Of the over six hundred performances I saw in 2013, Blake's two 9:30 Club shows are in my top twenty. His music is visceral, sonically sensuous, the songs beat driven, but not the usual straight-ahead danceable beats. I've never heard anyone play like his drummer, Ben Assiter. This young British drummer's beats are angular, clicky, spare, and unexpected. He's one of two old friends who accompany Blake onstage. Rob McAndrews, the other, plays guitar, though you'd be hard-pressed to identify his atmospheric, textured sounds as coming from a guitar. McAndrews and Assiter complement and punctuate Blake's soul-filled melodies, fleshing out their sound. But what's most mind-boggling about their show is watching Blake and band build their epic songs from such simple elements. In concert they re-create and expand on the recorded work by live-looping Blake's voice and keyboard, and adding similar digital mojo to the other instruments. These aren't premade or replayed loops and sequences. The result is fantastic, like watching the perfect magician.

Blake is relaxing with his laptop when I enter his dressing room. He's seated, but I distinctly remember his lofty presence (he's six foot five) from another preconcert meeting, in 2011 at SXSW. That show was only his second time performing in the States, and he was nervous, shy. Now, more than two years later, he is joking and vibrant, more confident, and for good reason. A lot has gone well for him since those early dates. His records are more successful now, not just in sales but as works of art.

I turn on my flash recorder and ask Blake if he remembers a musical moment that shook him, that made him want to make music. He responds immediately: "Trouble Blues." He first heard the song a few years ago while studying popular music—"pocket fluff," as he calls it—at Goldsmiths, University of London. He was in his second year and living with a group of fellow students. "I remember doing a piece of writing on something that required me to listen to *Night Beat*. And so I listened to [it] and I really had a moment. . . . With 'Trouble Blues,' I felt like I listened to something that would be a yardstick from which I could measure my own vocal ability." I view Blake as an electronic music pioneer, and assumed he'd pick some contemporary innovator. So I'm slightly shocked when he names *Night Beat* as his inspiration. In my mind, Blake's music is sonically restrained, bare, and adventurous, to me almost the polar opposite of Cooke's straight to the heart style—but maybe straight to the heart is where Blake is heading? Then again, *Night Beat* was a different Sam Cooke. In the six years or so that he'd been recording, Cooke had never made a blues album. He was spiritual when he sang gospel with The Soul Stirrers and upbeat in his string of secular pop hits, including "Another Saturday Night" and "Twistin' the Night Away." Whether he would have continued down this path and become a great blues singer, we'll never know. Sam Cooke was shot dead about a year and a half after recording "Trouble Blues."

Cooke inspired generations of musicians that followed. You can hear his gospel-infused soul in the voices of Aretha Franklin, Stevie Wonder, and James Brown, as they blend the spiritual with the secular, praise with pleasure. Throughout his career, Cooke mixed business with music making, managing his own affairs and racking up thirty hits in his eight years of pop recording. You might consider this an early model for what is now commonplace, musicians not only writing and singing their own songs, but promoting and marketing them as well. Around 1950, before he became a soul singer, Cooke was a bit of a heartthrob in the pioneering gospel group The Soul Stirrers. In Peter Guralnick's book *Dream Boogie: The Triumph of Sam Cooke*, the author describes young girls rushing the stage to get close to him. Back then it wasn't acceptable for gospel singers to make popular music, so Cooke recorded his first pop song under the alias Dale Cook. But his clear and rousing voice was too distinct to fool anyone. From there he went on to write many of his thirty hits, also unusual for the time.

Tragedy entered Cooke's life, though, with the death of his eighteen-month-old son, Vincent, who wandered away from his mother and drowned in their swimming pool. Afterward, Cooke blamed his wife, Barbara, for the death of their child, and his extramarital affairs increased. Eighteen months after their son's death, Cooke was shot in the heart at a Los Angeles motel and found naked except for his sports coat and shoes. The story of his death is a complicated one, involving money, sex, and alcohol, and the music world deeply felt his loss. In the time between his son's death and his own, Cooke released *Night Beat*. However, his most lasting achievement, and arguably his most remarkable song, "A Change Is Gonna Come," wasn't released until after his death. Inspired by Bob Dylan's "Blowin' in the Wind," Cooke's 1964 recording became a seminal song of protest and an anthem of hope for the civil rights movement. Tragically, he would never know its impact.

Almost fifty years later, across the ocean in London, a young James Blake dimmed the lights of his room at school at around 10 P.M. and played *Night Beat*. Usually he listened to Joni Mitchell's *Blue,* Bon Iver's *For Emma, Forever Ago,* or music by Joanna Newsom—basically, he tells me, "people with incredible voices." What astonished him about "Trouble Blues" was simple, really—it was "just the humming." Sitting across from me in the dressing room, Blake breaks into song and hums this mournful, melodic tune, the opening of "Trouble Blues." But I immediately recognize it from another song. It's the same hum you hear during the opening of "Retrograde," from Blake's album *Overgrown*. In that instant the connection, the introspective soulful expression, is suddenly clear. Blake notices the smile on my face and says, "In some subconscious way, maybe I filtered that into 'Retrograde.'" Indeed he did.

The opening to "Retrograde," sonically one of the most incredible songs from any artist in 2013, echoes the soul-filled yearnings and melodic lines of "Trouble Blues." It's easy to compartmentalize music, and it's common to compare artists of one generation to their contemporaries, but when two similar sounds are from such different places and periods, the connections aren't so obvious. Both songs are about a lover and a longing for spiritual peace. In Cooke's song, his woman has left him, and Billy Preston's organ and his voice combine to form a near-perfect outpouring of heart and soul. In Blake's case, it's distance and time that separate him from his lover, and the rising and falling lines of the synthesizer symbolize the two lives diverging and converging. For me, the connection between these two songs separated by fifty years is incredibly poignant, further evidence of the lives that Sam Cooke continues to touch long after his death.

As a dedicated young artist, James Blake was inspired by the music he grew up with but was also eager to find his own voice, his own unique means of expression—rarely an easy process. When he first heard "Trouble Blues" he was living with a group of college mates, and his attempts to sing outside his comfort zone and ability made for some awkward sounds. It's like a kid learning a violin; they'll make awful squeaks at first, and it's natural for them to be self-conscious about it. It wasn't easy for Blake to learn to sing while living in a group home. He'd attempt to shut his door and record, but was constantly aware of his housemates or anyone listening. He tells me, "I mean, they could hear through the walls and everything." It's one thing to sing in front of thousands once you've mastered your style, but discovering your limits and strengths can be embarrassing, and privacy, while imperative, was not always possible. "I still can't write and be completely honest knowing that there are people listening. It's quite unnerving."

Inspired by Sam Cooke's bluesy, yearning sound, Blake took his singing to the next level, and it soon became the perfect foil for the electronic sound he was creating. This is music that could exist only in the twenty-first century. You simply couldn't produce the sort of deep bass and complex textures that are common in his music until now. I've been an electronic musician since the late 1970s and have often noticed that my own music comes to life with the addition of a singer, an acoustic guitar, or some other organic element. It becomes more memorable and potent.

In my twenty-six years of producing music stories for NPR, I've come to a not-so-surprising conclusion: people who make music at a young age often have parents who are either musicians or in some creative field. James Blake grew up around a singer and performer. He and his dad share the name James Litherland; the senior Litherland played guitar in the British progressive rock band Colosseum in the late 1960s, then later with Mogul Thrash. Litherland's progressive rock style took a turn toward the blues during the late seventies. Then, in the early eighties, technology enabled him to set up a home studio and create professional-sounding recordings without a huge amount of money. Basically, with the advent of electronic drums and computers with MIDI (Musical Instrument Digital Interface), which is a way to connect computers to instruments, it was possible to sound like an entire band without the use of other musicians. Blake's father was a musical pioneer in his day—the apple doesn't fall far from the tree, I guess.

"He was doing it. And he was making his own albums. So in England, he may have been one of the first people to do that." Blake picks up his laptop and searches for his father on YouTube and finds "Where to Turn." He plays it for me and I'm shocked. It's basically "The Wilhelm Scream," a song I recognize from Blake's first solo album. I didn't know his father was a musician until this conversation, or about this video of his dad singing a song Blake would later record and make famous. The opening verse from "Where to Turn," recorded about fifteen years ago, has the same lyrics and phrasing that define Blake's sound. It's eerie, hearing this early rendition. I think of Blake's music as unique, just as every generation views its music as separate from what came before. Certainly the electronic beat makers must feel solitary ownership of their music, creating odd sounds with laptops, rubbery backlit controllers played through powerful subwoofers capable of vibrating an audience to their core. And there *is* newness there, but not entirely. The synthesizer can sound remarkably like something as old as a jaw harp, or the sound the pygmies in New Guinea made when they blew air through the wings of a sago beetle. These sounds precede the electronic dance music we hear today, and if the pygmies are a good indication, they've fascinated humans forever. In the case of James Blake, there's still freshness to his restrained twenty-first-century electronics, and despite its forward-reaching sound, his father and Sam Cooke clearly connect his music to the past.

In our time together, I discover many connections between Blake and his dad, most notably their similar passion for making music in a home studio. His father comes to his shows, though they don't make music together. "We're very individual," Blake says. "We get on great." You'd think his dad as a blues musician would have turned his son on to Cooke's blues record, not only his popular hits, but *Night Beat* was a critical success only, not a commercial one, and it's likely his dad never knew it existed.

What isn't odd, given his father's passion for the blues and how well that sort of soulful voice works with electronics, is that it's the album Blake found most inspiring when developing his singing. "I felt like [my voice] was something that could grow. And now I feel like I'm getting somewhere, where, you know, I could do something. I could sit and I could put myself amongst my favorite singers. At some point, I'm not saying that I am already, but I'm saying—I feel vocally, now, I'm getting to a point where I'm solid. And even though my voice sometimes falls off the note—or it feels like it's going to fall off the note—I feel like I've developed a sort of character. I've developed how I want to sing, which now comes naturally to me."

All that happened in the span of four years. In many ways, Blake had to sacrifice what most people view as a normal life to get there, including not seeing much of his friends. "I think only now that we're talking about it am I realizing exactly what I've done to cut myself off from the rest of the world so that I can do it. And it has turned out to be worth it."

COLIN MELOY

I am confident that singer-songwriter Colin Meloy will choose a Shirley Collins song as the piece of music that changed his life. I'm just not sure which one. He might pick one of the suite of songs from *Anthems in Eden*, a groundbreaking 1969 British folk record by Shirley and her sister Dolly Collins, with an odd consort of instruments, including electric guitars and alto, tenor, and bass sackbuts. Colin and his band The Decemberists excel at running songs together into suites, perhaps most successfully on their albums *The Crane Wife* and *The Hazards of Love*. Another tip-off in favor of him choosing the legendary Shirley Collins: the EP of traditional songs associated with Collins that he recorded solo in 2006. Then again, he's also made solo recordings of songs by Morrissey, The

Colin Meloy with The Decemberists at the Newport Folk Festival in 2015.

SPRINGDALE PUBLIC LIBRARY
405 S. Pleasant
Springdale, AR 72764

Kinks, and Sam Cooke. It would be especially odd if he chose Sam Cooke, since a few days earlier I spoke with James Blake about that very artist.

I meet Colin backstage at the historic Lincoln Theatre in Washington, D.C. He is on his fall 2013 solo tour. We've met a number of times, including when he toured with those Shirley Collins tunes and then again in Austin, Texas, when he premiered *The Hazards of Love* live at SXSW, and later at my desk with The Decemberists for one of my favorite Tiny Desk Concerts. He always seems chatty and relaxed on these solo jaunts, but then he always has a gracious demeanor, even while playing high-pressure, big-production shows and singing songs of murder, shape-shifters, and dead babies with his band. I enter his small dressing room, turn on my recorder, and discover that Colin's choice couldn't be further from my folky assumption. It's a song by Hüsker Dü, an often loud, brash band from Minnesota. So instead of imagining the connection between Colin's and Collins's versions of British balladeering and storytelling, I find myself attempting to connect Hüsker Dü's and Colin Meloy's creative spirit, and it's a bit of a short circuit.

Colin Meloy grew up in Helena, Montana. He was four years old in 1979, when singer/guitarist Bob Mould, bassist Greg Norton, and singer/drummer Grant Hart formed Hüsker Dü in St. Paul. Colin's sister Maile was a few critical musical years older than Colin and turned him on to bands as a kid, particularly synth-pop ones from England like Depeche Mode and Yaz. Then, in fifth grade, Colin discovered Scritti Politti, a postpunk band Green Gartside had formed in the late seventies. Gartside was an art student, who, like so many other British teenagers, was inspired by the punk scene. Basically, between 1976 and 1977 punk burst open like a seedpod, giving birth to a ton of new bands brimming with a combination of hope, desperation, and energy. Like so many youthful bursts of wonder, time and experience changed these bands, and by the time

Colin heard Scritti Politti in the mid-eighties, they were more in tune with electropop, which had become the new "outside the box" sound for teens and those young at heart.

Colin's face lights up as he talks about Scritti Politti. There's a bouncy sparkle in their music, at least in the Scritti Politti he knew. Back then his uncle Paul, a college student at the time, took on the role of educating Colin and his sister about music. Uncle Paul called Scritti Politti "Wham! for smart people," referring to the popular and sexy pop duo of George Michael and Andrew Ridgeley. It was an eye-opener for Colin. "Scritti Politti was the first band that I sought out myself and bought the record, *Cupid & Psyche 85.* I just wore it out listening . . . and thought of it as just kind of pop music. And only later did I understand that Green Gartside had been kind of an anarchist punk in London in the late seventies, early eighties."

Great songwriters are often music geeks as well. In my conversation with Colin, it's clear that he is, and I'm sure we could spend the next hour talking about Scritti Politti, but I push him toward his Hüsker Dü moment. It turns out that Uncle Paul steered him there as well. Uncle Paul was the youngest brother of Colin's mother and a student at the University of Oregon. He was ten years older than Colin, who was twelve at the time. For their family Christmas in 1986, Uncle Paul sent two cassettes, one to Colin and one to his sister. Colin's sister's cassette was a compilation of mostly "college rock" bands. Back then the term "college rock" was replacing the term "new wave" because college radio stations were pretty much the only ones that would play it, plus every generation feels the need to coin their own term for underground, alternative, indie, etc. Colin coveted his sister's new cassette, filled with the music of R.E.M. before their big breakthrough. If you listen closely, you can hear the sound of mid-eighties R.E.M. all over The Decemberists' *The King Is Dead,* with its big strong choruses and shimmering twelve-string guitar. In fact, The Decemberists once covered R.E.M.'s "Cuyahoga," from *Lifes Rich Pageant,* in a KCRW studio session. That cassette from Uncle Paul also had another jangly band from Georgia that Colin loves to this day, Guadalcanal Diary, as well as The Replacements, a Minnesota band like Hüsker Dü, and the seminal eighties British band The Smiths.

Colin's tape from Uncle Paul consisted mostly of demo recordings from a University of Oregon bar band, Coos Bay. Colin liked their music, but he found his life-changing moment at the end of the cassette. Among choice cuts like R.E.M.'s "Superman," Guadalcanal Diary's "Pray for Rain," and the Beat Farmers' "Happy Boy" was Hüsker Dü's "Hardly Getting Over It."

"I would say that 'Hardly Getting Over It' hit me so hard, and that's off of Hüsker Dü's record *Candy Apple Grey*." When I ask him what it was that hit him so hard, he tells me it was the song's melodic quality, and that Bob Mould's voice had an "aching sort of sear to it," and that the arrangement was simple and sad. He was just moving into his preteens when he discovered them, and "simple and sad" appealed to him. "I went and sought out all those records. I sought out Guadalcanal Diary's record. I sought out R.E.M.'s record at the time, which was *Lifes Rich Pageant,* and then *Candy Apple Grey*. And I remember going home with *Candy Apple Grey,* the record that had 'Hardly Getting Over It,' this beautiful, aching, gorgeous acoustic song."

Colin remembers buying Hüsker Dü's cassette at Pegasus Records in the Capital Hill Mall in Helena. As much as I'm thrilled with the ease and availability of music these days, there is something more significant about the physical act of buying an album with your own money and staring at its cover art—it becomes a memory. I trust you won't remember where you were when you bought your first or even your latest digital download, and—frightfully—you might not even know what the cover art looks like. Colin forms his hand as if holding a cassette tape: "I came home and put it on my little Sony Sports boom box. And the first song, for those who know, is a song called 'Crystal,' which is as hard as anything that is on [Hüsker Dü's earlier album] *Zen Arcade*. It's just like blaring, screaming hardcore. And I was really dismayed initially. But suddenly—I think I listened to it again and then pressed through until I got to 'Hardly Getting Over It.' And then it all started to make sense. This vast spectrum of music was played out for me [by] this single band. This songwriter in particular, Bob Mould, could be all of these things and do them well and convincingly, and beautifully. . . . It took a while before I could actually listen to 'Crystal' all the way through. But eventually, I came to really love it, and loved the really crazy stuff and then dug deeper. But I feel like that was a real eye-opening moment."

Colin wasn't the only one dumbfounded by these seemingly polar-opposite forms of music from the same band. Fans of the hard stuff were confused by Hüsker Dü's shows, which would open with their pounding, loud material and end with Bob Mould solo on his twelve-string guitar. "And people would just freak out and get so angry. That was kind of as they were transitioning away from just being an underground hardcore band and into the band of their heyday. I think that took a lot of guts." And there it is: the connection between what an artist is drawn to—even before they become artists themselves—and what they create. The Decemberists embody that split between pretty, jangly, romantic songs, such as "O Valencia!" or "The Engine Driver," and intense progressive rock like "The Island: Come and See/The Landlord's Daughter/You'll Not Feel the Drowning" from *The Crane Wife*. Fearlessness is what attracted Colin to the song that inspired him. He and his bandmates create challenging music and also pretty literary ballads—the Shirley Collins variety—and sometimes intertwine both elements in the same song or a suite of songs. As a listener, I love and admire that sense of adventure. It's what keeps me coming back to The Decemberists, always waiting for their next surprise, their next story to unfold. "I think the bravery that Bob showed in really following his whims, be it loud or quiet, despite his audience, finding his own voice and following it, I think is the thing that has most affected me and hopefully is something I've done in my music." Colin tells me that he doesn't think the sound of Hüsker Dü shows up in his music, but the chance taking and bravery most certainly does.

TREY ANASTASIO

Phish fans, please forgive me. Of all the artists in this book, Phish is probably the most popular band that I don't really know. Their music, though filled with twists, turns, brilliant playing, and adventure, has never spoken to me (again, forgive me), yet I'm fascinated by their dedication to their fans, and vice versa. To better understand what others love about this music, I wanted to speak with their guitarist/singer/guiding force Trey Anastasio. I never expected our lively conversation to center on Leonard Bernstein and Stephen Sondheim's *West Side Story.*

Trey Anastasio having a ball with Phish at Merriweather Post Pavilion in Columbia, Maryland.

Trey is a nickname; he's the third in a line of Ernest Joseph Anastasios, after his grandfather and father. "My dad, being an Italian, one hundred percent Italian, absolutely had to name his son after his father, right? That's the way you do it. And my mom didn't like the name, so she said, 'You can put it on his birth certificate. I'm going to call him Trey.' So no one's ever called me anything but Trey."

His dad made SAT tests in Princeton, New Jersey, and did so for thirty-five years. His mom, Dina, edited *Sesame Street Magazine* and is a children's-book author. "My mother grew up going to every Broadway show in the Golden Age of Broadway. And she told me it wasn't that hard back then. It was cheaper than a movie. That's what you did, I guess. But she used to play this stuff all the time. She has original copies of vinyl that she bought. So when I was a kid, I remember she gave me a stack of her original Broadway cast recordings on vinyl . . . it was *Oklahoma,* it was *Gypsy,* it was *Carousel,* it was *West Side Story.* I remember being in fourth grade and my mom had given me a record player, and I listened to all these Broadway recordings, and the one that got me was *West Side Story.* I used to listen to the whole thing, but the thing that used to kill me—well, there were two. One is that song 'Something's Coming.' I remember listening to it over and over again, and what I first heard was that when he sings about the wind, Leonard Bernstein made the wind with the orchestration. And I remember thinking there was some kind of magic in the music that I couldn't figure out."

Trey then breaks into song—no guitar, just his voice: "'A boy like that will kill your brother. Find another, one of your own kind. Stick to your own kind.' And then he dies, Tony dies, and she's leaning over his body, and they play 'There's a place for us' ['Somewhere']." As he sings, I'm bombarded by my own memories. Musicals filled my home, too, all the ones he mentioned and more, but I was nearly allergic to them, except for *West Side Story.* The *Romeo and Juliet–*

inspired tale, set on the Upper West Side of New York, pitted Puerto Ricans against Caucasians and featured, of course, the modern lovers Tony and Maria. The story of street gangs and love was good, but the music of Leonard Bernstein was unforgettable. Trey puts it best; there *was* magic in that music. As Trey continues, he becomes pretty animated, waving his arms and singing the woodwind melody to "Somewhere." He says, "This is the part that used to kill me—it goes [he begins to sing the orchestration] boom, the basses are low, and then it modulates up, but the basses don't. So it's, like, to a key where it's dissonant. You know, Leonard Bernstein was right on the tail end of all that stuff that was going on, which was like the liberation of dissonance, which, of course, very quickly went too far, in my opinion. In a lot of people's opinion, I think. There was a moment where you lost melody to this math. But he was right at the cutting edge, and he was writing for a popular art form. Even though he was rebellious against it, he wanted to be taken seriously as a composer, but he was writing popular songs. But he put that stuff in there. And so at the end when they're doing, 'There's a'—do, do, do, do, do—'somewhere,' boom. [Trey does his best orchestral imitations, timpani included.] And it's like a minor third and then, 'Somewhere,' boom, and then it's like a—then it goes up again [Trey sings the highest high notes] and eventually it's—I'd have to go back and sit at a piano, but like a tritone away from the bass. And it feels completely unhinged and unsatisfying and the play ends. And it's just heart wrenching."

Trey understands musical form, and his ability to articulate it is unusual among the musicians I meet. Most are able to create and talk about the emotion of making music, but not the craft of making music. He tells me, "I read a book about Debussy's life as a child. He was in Paris at the time, had great schooling. They had great education. So every kid that was interested in music had to learn everything. Well, apparently, he was a very rebellious guy. All his teachers wrote—when he was fifteen, sixteen years old—'This guy's never going to go anywhere. He keeps trying to break all the rules.' But he knew all the rules, because everyone had to know all the rules. And the guy went on and reinvented harmony—reinvented harmony!—and reached what a lot of people would consider to be a level of beauty that no one's ever achieved since. And I would agree with that. That era, to me, Ravel and Debussy, is as good as it ever got. But you know, when I think about Leonard Cohen or something like that, he's clearly straddling that razor's edge between simplicity and literacy. I believe that's what it sounds like to me. I mean, I don't know, but he [Bernstein] is operating on a higher level, he didn't just stumble into it."

Back in 1988, at Vermont's Goddard College, Trey's thesis was a musical suite and concept album, *The Man Who Stepped into Yesterday.* (Songs from that unreleased record can be heard at Phish concerts; fans also know it from bootlegs.) Around that time, he and some friends from the University of Vermont began playing together.

Phish's success is nearly as much about community as it is music. The band, including Jon Fishman, Mike Gordon, and Page McConnell, gives so much to its audience, everything from Rollerblading around while wirelessly playing guitar, to handing out boxes of macaroni and cheese to serve as percussion shakers, to bubble machines, to beach balls that elicit a musical response onstage when they hit the crowd. There are also rubber chicken props and vacuum cleaners instead of woodwind instruments. On Halloween the band wears "musical costumes" and performs entire records by other bands, sometimes chosen by fan votes. One year they performed the Beatles' 1968 double album, known as *The White Album,* in its entirety. Another year, accompanied by a horn section, they performed The Who's rock opera *Quadrophenia.* They've also covered Talking Heads' *Remain in Light* and Pink Floyd's *The Dark Side of the Moon.* Their ability to re-create classic records nearly note for note speaks to their craft, joy, love, and appreciation for the musicians that have inspired them, and for their dedicated fans and the loving community they spontaneously create.

My earliest encounter with the music of Phish was a funny one. As director of *All Things Considered,* beginning in the early 1990s, I selected the music between the news stories. We call them "buttons," because they hold the show together, tying one story to the next. Part of my job was to sift through the many musical submissions sent in by publicists, record labels, and individual artists. One of those CDs was from Phish, a record called *Rift.* I distinctly remember skipping through to find instrumental break music, and breaking out laughing when I heard their song "All Things Reconsidered," a two-and-a-half-minute reimagining of the *All Things Considered* theme. Needless to say, after that day, the song was in heavy rotation during my shifts.

When I recently invited Trey for a Tiny Desk Concert, he was gracious and said he was humbled to perform for the many employees at NPR. If you watch the video, you can see him choke up a bit as he says, "It's funny, I want to say—my wife and I raised our kids in an old farmhouse in Richmond, Vermont, such beautiful memories of that time when the kids are running around. One of those things about that house is that we had a radio in the kitchen. We just left it on NPR. It was pretty much on VPR, Vermont Public Radio, all the time. It just was going when I made my coffee. The kids were running around, growing up. I sometimes would come down in the middle of the night and it would still be on. And what I was thinking was, for my wife, Sue, and I, you guys entertained us for so many years, so it's really an honor to be able to come in for about two minutes and actually do something for all of you . . . you're part of the fabric of our life, so thank you, I want to thank you for that."

These words are from a man with a good heart, the same good heart that keeps him and his band so generous to their fans and listeners. They're also from a man whose life went dark for a while, and who's grateful to the police officer who caught him meandering over the center yellow line in his car in 2006. He was arrested for driving while intoxicated, and for possession of heroin and other drugs, all part of a downward spiral that had begun a few years prior, during which he disappointed his bandmates and forced Phish into a nearly five-year hiatus. After fourteen months of treatment and community service, he came back healthy.

Phish's 2009 album, *Joy,* their fourteenth, marked Trey's return. Then in 2013, he was nominated for a Tony award for scoring *Hands on a Hardbody.* Based on S. R. Bindler's documentary of the same name, the show is about ten desperate families who enter a contest to win a new pickup truck. Trey worked on the score with lyricist and songwriter Amanda Green, who, incidentally and coincidentally, at the age of nine played the role of Maria in a summer camp production of *West Side Story.* Trey also worked with Pulitzer Prize–winning playwright and screenwriter Doug Wright, who wrote the book for *Hands on a Hardbody.* "This is what I learned sitting next to Doug and Amanda. . . . You have to come to the character. You can't spoon-feed the audience. You can lose them this quick [snaps his fingers quickly twice]. And that you can't spoon-feed the audience this information—tell me if this sounds like it makes sense. [Doug] would say that—and it's a balancing act—but sometimes sitting in the audience, you might know that the character is walking himself into a trap. The character doesn't even know. You know, and the writer knows, which means that you're being valued as part of the audience. . . . So then, I was driving along, and one of these many great Paul Simon songs came on. This has happened to me a couple of times with his stuff, any of them. [The song was] '50 Ways to Leave Your Lover.' You know she's trying to screw him. Paul Simon knows, but it's like he [the character in the song] doesn't even know. . . . It's like, tell me again. 'Let's just sleep on it tonight.' You know? And I realize that as a songwriter, he's operating on the level that Doug is trying to explain to me."

As Trey tells me this story, a part of me wonders how this could apply to a jam band guitarist. Then I start thinking about the nature of improvisation, which is about to be my next question in an attempt to connect the dots. Almost on cue, Trey says, "I mean, Sonny Rollins, let's talk musically instead of lyrically," and he begins to connect the dots for me, the lessons he learned doing Broadway and how they apply to playing music in a band. The short of it is this: When you practice enough to become really adept at something, it becomes part of your DNA. You don't even have to think about it anymore. The ability to think deeper and on a higher level just happens. It happened with Bernstein and Doug Wright, and I'll say it happens with Trey Anastasio. He continues, "Herbie Hancock recorded in my barn, and I got to do a song with him. He played the piano. We got to sit up one night, just me and him, and play—which was the greatest thing that's ever happened. And he was childlike in that he was such a good listener. We would kind of jam, but very, very simple, simple, simple, simple ideas. Not at all the tyranny of jazz knowledge. It didn't sound like that at all. But the forty, fifty years of learning everything there is to know about harmony, and then forgetting it, was in there. I don't even know how he was doing it. Nobody but Herbie Hancock could play like that. And he would tell us stories like, 'Oh, I was in France in 1950 and there was this piano player that we all idolized, and I asked him what he was doing with his chord voicing, and the guy would say, "You listen to the soloist and you try to create a chord with as many interpretations as possible. So when you play a note, I want to play a chord that could be a C-sharp minor chord, or you could look at it as an A-flat chord, and the reason is because I want to open doors for you, as opposed to close them."' That's a very high level of thinking."

For members of Phish and for the kind of music they create, music that evolves and changes on the fly, the key is listening.

"I feel like after thirty-one years of that band and then the other [Trey Anastasio Band] that all I try to do is listen. Like *all* I try to do is listen, and that means the audience, too. . . . There are moments when something is very simple and beneath that conscious mind—boy, it's hard to talk about this stuff without it sounding like a bunch of hooey—but it does make you feel it sometimes, that the thinking mind does go away . . . it's like martial arts or something like that. It takes an enormous amount of discipline to get to [that] point."

All the while he's talking about the play and improvisation, I can't stop thinking about his mom handing him that stack of Broadway original cast records. Parents, take that to heart. When it comes to our children, the simple gestures are the important ones, and you never know what will stick. Trey tells me, "My daughter was sidled up next to Doug [Wright] throughout [the] whole process because it took about six years—and now that's what she wants to do." The seemingly simple act of passing what you love to someone else has now impacted two generations of Anastasios, and who knows how many to come. I imagine a future Ernest Joseph Anastasio's birth certificate being ignored.

JENNY LEWIS

Jenny Lewis was raised a little differently. First of all, she grew up in Las Vegas, and her babysitter was a female Elvis impersonator. Ellis was her name. "We lived in a very modest one-bedroom apartment and she would listen to Elvis to get ready for her act. So my earliest memories are of hearing the Sun Records[-era] Elvis . . . it has such a spooky quality to it. It felt otherworldly. It felt like music beamed in from Mars."

This singer, known for the country-rock-flavored band Rilo Kiley and for her solo odd-edged pop, comes from a long tradition of performers. Her grandmother and grandfather danced in vaudeville, and her grandfather sang in his own act that toured with Bert Lahr

Jenny Lewis on stage in her Gram Parsons–inspired rainbow suit, designed by Adam Siegel, at the Newport Folk Festival in 2014.

(best known as the Cowardly Lion from *The Wizard of Oz*). Then her mother and father had a lounge act in Las Vegas called Love's Way. They split when Jenny was young, and her dad, Eddie Gordon, played harmonica in a band led by Johnny Puleo, known as "the little guy with the big talent" because Puleo was a little person. Eddie played for the pope, President Kennedy, and television stars like Milton Berle, Ed Sullivan, and the Smothers Brothers. Jenny's mother, Linda, was a singer in Las Vegas who owned a substantial record collection filled with the likes of Tammy Wynette, Dusty Springfield, Bette Midler, Laura Nyro, Dory Previn, Roberta Flack—all strong female voices. As a kid, Jenny liked to emulate another woman in her mom's collection: Patsy Cline. And then there was Barbra Streisand—every Sunday was Barbra day. Jenny was born Jewish, and I think it's not unreasonable to say that many Jewish kids heard a lot of Barbra growing up. I know I did. But Saturday was different; that was the day her mom played Lou Reed. Jenny was too young to understand what "Walk on the Wild Side" meant, but she knew she liked it.

When she was four years old, Jenny moved with her mom and older sister, also a singer, to the San Fernando Valley, in California. She formed her first real musical obsession around age nine, for Musical Youth's single "Pass the Dutchie." She thought it was about a Dutch oven, unaware that the original version by The Mighty Diamonds was called "Pass the Kouchie." A kouchie was a spliff, a joint of marijuana. Musical Youth had sanitized the lyrics, changing all the drug references into food references. That said, Dutchie or kouchie, the song was catchy. "I listened to it over and over and over again. I still love reggae music and Jamaican music, for whatever reason it just felt so good listening to that song."

Jenny was a child actress, not a terribly famous one but a breadwinner nonetheless. Her first role was in a Jell-O commercial. Then she appeared on television shows such as *Baywatch*, the new *Twilight Zone*, *The Golden Girls*, *Roseanne*, and *Mr. Belvedere*. There were movies, too, like *Big Girls Don't Cry, Pleasantville, Uncle Tom's Cabin,* and *Sweet Temptation.* Growing up on set made for some unusual company and unlikely friendships. One of her big musical influences was actually actor–teen heartthrob Corey Haim (best known for the film *The Lost Boys*): "When I was ten years old he gave me a cassette tape that had Run-D.M.C. on one side and the Beastie Boys on the other side. And that completely changed my life forever. I had never heard hip-hop. And it just spoke to me on such a deep level." Following that introduction, this ten-year-old self-described "white girl from the Valley" fell in love with hip-hop. She loved how the lyrics of the Run-D.M.C. song "Peter Piper" twisted the Humpty Dumpty and Peter Piper nursery rhymes in unimaginable ways. "And the Beastie Boys, it just felt like you were listening to the coolest kids that ever existed. It definitely changed what I would listen to for the next five or six years. Exclusively hip-hop. Only hip-hop."

A few years later, in 1988, *Yo! MTV Raps* launched, with rap videos, live performances, and interviews. "I remember getting on the phone with one of my best friends at the time, and we'd watch *Yo! MTV Raps,* and then we'd fall asleep on the telephone. And then wake up the next morning before school, like: Are you still there? Wasn't Big Daddy Kane amazing?" Rap filled the commercial airwaves as well. "KDAY, that was like the hip-hop underground station in Los Angeles. You really felt like you were in on something. It was like a big secret, you know. Like, you had to research the hip-hop acts before they became big. And then I got into kind of underground West Coast hip-hop, like Freestyle Fellowship, Del the Funky Homosapien, and Souls of Mischief. And I would go by myself to these shows when I was a teenager. And I actually had a moment with one of the guys in Freestyle Fellowship, where he was rapping and there was, like, a big circle of people. And I was really the only white girl there. And he did a freestyle and kind of singled me out in a not-so-positive way. And I just felt so betrayed because I was the biggest hip-hop fan. I was such a fan. And I was so happy to be there. And I loved the music so much. And I just felt like, man, maybe I can't be an MC. It dissuaded me because I really did—I wanted to be an MC."

Jenny wasn't entirely dissuaded, though, and spent a lot of time alone in her room creating her own kind of hip-hop with her Casio keyboard, its rhythm set to the marching beat preset. "I had one experience at another kind of freestyle session in the nineties, where Biz Markie was, like, guesting at this club in L.A. called the Gaslite. And it was kind of like an open freestyle-type session. And he laid down a verse, and then I grabbed the mic. This is my only time doing this in public, and I kind of destroyed the place. And that was the birth and then the retirement of my hip-hop career."

Jenny owned a little pink Sony cassette recorder with a built-in microphone. The first song she ever wrote was on that machine, the same one she used to play The Cure's singles collection over and over again. In fact, she recorded her first song right onto that cassette, covering the little tabs with Scotch tape to enable the machine to erase what was on the tape and record her song over it. It was set to her Casio's samba beat. "I just remember that being a kind of pivotal moment where listening to music became making music on the same little contraption."

Not long afterward, in 1993, Jenny met fellow teen actor Blake Sennett and everything changed. They fell in love, and by their early twenties they started writing music together and formed Rilo Kiley, whose first record was released in 1999. Rilo Kiley had a sort of country flair. You could hear it in Jenny's voice. The influence of her mother's record collection, from Patsy Cline to Barbra Streisand, can certainly be found in those early recordings.

When Jenny started her solo career in 2006, not only were her songs influenced by her mom, but her parents became their subject matter. And there were words, lots of words. I first met Jenny that year when I interviewed her for a live webcast of her concert at the 9:30 Club, supporting her first solo album, *Rabbit Fur Coat*. She talked a lot about her love for hip-hop then, and frankly, it surprised me. But as I listened to her music that night I could hear how hip-hop seeped into her country-ish sound. It was all in the wordplay. She'd overwrite, cramming more words into her songs than she could sing. She told me that she'd also write these call-and-responses for her two fabulous partners, the amazing country-singing sisters The Watson Twins, so that she could pack more lyrics into one verse than she could sing on her own.

Eight years later, in 2014, in the very same dressing room of the very same club, we meet again to talk about the music that changed her life, and she keeps coming back to hip-hop. She is touring with a full-on rock band with some country tinges for her third solo record, *The Voyager*. She wears a knockout pantsuit, perhaps inspired by those made famous by country-rock pioneer Gram Parsons. His distinctive outfits, often white and decorated with crosses and roses, marijuana leaves, and more, were known as Nudie suits, created by Ukrainian designer Nudie Cohn. Jenny's suit is similar—both cosmic and country, with its airbrushed waves of color—and there are stars on her shoes. It's funny, but in some ways her clothing choice represents her musical split as a lover of both country and hip-hop. Onstage she wears the cosmic pantsuit, but for our conversation backstage, she chooses a red tracksuit (she tells me she tours with twelve of them). It's a style, she admits, that comes from her love of hip-hop culture.

Jenny and I talk for a while about her mom's records and Corey Haim's cassette. And just when I think she might not have one moment, that her musical experiences are too numerous and broad, she tells me about A Tribe Called Quest and the record, or in this case the cassette, that changed her life at age fifteen: "I used to actually go to raves at this time, in the early nineties. And it would be like a carful of kids, teenagers. And I remember coming home from a late-night rave, [at] like five in the morning. I don't know where our parents were at this time. But we were listening to that cassette on repeat and 'What?' came on. I was like sitting on someone's lap in the backseat." The album was *The Low End Theory*, and the song that knocked her out is a series of thought-provoking questions:

What is a poet? All balls, no cock
What is a war if it doesn't have a general?
What's Channel Nine if it doesn't have Arsenio?

"I think it's the simplicity and the wordplay. And it was something that I could learn after hearing it once. But it was so clever, the lyrics were so smart." *The Low End Theory*, A Tribe Called Quest's second album, was a groundbreaking record not only for its sound, one that's relatively spare and features the great jazz double-bassist Ron Carter, but because it forged a bond between hip-hop and jazz. For Jenny Lewis, though, sitting on someone's lap in the backseat, and for many teens of the day, its power lay in its authenticity. She says, "This is real. This is the real shit." I could say the same about some of her songs, and after speaking with her, I'll never listen to "Rise Up With Fists!!," "Acid Tongue," "Asshole," or "Just One of the Guys" without thinking about her influences. It's all about the words for Jenny.

DAVE GROHL

God Bless Aunt Sherry. Without her there would be no Nirvana or Foo Fighters. And a brilliant ambassador for rock? We might still be looking for one.

Dave Grohl—drummer for Nirvana, singer, songwriter, and guitarist for Foo Fighters, and participant in hundreds of other projects—grew up in Washington, D.C.'s suburban backyard, Springfield, Virginia. His mom was a schoolteacher, his dad a news writer, speechwriter, and musician. The apple didn't fall far from the tree. Like his mom, he's a teacher, and like his dad, a public speaker and musician. For a kid born in 1969, D.C. was a brilliant place for hard-hitting music, though Dave didn't discover that fact until he visited his aunt Sherry. "First show that I ever saw was in Chicago. I went to . . . visit my relatives that lived in Evanston, Illinois. I think I was, like, twelve or thirteen years old. . . . I got there to Chicago, and my cousin Tracy had turned into a punk rocker, and I was so blown away. I had never seen a punk rocker in my life. It was like seeing Spider-Man or something. I was like, This is so cool. . . . That night she was gonna go see this punk rock band at a club—a band called Naked Raygun—and the club was called the Cubby Bear. It was right across the street from Wrigley Field. . . . I think my aunt Sherry pressured her to take us with her . . . I think she said, like, 'Well, Tracy, maybe the boys want to go to the show.' And [Tracy] looked and was like, 'Oh, God, they're gonna get their asses kicked.' And that was the first time I ever saw a band. And it was this punk band in a tiny club. I'd never had my belly up against the lip of a stage as a singer was on top of my head with, like, a hundred-and-forty-decibel guitar in my face, you know? I mean, that is a life-changing event, where you're just like, 'This is the most—this is so real. I never want anything—everything else is not real.' You know? And so that really, it just turned me, man. Like, that was it. And I went record collecting. I went to Wax Trax [in Chicago] and bought all these records. And it's funny, because when I was there, I bought a lot of records of bands from here [D.C.]. I'd pick up a Minor Threat record and look up the address on the back, like, Wait, that's where I live. Or a Scream record, which is really where I live. You know, Bailey's Crossroads was the P.O. box. And I came back from that to my friends [and] our little neighborhood band that played Rolling Stones covers and I'm like, 'No, no, no, you guys. We can write *our own* songs, and we only need three chords!' And they're like, 'No way, Dave.'" Like I said, God bless Aunt Sherry.

At that time, in the early eighties, the D.C. scene was thrilling. Before then, club owners' business model was based entirely on bar sales, so they'd kept the under-twenty-one crowd out. The 9:30 Club was one of the first major venues to change that policy, by allowing underage kids in and scrawling a big *X* on their hands to alert the bartenders not to serve them alcohol. I remember going to the 9:30 Club's three-bands-for-three-bucks night. The bands and the fans were young, real young, not like the twenty-plus-year-olds who followed Tiny Desk Unit back when the club opened in 1980.

When Grohl sits down to speak with my *All Songs Considered* cohost, Robin Hilton, and me at our NPR office in the fall of 2014, I hand him his tea in a 9:30 Club mug. "You guys thought you were so cool with your 9:30 Club cup," he says with a big grin. I tell him that I was in the first band to play there, and he lights up. "You were in Tiny Desk Unit? Are you kidding me? Oh my God! No way!" D.C. was heaven for kids like Grohl and guys like me, in my late twenties, who were desperate to be in a band. It was also relatively easy to become a big fish in a small pond—the community was hungry for new music; the clubs were new, few, and looking for kids to become regulars. Like the punk scenes in England, New York, Chicago, and Los Angeles, D.C. was wide open for kids eager to make music. So when Grohl returned from his visit to Aunt Sherry's, it was as if the stars had aligned. "The first thing I did when I got home was go to the Rock Against Reagan concert on the Mall." It was during the long Fourth of July weekend, 1983, at the foot of the Lincoln Memorial. "*That's* my Woodstock. You know? Like, that was what changed my life, because I thought at twelve or at thirteen years old, I was in the middle of a revolution. And it was musical. So you have, like, seven hundred thousand people that come in from Maryland and Virginia with coolers full of Southern Comfort. And . . . they just want to hear, like, The Beach Boys. Watch the fireworks. And there's Dead Kennedys in the middle of all of that. Like, yeah, man! Totally changed my life."

But for a kid in the suburbs, finding a band wasn't so simple. He'd set up pillows on his bed as if they were drums and pound them until, as he said in his 2013 SXSW keynote address, "there was literally sweat dripping down the Rush posters on my walls." What you hear when you listen to Grohl speak, whether it's a keynote address or a casual conversation, is utter determination. He still possesses the drive and passion he put into pounding those pillows so many years ago, and tells stories in ways I've never heard from any other musician I've interviewed. Eventually, Grohl found a neighborhood band and then another and another, all inspired by the local punk scene—bands like Bad Brains, Minor Threat, and Scream.

Then, at the age of seventeen, this son of a classically trained musician and a schoolteacher dropped out of high school. "I think from an early age, they understood that this was something that was not going to leave me. Nobody really wants to see their child give up school, but I think that my mother always thought that it wasn't necessarily the kid that fails the school. Sometimes it's the school that fails the kid. And for someone like me, whose brain might not work like everybody else's, that it might be better to find another way to become myself. Because it wasn't necessarily happening there. So it wasn't easy. I mean, I worked at Marlo's Furniture Warehouse for a while, worked at Tower Records for a while, and did my thing. But, you know, I'm thankful that they understood there was something inside me that was gonna help me make my way out. And if there was a way that I could hitch that thing and take a ride, that it wouldn't be a bad idea."

Remember the Scream record he found in Chicago, the one with the Bailey's Crossroads P.O. box on the back? At age nineteen Grohl became the band's drummer, playing on their fourth album, *No More Censorship,* and by twenty-one he was touring Europe. Then, in 1990, Scream broke up unexpectedly. "I found myself stranded in Hollywood without a cent to my name and no way home, crashed out in a Laurel Canyon bungalow with a bunch of female mud wrestlers." Then he found Nirvana, and the rest is legend.

Thirty years later, Dave Grohl is hosting and performing at a five-hour show to celebrate the music of Washington, D.C. There's punk and go-go, all part of the Foo Fighters' new album and HBO project

Sonic Highways. Both focus on and explore the relationship between geography and music in ten American cities. One of those cities is Chicago, the place where it all began for him at the Cubby Bear: "That moment where my belly was up against the stage and the lead singer of Naked Raygun was on top of my head, that was that moment that lit that fire in me." Grohl spent a week in each city as part of the *Sonic Highways* project, interviewing artists about their town and gathering inspiration for his band's new album.

For him, music is distinctly linked to location, Grohl tells me: "When you go to a city and spend a good six or seven days there, talk to all of the people, not just about the musical history, but the culture of that city, and how it's influenced everything about that place: the food, the accent, the music. You know? Maybe music has an accent. Maybe that's what it is. Like, every city you go to, like, Oh, man. That sounds like Athens, Georgia. Listen to Pylon. Listen to R.E.M. . . . As you go around the country, you find these little communities where people would get together and it would, like, germinate and then grow into something that would become a regional movement. And I think it's beautiful, and amazing, and also, an interesting discussion now—as everything's interconnected—how do those things happen? This is one of the things that we talk about in the D.C. episode. The city was really sort of divided in a lot of ways. Not only was it racially divided, but it was kind of musically divided. But then, also, you know, you've got the richest city in the world and the poorest. And a homeless population . . . you've got someone—a homeless man—sleeping at the base of the Lincoln Memorial steps. And you're like, How could this possibly happen? So I think that music is such a beautiful language and a communicator—connector—[and] that somewhere in between Trouble Funk and Minor Threat, there's that place where it's really healing."

Historically, the Chicago music scene is perhaps most connected with the blues, so you might wonder what a band like Naked Raygun, with blistering songs like "Surf Combat," which focuses on napalm and horror, has to do with the blues. But musical communities often form as a reaction to their environment. For instance, when Dave Grohl interviewed the lead singer of Naked Raygun, Jeff Pezzati, in 2013, he asked him if he liked the blues. Pezzati's response: "No, man. It's too repetitive and it bums me out." When I mention this to Dave, he agrees and says, "Yeah, I mean, I think that a lot of those punk rock scenes or communities, they were definitely a reaction to the musical climate at the time."

Chicago's music, including the blues, continues to influence Grohl. After recently interviewing a number of musicians there, he was inspired by Buddy Guy, one of Chicago's blues legends. As a younger man Buddy Guy was so determined to play, he would construct instruments from pieces of his screen porch, or buttons and a rubber band, or a string nailed to a board strapped across a glass bottle. "Something from Nothing," a recent Foo Fighters song, is the result of Grohl's meeting with Guy. "He'd, like, take a wire and make a guitar, and he didn't even have a radio. He was just hearing music in his head. He started playing it. When I interviewed him, he told me that once he found a chord, he kept playing it. He didn't want to stop playing it until someone heard him playing it, so he just walked until he found someone. And he played the chord till his fingers were bleeding, man. . . . You know, it's funny. It doesn't matter if you're Chuck D, or if you're Dolly Parton, or you're Willie Nelson, or you're Gibby Haynes from Butthole Surfers. Everyone has had the moment in their life where they just go, [snaps fingers] 'Okay. I'm gonna do this.' It doesn't matter what it is—it could be seeing Roy Orbison. It could be seeing Naked Raygun. You know? It could be seeing *American Idol*. Whatever it is, you see it, and it makes you—it just lights that fire. As a drummer, growing up here—I mean, oh my God—because D.C. had its roots in this rhythm that was the rhythm of the city. Now, this is something that influences every city. Like, even, you go to New Orleans, man, they're like the sound of the paddle wheel in the river. Those things, by osmosis, make their way into you. And growing up here in Washington, D.C., I was playing crazy punk rock music. But you walk down the street and you see a drummer with paint buckets tearing it up, it's inevitable that that's gonna make its way into what you do." And for Dave Grohl, guitarist, drummer, singer, songwriter, and ambassador of rock and roll, it most certainly did.

CAT STEVENS

When I was seventeen years old I worked at a summer camp in upstate New York, Camp Greene Hollow. I was a counselor for five-, six-, and seven-year-old boys. These kids, many away from their parents for the first time, were my responsibility for about two months, and I'd never taken care of a child in my life. It was daunting. The kids cried, wet their beds, and held their teddy bears, but in time we had a ball. It was 1970, and I wore my hair long and parted down the middle, with my homemade macramé necklace around my neck, and to no one's surprise, I loved music. I brought an armful of records to camp with me and taught a rock music appreciation class to those kids (I smile as I write this). We listened

After his Tiny Desk Concert at NPR, Robin Hilton and I had to take this picture with a man we both deeply admire, Yusuf Islam (aka Cat Stevens).

to The Beatles, Dylan, Donovan, The Doors, and many others that surely went over their sweet little heads. The camp, in Hunter, New York, wasn't far from Woodstock, which the year before had become famous for giving its name to the iconic music festival, though the festival actually took place a good sixty miles away in Bethel. The town of Hunter was a haven for hippies and musicians, and I felt a kinship with its residents—even though I distinctly recall getting swindled one Saturday night when I tried to buy hashish. I ended up with a ball of bubblegum and crushed incense.

I returned home that August much wiser, thanks to those kids, and I had learned to care for others more than myself. I was about to enter my final year of high school in Bethesda, Maryland. Two years prior, my family had left Queens. I didn't have lots of friends in Bethesda and missed my New York stickball buddies. I was lonely, and music became my best friend. I bought a lot of records.

Five years earlier, in 1965, The Beatles had inspired me, like a thousand other teenagers, to pick up the guitar. When my guitar teacher told my mom I had no musical ability, I was crushed and stopped playing. But with the fifty dollars I made as a counselor at Camp Greene Hollow, I bought a nylon-string guitar, determined to learn to play. It was cheap and hurt my fingertips, and in some ways, my teacher was right. It was hard for me to get my hands to do what my brain wanted. However, I don't believe it's ever okay for a teacher to tell a kid in love with music that they have no ability.

That November Cat Stevens released *Tea for the Tillerman*. I bought the record for its beautiful cover, a watercolor painting of a jolly, bearded old man sitting in the forest sipping tea while children climb a tree as the sun sets. It was an intimate album, a different sort of music for me. At the time "soft rock," as it was called, seemed a psychedelic phrase, and the term later became pejorative, though it's still an apt description—rock that is soft in both heart and sound. I loved *Tea for the Tillerman* and learned to sing and play almost every song on the album. "Father and Son" is the one I recall playing most. It's about a conversation between a father and son, in which the father tries to persuade his son not to go to war. When the album was released, this story felt highly personal, as I was about to become eligible for the draft during a time when kids right out of high school were fighting a war in Vietnam, and the ones I knew had either died or returned home dramatically changed.

Now, forty-five years later, at my desk at NPR, Cat Stevens plays "Father and Son." His son, Yoriyos, kneels behind me. I listen and think about my own son at college in Rochester. The song's familiar chords and lyrics bring to mind the passage of time, the loss of my own father, and my happiness at having a bright, wonderful child. I begin to cry.

Cat Stevens's life changed in 1976, when he nearly drowned off the coast of Malibu. He tells me that he pleaded for God to save him and shouted to the heavens, "Oh God! If you save me I will work for you." Then a strong wave swept him to shore and he dedicated his life to serving God. He studied the Koran his brother had given him and converted to Islam. In 1978, he took the name Yusuf Islam, stopped releasing pop music, and devoted his life to the Muslim community. Twenty-eight years passed before he released another album.

After the Tiny Desk Concert, Robin Hilton and I move into our studio with Yusuf Islam to chat. Yusuf is a charming man, happy and congenial. He was born Steven Demetre Georgiou and grew up above a café called the Moulin Rouge in West London that his mom and dad managed. His Swedish mother played simple lullabies with one finger on a small grand piano that barely fit in their tiny living room. His dad is Greek Cypriot, and Yusuf's half brother from his dad's first marriage played bouzouki and violin. All of this eventually crept into his music. Their area in West London was full of theaters, and he tells me that musicals were a considerable influence: "There was a theater and I used to stand in the stage door and listen to the music coming out. Gershwin's *Porgy and Bess* was very big for me because my sister had the record. And then *West Side Story* just blew it all apart. That was it for me. Well, me and my friends. And we just kind of made up a gang called the Belts. And actually I think [Leonard] Bernstein had the big effect on my music because . . . in the early days when I started doing it and making it, he was a model for me. And it was very staccato. I loved that. . . . One of the all-time classic songs for me was . . . 'Somewhere.' And that song was just like—it was everything to me. It was everything."

In a conversation I had with Trey Anastasio of Phish, we talked about this very song, and about the power of its orchestration. I find Stephen Sondheim's words particularly moving, especially in the context of this *Romeo and Juliet* story set on the Upper West Side of New York City. In the final scene Tony, the Romeo of the story, is shot and Maria, the Juliet, holds him in her arms as he dies. Yusuf connects this song to The Beatles, something I've never done. John Lennon and Paul McCartney wrote an early single, "There's a Place," which I owned on a 45 put out by a short-lived label called Tollie Records. Yusuf is sure Lennon and McCartney were inspired by "Somewhere," and Yusuf *loved* The Beatles. But it's the flip side of that single from his sister's collection that changed his life, their rocking, screaming cover of "Twist and Shout."

At first it's impossible for me to imagine how this particular tune influenced Yusuf's music, but it did. "I think I was about fifteen and my dad was kind enough to lend me or to give me eight quid, eight pounds to buy my first guitar, an Italian thing. I sounded awful. I said, I'm gonna give this up. . . . And then I picked it up again and you know what, it all started working. It was kinda like a thing which just became natural. I was perhaps trying too hard in the beginning. And then that's where it started and then I started transposing what I learned on guitar onto piano. So that's how I learned the piano. I was so bad at playing other people's songs that I started writing my own almost immediately. But 'Twist and Shout' was like 'La Bamba.' It's, like, three chords. It's very, very easy, so that's where I started."

Yusuf's sister, Anita, owned a diverse record collection, which wasn't unusual in those days, when the radio played all sorts of music on the very same station. "She had a kind of cross of classics and smoochy like Frank Sinatra, Nat King Cole, that kinda stuff. She had these classics like Beethoven and Tchaikovsky, and I loved those. And I used to love painting while listening to those records. I was watching all this landscape happening, a musical landscape, and I was just drawing as I listened. So it became a big thing for me to listen while I was drawing. And I think that kind of led, in some way, in the future, to me telling stories and painting with words and music. And that's kinda what I do."

I love the image of him painting while listening to music. His albums were all the more magic for those watercolor covers. "I couldn't get a grip of oils. They took too long to dry and so many other things, and it smudged, whereas somehow I got away with watercolors. . . . My first ambition, I suppose, before the musical one, was to be an artist like my uncle from Sweden, who was an abstract artist." When Cat Stevens was considering album art for *Tea for the Tillerman*, Chris Blackwell, the owner of his label, Island Records, had an idea. "He said, 'Well, why don't you do it?' Really? This is great to hear that from a music boss." And those covers helped define Cat Stevens. There was a lot of wonderful album art in the seventies, but the innocence of his watercolors set his records apart. The sense of unity between his paintings and his music felt whole, not abstract, and without pretense. He tells me that sometimes his painting inspired his music: "I learned, probably late in my life, that if you spun a disk with all the colors on it, it would turn white. And so that was the theme for my song 'Into White.'" That song on *Tea for the Tillerman* was a defining one, and there's much beauty in its poetry:

I built my house from barley rice
Green pepper walls and water ice
Tables of paper wood, windows of light
And everything emptying into white

The recordings were striking, with his guitar strumming that meshed perfectly with his partner Alun Davies's fingerpicking and, perhaps most of all, with Paul Samwell-Smith's sparse orchestration. "It was kind of a marrying together of my knowledge of—or my love of—classical music, and the simplicity of my demos, which is what I wanted to capture."

When Yusuf Islam returned to the recording studio in 2014 for his new album, *Tell 'Em I'm Gone,* he teamed with legendary producer Rick Rubin. Rubin is known for producing and popularizing rap and hip-hop, and for his later stripped-down work with Johnny Cash. According to Yusuf, Rubin's intention was to create a record similar to *Tea for the Tillerman.* "But I had all these blues songs in my pocket and I said, 'These are the things which interest me now.' Anyway, he kind of did an about turn. He turned around and he said, 'Okay. We can work with this.' And then somehow the musicians they picked were perfect, particularly Matt Sweeney, who had been working with a group called Tinariwen, so he had a kind of African bluesy approach. And one of the songs I wanted to really get under my belt was this song 'Take This Hammer,' which is sort of the title track of my album *Tell 'Em I'm Gone.* . . . Lead Belly was one of those first iconic blues players who I could play because it was very simple. All the chords were, like, three chords and that's it. . . . I had a kind of rule with this album. I wanted to get at least seven songs done in a week. And I just made everybody conform to that kind of timetable. And because of that it became live, very live. Otherwise you could spend a year—you know, you can—I didn't wanna do that. I just wanted to get it out because it had a live feeling. It had a kinda vital mood I wanted to get out, and that was it."

When Yusuf first told me "Twist and Shout" was the song that changed his life, I didn't see the connection between that song and his music. I understood it as a catalyst, the song that moved him to pick up a guitar, not as a source of inspiration. However, with the album *Tell 'Em I'm Gone*, his passion for spontaneity is clear. The Beatles recorded their version of "Twist and Shout" in under fifteen minutes. And *Tell 'Em I'm Gone* is filled with three-chord songs like that.

There's always been a simple sort of elegance to the music of Cat Stevens. A bit of strings here and there, some big drum sounds now and again, plus intricate fingerpicking. But its essence can be found in three chords, the same three chords found in Lead Belly and in Ritchie Valens's "La Bamba." They're also the same three chords I learned to play as a seventeen-year-old on my fifty-dollar nylon-stringed guitar.

STURGILL SIMPSON

"In a weird way, [for] a lot of time in my life, music felt like a curse because it was this thing I loved more than anything in the world. I just felt like I could never get anywhere with it. You'd pour your heart and all your effort into this thing and spin your wheels for years, playing in the same club in some local band, [and] it was just like, Wow, I'm really fooling myself with this. This is like a total delusional pipe dream. It's time to get a job. Mom was right. And then you go do that and you're more miserable than ever. But from the time I was three years old, I don't remember ever caring or . . . being so obsessively in love with anything else. I lost my mind

Sturgill Simpson at the newly opened City Winery, part of the Americana Music Festival in Nashville, Tennessee.

three or four years ago and decided to move to Nashville and be a songwriter. And now I'm sitting here talking to you."

That's Sturgill Simpson and the "here" is Washington, D.C.'s 9:30 Club, where in half an hour, twelve hundred people will come through the door to hear this talented country singer and songwriter. His musical obsession started long ago in southeast Kentucky: he remembers standing on the front seat of his mom's car listening to John Anderson sing "Wild and Blue." Sturgill was four years old and his mom played a lot of country music on the radio, but it was more than just the radio; in a sense music is in his DNA, as it is in the culture of Kentucky. "Both my grandfathers played music, mostly country and traditional bluegrass, so those are the first sonic imprints my ears ever received. My mother's father was in Jackson, Kentucky, which is southeast Kentucky, Appalachia, and my dad's father lived about forty miles down the road, even farther east, in Hyman. When I was around both of them it was a pretty great deal as a little child, especially Mama's father. He listened to a lot of old Marty Robbins, Merle Haggard—I remember they had one of those old—you know, the old wooden furniture-type record players . . . it sounded amazing. And so between his eight-tracks—he had an eight-track player fitted for that stereo and she had this old endless stack of 45s of old Motown and Stax and soul music. She loved that stuff. . . . '(Sittin' on) The Dock of the Bay' probably got played most." At age five, Sturgill was allowed to play any record he wanted. "I was a pretty methodical kid. So once I was able to touch that, whenever we'd go to my grandparents' house I went straight to the basement—because it just sounded so good. I'd give anything to have that in my house now." There were two songs he most wanted to hear as a child, Otis Redding's "(Sittin' on) The Dock of the Bay" and Bill Monroe's "Wayfaring Stranger."

Otis Redding got his start working with the incomparable Little Richard, and both artists were raised in Georgia. Redding is one of the greatest voices of soul and gospel. His sound has a good deal of guts and throat and a whole lot of sweat. Besides Little Richard, Redding was also inspired by Sam Cooke. Sadly, both died at a tragically young age: Cooke was shot at age thirty-three, in December 1964, and Redding died on tour at the tender age of twenty-six, in December 1967, when his twin-propeller Beechcraft plane crashed in a lake near its destination of Madison, Wisconsin. A mere three days before, Redding had put the finishing touches on "(Sittin' on) The Dock of the Bay." He was inspired by a recent houseboat stay in Sausalito to write it with guitarist Steve Cropper. The song is out of character for Redding, more pop than soul, reflecting his love for The Beatles' *Sgt. Pepper's Lonely Hearts Club Band,* which had come out a few months earlier, in June 1967. He recorded the original whistling melody at the end because he forgot the rest of the tune, though on the recording we all know it's performed by his bandleader, Sam "Bluzman" Taylor. Steve Cropper had trouble mixing the song, and Taylor's whistle helped end it. Like Sam Cooke's signature song, "A Change Is Gonna Come," Redding's biggest hit came after his death.

There's something so sad to me about the fact that Otis Redding never heard the finished version of his biggest hit. The wistful tones of the infamous whistle, along with the seagulls and crashing waves, made for a fitting, solemn farewell. Sturgill comments, "The opening stanza, where you have the ocean rolling and you can hear the seagull, that was like magic. I don't know why. And then when that bass line came in and they dropped the groove and he started singing—I was mesmerized. I would listen to that one over and over and over. Otis Redding . . . is still my favorite singer of all time."

Sturgill tells me almost everyone in his family plays an instrument: "Yeah, Grandpa would play an old Gibson." When he grew older, Sturgill picked up the guitar, too. "Through puberty I locked myself in my room and learned how to play the guitar. Like three or four years just disappeared. I went to the military and didn't touch one. I traveled in the military over to Asia and the West Coast

[with] girlfriends and friends. You get turned on to all these things you never would've probably discovered . . . [and] in that moment or period of discovery when I was out kind of like feeling the world, so to speak, I lost myself. I went to all the wrong parties, met all the wrong people. Next thing you know you're completely in this other realm of existence. I was across the country from everything I ever knew and understood and just sort of embraced it and ran with that. After I got out of the navy, stayed out in Seattle for a good year, [and] got into nothing good, and [then] kinda reached the point where, all right, it's time to go home. . . .

"Looking back on it, it's so easy to see, but when you're twenty, twenty-one-years old you don't realize when you've lost yourself. I was so laid-back in high school. . . . I came home after the navy and all my friends were like, Oh, who the hell is this guy, because they just wire you so tight. And I was just lost, man. I didn't know what to do with my life or anything. And I was driving—I'll never forget, I was driving an S15 GMC Sierra pickup and there's probably an NPR station or, like, WRVG . . . and they played a Bill Monroe song, 'Wayfaring Stranger,' and it was something. I remembered those sounds from my childhood. It resonated so hard. There was something in his voice and that song had feeling, it really felt like home, and I had to pull the truck over, and then all of a sudden I was like, I'm gonna learn. I don't know, it hit a musical nerve [or] something—I realized, I'm wasting my life. I'm not doing what I should be doing kinda thing. And from that point on, I'm talking early twenties, I became obsessed with old bluegrass and Appala-chian blues and country music. . . . I would search and dig [up] any-thing I could find. And I really just got into that. I started playing in my first band because of that."

The song Sturgill remembers hearing as a kid, and then once again as a young man, was by another Kentuckian, the father of bluegrass, Bill Monroe. His music is a mix of Irish and English storytelling songs, which found a home in Appalachia during the eighteenth century. It was dance music, too, with elements of jazz played deftly by Monroe on his mandolin. The breakneck pace of bluegrass is reminiscent of and inspired by Irish and Scottish reels and jigs. But Monroe also played ballads, and "Wayfaring Stranger" is one absolutely perfect, plaintive example. It's a tale about a lost soul who wanders on foot through a "world of woe."

I know dark clouds will hover o'er me
I know my pathway is rough and steep
But golden fields lie out before me
Where weary eyes no more will weep

It's not hard to imagine a lost soul like Sturgill, with deep Kentucky roots, hearing those lyrics sung in that high lonesome way Monroe made famous and experiencing a life-changing moment. The song touches my Brooklyn soul. Its sense of yearning is undeniable.

After that day, Sturgill bought a Martin guitar and became serious about songwriting. He played bluegrass with the Lexington band Sunday Valley and, for a year or so, attempted a solo career in Nashville, but his brand of straight country couldn't find an audience in the more pop-leaning locale. He drank a lot, and his drinking became a problem. Then a friend got him a job in a Salt Lake City freight yard, and he got sober and has been since. "I had a great job with the railroad, a good salary. I was like, I'm gonna quit this and gonna be a songwriter, because that's what I'm supposed to do." He lived with his then girlfriend, now wife, Sarah, who encouraged him to leave the freight yard, sell everything, and follow his dream. The year was 2012.

He made his first solo record, *High Top Mountain,* in 2013. The album's title refers to the cemetery in Jackson, Kentucky, where many in the Simpson family are buried. Sturgill self-funded and self-released it. Though it was recorded in Nashville, it goes against the polish of the current sound there, leaning more toward the traditional sound he loves, music akin to what outlaw country folks like Waylon Jennings were creating in response to mainstream Nashville in the sixties. You could call it a more "authentic" sound, and it's certainly a rawer sound than you're likely to hear on most Nashville recordings these days.

About a year later, Sturgill shifted the focus of his lyrics from drinking to thinking, and through that change found his audience. He told NPR's Ann Powers, "I just reached a point where the thought of writing and singing any more songs about heartache and drinking made me feel incredibly bored with music. It's just not a headspace I occupy much these days. Nighttime reading about theology, cosmology, and breakthroughs in modern physics and their relationship to a few personal experiences I've had led to most of the songs on the album." His next album, *Metamodern Sounds in Country Music,* wasn't so much a shift of sound as it was a shift of theme. It appealed to young listeners who normally dismiss country music for the same reason he changed his style—they're tired of songs about women and booze. I'm one of them. I seldom listen to modern country music, but his record, especially the opening words to "Turtles All the Way Down," simply fascinates me:

I've seen Jesus play with flames
In a lake of fire that I was standing in
Met the devil in Seattle
And spent nine months inside the lion's den
Met Buddha yet another time
And he showed me a glowing light within
But I swear that God is there
Every time I glare in the eyes of my best friend

The song was inspired by French philosophy, Dr. Rick Strassman's book *DMT: The Spirit Molecule,* Ralph Waldo Emerson's essay

"Nature," and Sturgill's experience on hallucinogens. It also came at the encouragement of his wife, who was weary of his philosophical rants. He told NPR's Rachel Martin about her frustrations: "'You're probably gonna drive yourself crazy, but you're definitely driving *me* crazy, so maybe you should get this out of your system and write some songs about it.' And I thought, That's a great idea."

The album's name is a playful twist on a 1962 Ray Charles classic, *Modern Sounds in Country and Western Music*. There's sweetness to the title, and it goes to the heart of Sturgill's music. The record opens with an old man's voice that sounds as if it's played on a timeworn phonograph (ironically, it was recorded on a cell phone). The man introduces the title and stumbles a bit through the opening words, "metamodern sounds in country music." I later found out it was voiced by "Dood" Fraley, Sturgill's grandfather, the man who gave him his musical education. Part of that education came from watching the country music entertainment show *Hee Haw* on The Nashville Network. Dood was raised on the Grand Ole Opry, which he used to listen to on his radio in eastern Kentucky. The Grand Ole Opry is the longest-running radio broadcast in history, and it helped Dood distinguish the great performers from the fakes. Sturgill tells me his grandfather thought of the program as magic coming out of a box. For anyone who makes country music, playing the stage at the Grand Ole Opry is the greatest honor. So when the day came and Sturgill played that stage, it was a huge point of pride. In the article "Sturgill Simpson on Playing the Grand Ole Opry," on the Saving Country Music website, he recounts his grandfather's reaction: "He told me, 'That's it, bud . . . that's the biggest honor in country music. That's what you've been working so hard for all these years, whether you knew it or not. If you never sing or record another note, you ain't gotta prove nothing else to nobody after that. Don't worry about what they're doing now, just go do it your way and I'll be right there with ya.'"

"Do it your way" is just what Sturgill does so well. And as we sit on the balcony before his show, a line forms outside the 9:30 Club, a venue more often associated with rock music. This isn't just another night. Sturgill has made country music believers out of nonbelievers. "It was like three or four months ago, all of a sudden some—I don't know what the catalyst was, because—I mean, up until six months ago, even when the record had just come out we were still hitting towns and hoping there'd be a hundred, hundred fifty people there. And then it was almost, I wanna say overnight, but it was definitely between one tour and the next, like, holy shit, what's happening here? And now we're selling out the 9:30 Club in D.C., and packing rooms in New York playing country music. I honestly don't know why this is happening."

I do, and I bet his grandfather does, too.

JUSTIN VERNON

"It really felt like I was lifting off the ground." That's how Justin Vernon describes the song that changed his life, a moment that happened mere months before our interview.

As a music journalist who's spent years speaking with a variety of artists, I've found that life-altering musical moments tend to happen during the formative years—teens, maybe twenties. With many musical milestones since he recorded Bon Iver's *For Emma, Forever Ago* in 2007, it's astonishing that music can still change Justin in such a profound way at age thirty-three, especially since it has always played a significant role in his life. "I played music with my brother a lot. And I sang with my sister growing up, and Mom and Dad were really musical. We always had music going on in the house."

As a teenager, Justin loved the Indigo Girls, the duo from Decatur. Emily Saliers and Amy Ray produced the first music that truly touched him. "I'll never point at anyone higher than Amy. She's kind of my musical living mentor, just her spirit, how she carries herself in her songs, and just a fever for music. I think it's always been a thing and it continues to be." Amy Ray has experienced Justin's passion for her music firsthand. "She's seen my chest tattoo with the Indigo Girls lyrics and everything." The lyrics from "Fugitive" tattooed above his left nipple read: I SAID REMEMBER THIS AS HOW IT SHOULD BE. Directly above is a tattoo of Wisconsin, Justin's home state, with the six counties he loves highlighted in red.

Eau Claire and its surrounding counties are not merely home base for Justin Vernon. They also represent an attitude, a sentiment, a place he thought he'd outgrown when he and his bandmates moved to Raleigh, North Carolina, in 2005. But he moved back in 2006, brokenhearted, bandless, and sick with mononucleosis. The backstory to *For Emma, Forever Ago* is often told: Justin seeks refuge in his father's Wisconsin cabin, finds his voice, not just his falsetto but his emotional connection to place and a way to express his feelings that goes beyond mere words. He recorded the album as Bon Iver and released it independently in 2007. In 2008 it was more widely distributed by Jagjaguwar, and it touched the hearts of many. I bet a thousand bands formed because of that album, and I distinctly remember the first time I heard its opening cut, "Flume," in the fall of 2007. Even though the words were a puzzle to me, the vulnerable emotion was clear and the simple acoustic arrangement felt timeless.

NPR Music presented Bon Iver at SXSW in 2008. After the show, Justin was upset because he had misplaced his fanny pack, which contained his few important possessions. The band and I took a stroll through the park across from the Parish, where they had just played, and talked about how the three friends came together. Sean Carey recalled spending hours learning the drum parts to *For Emma, Forever Ago* from Justin's MySpace page. Afterward, he approached Justin at a show, told him he knew all the parts, and wound up playing with him that night. Michael Noyce was one of Justin's guitar students and, in 2007, still a college student. Michael laughed at how Justin convinced him to drop out of school and come on tour. They were new at this then, and the band's success was still on the horizon, but I think they could sense that.

Bon Iver's self-titled second album was also created in a space with a deep personal connection for Justin, and it's no coincidence that his life-changing musical moment happened there as well. He and his brother Nate bought a dilapidated veterinary clinic in Fall Creek, Wisconsin, in 2008. On the site of an old swimming pool, they built April Base Studios. Justin has a lot of history in this area. The studio and clinic are only a few miles from where he grew up, a short drive from where he was schooled in jazz and religious studies on the University of Wisconsin's Eau Claire campus, and near a bar called Joynt where his parents first met.

The studio became their special place, a home as much as a creative space—and not just for Bon Iver. When Justin had his life-changing moment at April Base, he was working with a band called The Staves, a trio of sisters from Watford, England. It was the tenth record he had worked on within an eighteen-month period, and he was pretty burnt out. "This particular project kind of came along at a very interesting time. They wanted to make a new kind of record for them. They wanted to just try out some new ideas, and try to kind of spread their wings a little bit in the studio. So over the course of a year and a half they would come out for ten days at a time, you know, four or five times, and just kind of write in the studio. And we ended up creating a special bond."

The Staves were struggling with a song called "No Me, No You, No More" and working with Justin when something magical occurred. "I couldn't quite understand just what didn't hit me right about the guitar part, and so we just kind of ended up making a loop off of one of the girls' voices, just kind of a drone note. And they just sat in the control room, just started working through an arrangement. They went out on the mics, and they just sang the entire thing to a drone with no click track. It was just one of those magical moments like that. I'd say this has probably only happened two or three times in my life. At certain moments when they were doing this take, it felt like I was kind of out of my body. At that moment, I realized that there are certain people that you come across in your life, and with this particular experience, these people seemed to be people I was meant to know, and our friendships have grown to be so special—one-in-a-lifetime type friendships. But that particular moment just took me away and really reminded me of so many of the things you forget about when you're out on tour and you make records. The Staves were just another record that I was making in a line of . . . records that I wanted to make, and to kind of just be picked up and removed from the earth for a second—that was pretty incredible."

There are a few things I want to unpack here. Let's start with the song. The stark tone he describes strongly underpins the lyrics about a love dissolved. It opens with these words:

I can't go back to life before
Before I knew
that you didn't love me no more
You didn't need me no more
You didn't love me no more
You didn't want me at all

Touching lyrics for anyone who's ever had their heart broken, and the clarity of the simple arrangement, as sung in the sort of stunning harmonies only sisters can conjure, makes me understand what Justin must have heard that day. Unlike the guitar or piano, vocal harmony is human, relatable. Not everyone has picked up a guitar, but the majority of us have put our voice to a song, at least in the shower or car. When we hear singing this pure—for most of us, unimaginable and unachievable with our own mediocre voices—it strikes a resonant chord deep inside. "I think there are very few people that are creating new kinds of harmonies. I think Gillian Welch and Dave Rawlings are a set of people that really push different harmony structures and vocal movements that don't really make any traditional sense. And I would say that the girls—The Staves—are also in that category. Doing new things with voices that just kind of bend the mind."

Perhaps you've never been lifted out of your body while listening to a song, but you've likely noticed how music can manipulate the sensation of time, how a few minutes can hold the weight of an hour, and how an hour of listening can pass in what feels like minutes. I've lain in bed and listened to Bon Iver's *For Emma, Forever Ago* and experienced a similar reaction. His voice possesses a sense of purity and yearning, and his falsetto hits a height that, at least for me, is unattainable. Most people who listen to Justin's songs, or one as wonderful as this one from The Staves, are unlikely to have an out-of-body experience. It's a rare occurrence and as much about the marriage of sound, texture, lyrics, and rhythm as it is about the listener's state of mind.

It wasn't the song alone that evoked Justin's intense emotional response. It was also the community he formed, the people he brought into that session and place. "This experience making the record with these people here, it just kind of hit every note of why it's important to have friends, and why it's important to believe in people that you meet, and that you care about," he says. "This Staves record, and this song, it proved to me that I'm here for more reasons than just to spit out my own music. There's more to life than to understand these things, and that music's . . . kind of a cloth to wrap around these things to give it a nice setting, to understand it a little more in a framework. But it's all so magnificent and sort of huge that it's hard to fully grasp.

"It actually made me wanna change the way I think about how

music should be done as a job. I was technically the producer, but what was also so meaningful for me, Bob, is that, as a producer—I don't really like that term. I think it's a little strong, and I think it's a little hierarchical—but the girls came into this space that I've created with my people around here in Eau Claire. And so I think just allowing them to be in a space, and have them feel comfortable and have them spread their wings, and to experiment rather than just say, 'All right, time to make a record,' I think giving them that runway was probably my greatest skill. I mean, I didn't really do much in that sense. I collected them, I gave them the space but, you know, I think we just tried to rally around them and champion what they were trying to come up with."

During our conversation, I half-jokingly mention to Justin that he should open a musical hotel and act as the host. Truth is, that's not too far from what he did with The Staves. "This work is personal. For me, it's like, I love music so much, you know? I have a kind of undying thirst to create it and be a part of it and everything. But this record made me slow down so much, because even [with] all the amazing people I've worked with over the years, there was just something extra rewarding about having a band like The Staves come in, and have as much success in making a record. And me being, like, a role player, it made me feel really good about myself. And, you know, I do the Bon Iver thing naturally . . . but it often can be kind of distracting for me if I go on tour and everyone's just kind of there to see your show, and they want to talk to you, and tell you how much my music has helped them. . . . I don't do well in that scenario as much. I'm not looking for that particularly. But in this instance, I just felt like I was in the perfect place. It was a perfect use of my skills and my personality. And then to just meet people . . . there's a lot of camaraderie here. During the December session, there were probably eight people living here. We were eating together every night. The whole thing." I'm curious to see what becomes of this studio space. Will Justin's embrace of the communal creative vibe prove to be merely a momentary reorientation, or will we find in the years to come that his touring slows and his connection to Wisconsin manifests in more significant ways? On the day we speak, in November 2014, Justin is preparing to host thirty-eight people for Thanksgiving dinner, including cousins, aunts, uncles, and grandkids. Hotel April Base? Concierge Justin Vernon at your service? We shall see.

CAT POWER

The Sixth and I Historic Synagogue is not only at the intersection of Sixth and I Streets in Washington's Chinatown, it's also at the intersection of religious and secular culture in the city. This beautiful turn-of-the-century building is where I meet Chan Marshall, aka Cat Power.

Built in 1908, the synagogue was recently in disrepair and up for sale, almost gutted and turned into a nightclub. But these days, thanks to some crucial caretakers and recently discovered 1949 wedding photos, the synagogue is accurately restored. Ask any musician who has played this venue and they'll probably tell you it feels like stepping back in time.

I imagine its long wooden pews and stunning domed ceiling to be the perfect location for an enchanting conversation with Chan Marshall. She's performing solo on a cold autumn evening in November 2013. Instead, I meet her in one of the fluorescent-lit offices, which also serves as a temporary holding pen for her dogs. To escape the noise of the animals—and so she can smoke—we take our conversation behind the synagogue to the unlit, ugly, concrete rear of the building.

Charlyn Marie Marshall grew up in Atlanta. She was born in 1972, so I'm guessing that the song that changed her life will be something from the mid-eighties. But frankly, as someone who listens to and loves her range of styles, I think her choice could be anything. She has expressed a love for free jazz, and it certainly influenced her early performances, around 1992. She created her first recordings with Sonic Youth drummer Steve Shelley, in 1994, so there are punk and experimental elements to her music as well. After that, she made a fairly atmospheric record with members of the fabulous Australian trio Dirty Three. Then, in the late 1990s, she performed cover songs by artists as diverse as Bob Dylan and the Britpop band Oasis. In 2006, for her seventh studio record, she assembled a group of veteran studio musicians to create original music inspired by southern soul of the sixties and seventies. That album, *The Greatest,* was recorded in Memphis and is easily her most accessible. To make her musical influences even harder to pin down, she recently released an album filled with synthesizers and pop flair. *Sun* has become my favorite Cat Power record of all.

Chan Marshall seems unsure and nervous, jittery, as we hang outside in the dark concrete yard talking about music. She's been through a lot lately. A long relationship with actor Giovanni Ribisi came to an end, and then he quickly married someone else. Hospitalization and a canceled tour followed. But she's always been an artist who loves to talk. Our first meeting, in 2006, was in the dressing room of the 9:30 Club. It was just before NPR Music webcast her performance of *The Greatest* with a big band, and I took her hyperchattiness as preshow jitters. During that interview, she talked nonstop, to the point of not wanting me to leave. She'd say,

"Ask me something else, ask me something else," when I needed to get on mic for our broadcast and she *really* needed to get onstage for her performance. I have a similar experience this night, though she seems more scattered than I recall—that is, until she begins to talk about the first song she heard that really reached out and touched her, changed her.

She was living with her dad in an apartment in the suburbs of Atlanta. She remembers being home from school; maybe she was sick or maybe it was a holiday or a snow day, she's not sure. It was 1986, January 28, to be precise, the day the space shuttle *Challenger* exploded. She was watching PBS: "And there was file footage of Aretha Franklin from around, uh, '60. I wanna say '64, I'm probably wrong. And she had this eyeliner like Cleopatra, she had her hair all done up on her head, you know, coiffed high. And she was wearing this V-neck brocade dress or whatever you call it. Empire waist. But she was playing at this huge, like, seated classical place. And she sang and I remember she was sweatin' and the lights were just on her face and she was singing. . . . I'd heard of her before, you know. But she sang 'Amazing Grace' and that was the first time, 'cause I've sung it in church with my grandma and stuff. But hearing that song [like] that, I just started crying. I mean, it was probably a combination of my life thus far or whatever and watching her . . . her spirit come out like that. That was when I knew there was messed-up stuff. Or I knew there was, you know, contemplation you don't really ask about and stuff as a kid, you don't really get answers. . . . But that's when I knew that I was probably pretty much alone in that. There was a possibility of hope in that, in seeing that."

To feel hope at a moment when she found herself alone had a significant impact on Chan. During her childhood, she went eight years without speaking to her mother, always shuffled between her grandmother and dad, with never enough time in either place to make friends. The sense of hope was sparked by one of America's most beloved singers of soul and gospel music, Aretha Franklin, and "Amazing Grace," just about the most famous song in the English language. When Chan speaks of the experience, I can see the pain on her face but also her smile.

It is rather chilly behind the Sixth and I Synagogue, and Chan has the warmer, furrier hat. As we talk about that magic moment, a streetlight pops on and then a distant church bell rings out, odd for a Wednesday evening in Washington. There is mystery in Chan and in the way she speaks, flitting from one idea to the next. I struggle to connect her statements as they pour out. The entire exchange feels quite surreal to me, though I somehow suspect these conversations are the norm for her. For example, when I ask her if that song made her want to make music, she responds, "It released something in me, even in the lyrics, they say, you know, it was a huge release in that song. It brought . . . a kinship for whomever, whomever she was singing to. . . . There was, like, an ancient camaraderie going on there, I'm not sure what; it was just like this human survival pathos that lives in us all but a lot of us get deformed through media."

What happened for this fourteen-year-old girl is at the heart of what media does best, and in this case did: it disseminates information to many but touches us on a one-to-one basis. Aretha Franklin may never know she did that for a young woman in Atlanta. Not only did she touch people's hearts at the time of her performance, but because it was videotaped, she's able to do it again and again, which is exactly what records do—and what a live performance does, when it works. But on this night, at the Sixth and I Synagogue, I don't think it does. Chan is as nervous and unsure of herself onstage as she seemed during our backyard conversation. She forgets words, abruptly stops singing in the middle of songs, and sometimes begins playing but is unable to remember the chord sequence, or even what instrument to play it on. I've seen her play great shows but, all in all, concerts tend to be a bit of a crapshoot with her. She wears her heart on her sleeve. On some nights those raw emotions make for a brilliant performance; on others, they create a bit of a mess. She's got a lousy reputation for stopping shows, walking off, canceling tours. She's in a perpetual battle with alcoholism and self-hatred. When I ask her how long she has owned the Silvertone guitar in her dressing room, she tells me it's new, that she broke her old one in Paris around her twenty-eighth birthday. She whispers to me, "I wanted to jump out a window." But she made a choice and instead of hurting herself, she hurt the guitar, though she wound up smashing it *against* the window rather than hurling it *out* the window.

By her own account Chan Marshall is a broken person, who at times exhibits great strength. Her recent album *Sun* is an astonishing achievement, one that didn't come easy, I know. It had been six years since her last record of new songs. Oh, she finished a new album project in that time, but when she played it for a friend, she was told that it sounded like the old, sad Cat. So she started all over again. *Sun* is the perfect title for what she ended up with, the perfect antidote to the old, sad Cat Power. And with her latest triumph, I think it's fair to say she once was lost, but no more. She's found hope, the kind of hope one feels when music fills the spirit. It's the spirit she heard when Aretha sang "Amazing Grace." "That saved a wretch like me" is a line that seems to propel Chan Marshall. She can rise above the despair, the loneliness, but it's a constant battle—and just when all things seem triumphant, they can easily fall apart. She's more fragile than most, I think. If only in those disheartening moments, like now, onstage on this early autumn night, she could marshal the power to sing "Amazing Grace," to summon some of what Aretha gave her. I trust I will live to see that day: she's got the power.

JACKSON BROWNE

I'm in the back room of a record store with a box cutter in my hand. It's the winter of '72 and I'm opening the week's new releases at Waxie Maxie's in Rockville, Maryland. I make about $1.75 an hour, working forty-eight hours a week while putting myself through college. I'm a record store clerk and I love my job. I'm stunned by what I see when the box opens: a silk-screened photograph of a guy with his long hair parted in the middle, who looks exactly like me.

The image was of Jackson Browne and it was his first album. I don't think I'd ever heard of him at the time. I showed my mom his photograph in *Rolling Stone* and recall her saying, "What are you doing in that magazine?" I was a nineteen-year-old hippie-ish guy, studying psychology in college, and hoping to avoid the draft. Jackson Browne was a twenty-four-year-old budding singer-songwriter with a sharply written and catchy debut album. I must admit, though, I wasn't a fan. I was listening to heavier stuff at the time—Led Zeppelin, Jethro Tull, and the still fairly unknown English band Pink Floyd. I would sooner listen to Pink Floyd's 1971 album *Meddle,* especially the twenty-three-minute cut "Echoes," which filled side two, than Jackson's country-flavored rock. Still, my workmates loved Jackson Browne, and his album was a smash hit. We sold many copies of his single "Doctor My Eyes," for seventy-seven cents (plus four cents tax). In those days, before bar codes, we handwrote every sale on a slip of paper to track our inventory, and forty-four years later I still remember the label and number for his album (Asylum 5051).

I heard a lot of Jackson Browne in that record store. When his second album, *For Everyman,* came out, we put it on the store speakers. It opens with "Take It Easy," the hit he wrote with Glenn Frey of the Eagles. Frankly, when I heard it I became even less interested in him. I couldn't bear the Eagles. Despite the nice harmonies, my twenty-year-old self found their L.A. sound vapid. Not fifteen minutes into Jackson Browne's second album, though, cut five played, and permanently flipped my perspective. I knew the tune, the words, but what the hell was Jackson Browne doing covering "These Days," a song by Nico of The Velvet Underground? A little research revealed my cluelessness. Not only did Jackson Browne write that song when he was only sixteen, he also played the rhythmic, fingerpicked guitar that sits so eloquently beneath Nico's sad voice on the version I loved. There are two other Jackson Browne songs on Nico's 1967 solo album *Chelsea Girl.* In fact, the German singer and the Los Angeles songwriter were an item back in 1967, when he was nineteen and Nico ten years his senior. "These Days" is one of the best ballads of regret I've ever heard, and it's shocking to think Jackson was only a teenager when he wrote these lines:

I'll stop my dreaming
I won't do too much scheming these days
These days

. . .

Please don't confront me with my failures
I had not forgotten them

Jackson Browne and Nico met in New York. Jackson had moved there with some friends, traveling cross-country in a Rambler American station wagon. He tells me, "It was 1967, there was snow on the ground. I was wearing penny loafers. I had fifty bucks and that was it." In those days, Nico was hanging around Andy Warhol, starring in his movies and making gritty dark songs with The Velvet Underground, which went mostly unheard at the time but would eventually (and continually) influence the musical landscape long after the original group disbanded in 1970, and after Nico died in 1988. Browne's songs on *Chelsea Girl* sit well beside those written by The Velvet Underground's Lou Reed and John Cale. Jackson remembers meeting Nico when he went to see his friend Tim Buckley play in a New York club. She was the opener. "She sang in a bar called the Dom, which was filled with Andy Warhol's art crowd and people that came to gawk at them. There was a bit of an installation and it had some films on the wall. They didn't really have any paintings up, but they had Nico singing." Soon Jackson was accompanying her.

Jackson Browne was born Clyde Jackson Browne to an American serviceman, writer, and Minnesota native who later became a teacher. Like Nico, Jackson was born in Germany. His family moved to Los Angeles when he was about three years old. Both his mom and dad played piano. His dad was famous for the jam sessions he held with jazz musicians in their Highland Park home. According to Jackson, "My grandfather built his house in the countryside, between Los Angeles and Pasadena, and now it's completely engulfed by sprawl—a beautiful house that was really unique in that it resembles a Spanish mission. It was made up of river rock." You can see the house depicted on the front cover of his second album. "We had a chapel and a dungeon, all built around the courtyard. When the place would fill up with players . . . imagine forty people with instruments all standing around the piano and jamming." The music was Dixieland, songs like "Basin Street Blues." Back then Jackson played trumpet, but unlike his dad and his friends, who would improvise during the session, he'd compose parts for his instrument, something that didn't fit their free-form style.

When Jackson began choosing his own music, he tended toward folk, which his dad fully supported. "It was probably about '60, '61, and my dad was teaching high school. Every day he'd come home, take off his suit, his jacket, and his tie, and he'd fix himself a drink, and he'd sit down and start playing records." This was the early 1960s, and the folk scene was particularly rich in Los Angeles. "When I got involved in folk music, he weighed in with his own opinion—he took me to see Lightnin' Hopkins!"

There were two main clubs in L.A. in the 1960s, the Ash Grove and the Troubadour. You could see Lightnin' Hopkins or Gary Davis at the Ash Grove, and the Smothers Brothers at the Troubadour; basically, the more commercial acts were found at the Troubadour and the raw stuff at the Ash Grove. "Yeah, I love Lightnin' Hopkins. They ask Lightnin' why he drinks whiskey. [Jackson does a growling Lightnin' Hopkins impression:] 'Because whiskey give me a plenty of nerve.' I like Lightnin' Hopkins because there was the confidence, like telling the truth. He had these really great shades with gold rims and some gold teeth and he'd play the electric guitar with the DeArmond pickup on it. I remember the feeling. This was the beginning of the civil rights movement, too."

Jackson is referring partly to the racism that pervaded Orange County then. "One night we took Sonny Terry and Brownie McGhee [two southeastern black blues musicians] out to eat after their show at this club. 'We' would be my friends Steve Noonan and Greg Copeland and me, and a bunch of girls, and we're all eighteen, nineteen, sixteen maybe. We got this amazing ration of hate. We saw firsthand what it was like to [be] black in Orange County. These late-night, older men in the diner were like, 'What are you doing eating with them?'"

Jackson's activism had begun a few years earlier. "I joined the Congress of Racial Equality. I was a member of the CORE when I was fourteen, fifteen, and did attend demonstrations. In fact, one of the first really cool parties I ever went to was when everybody, [including] my sister, had gone to San Francisco to demonstrate against [Barry] Goldwater. A lot of people from SNCC and CORE and NAACP and my sister came back with a bunch of black friends. . . . I remember this incredible record party and people were dancing. It was wonderful because it was completely racially mixed—everybody let their hair down; it wasn't a meeting where people are going to speak and talk about integration and civil rights, it was simply a party. It was just glorious. From then on, I think I would always gravitate to those parties where people were going to get out of the box that they'd been put in."

Much of the folk movement in America was shaped by black culture and racial injustice. Folk music, particularly the kind played in coffeehouses and small clubs, is directly linked to the blues of the past—and Bob Dylan's music is a direct descendant of this melded sound. Many songs shaped and inspired Jackson Browne, but it was a Dylan song that changed him most. "'Don't Think Twice' was a hit song by Peter, Paul and Mary. It sounded really neat. I like the way they sing. It's very fresh sounding, actually. It's that sound of a woman's voice, but the lyrics were so great. I really liked it, but when I heard Bob Dylan, it's just, like, this is a whole other thing.

"I'd say that listening to Bob Dylan probably had the biggest effect on me of anybody. I loved Ray Charles; *Modern Sounds in Country and Western Music* was a really wonderful integration of white Western culture and black R&B culture. I didn't think of it at that time because it was a pop record. I didn't think how groundbreaking that was, even though I was immersed in the civil rights movement. But I didn't learn to play those songs. Bob Dylan was something else; you could learn one of the songs. I remember reading him say something about [how] he played folk music because you could do it by yourself. I thought, That's pretty smart, because really it's very hard to organize a group. I learned to play 'Don't Think Twice, It's All Right,' and it was a certain way of fingerpicking that I play now. It's just thumb, finger, thumb, finger, thumb, finger, thumb, finger . . . it's the building block of any fingerpicking arrangement. My own version of that became my own way of playing. I don't really play it like he played it. It was a point of departure for me both as a songwriter and as a guitar player. I think that was a moment where the road rolled out ahead of me. I thought, This is something to learn how to do, and I began playing Mississippi John Hurt songs and Reverend Gary Davis songs, and I began writing my own songs, really, not very long after that." Jackson played on guitars borrowed from his brother Severin and his sister's friend Tina. His sixteen-year-old fingers must have picked the pattern that became "These Days," one of his greatest songs, on one of those borrowed guitars.

Fast-forward to 2014, and Jackson Browne is singing at my desk. He's about to turn sixty-six, and I can still see my face in his, only he's kept his hair and I've lost mine. His demeanor is friendly but focused. For his final song, he begins to fingerpick. It's a familiar melody that takes me back to my teen years. In it he references "These Days," which he wrote fifty years earlier and Nico sang. This song is titled "The Long Way Around," and it's from his fourteenth album, *Standing in the Breach*. Its lyrics are Jackson's reflections on these twenty-first-century days:

> I don't know what to say about these days
> I'm seeing people changing in the strangest ways

Even in the richer neighborhoods
People don't know when they got it good
They've got the envy, and they've got it bad

This song encompasses everything I've come to love and respect about Jackson Browne. The lyrics are from the heart, and sung with clear compassion about a cause he cares for deeply. These later lines showcase his ability to mix politics with poetry, which few song-writers can do with any success, but it's something he's been doing with extraordinary prowess since his early teens:

It's so hard keeping track of what's gone wrong
The covenant unravels, and the news just rolls along
I could feel my memory letting go some to two or three disasters
    ago
It's hard to say which did more ill
Citizens United or the Gulf oil spill

When Jackson walked into NPR, saw the Tiny Desk area and the folks gathered for his acoustic set, he told his bandmate Greg Leisz, a friend he's known since high school, that it reminded him of days spent on the quad, where people would sing topical songs and write lyrics about present-day events. For him, it all snaps back to that time, the time he heard that Bob Dylan tune, a time when folk music was clearly defined and changed lives. "The whole world changed right at that moment because of folk music, because it embodied the values of the Beat Generation as much as a forward-thinking, political way of expressing what you felt about the present world and what needed to change." Fifty years later, Jackson Browne epitomizes that ideal, singing topical songs, playing sessions with younger musicians both on- and offstage, and generally passing his knowledge along to the next generation.

MICHAEL STIPE

Every singer on every stage, every song, and every record can touch a heart, inspire a dream, and change a life. There's a prepubescent vessel out there unknowingly waiting to be carried away by an idea, an image, a lyric, a melody—just ask R.E.M.'s Michael Stipe.

Michael Stipe was born John Michael Stipe in the first few days of the 1960s. His passion for music came from the AM radio airwaves and from cereal boxes. During our conversation, Michael tells me that when he was around age eight, "bubblegum music" was his thing. I laugh; as an older kid in the late sixties, I couldn't stand the overly sweet pop, and always found the term "bubblegum" pejorative, so the very idea of someone liking it feels strange. "No, man, it's fucking awesome music. It's the best. And it came out of doo-wop. Bubblegum is like hip-hop. It was about making hits. And it was about something that people wanted to sing along to. . . . Great songwriters . . . were writing for The Archies and The Banana

Splits, I think. . . . I didn't know that at the age of eight. I just knew that that was the influence that I had as a young boy."

Michael is right. Those manufactured hits were created by famous behind-the-scenes songwriting teams. Folks like Jeff Barry and Ellie Greenwich were essential to the early sixties girl groups. They cowrote "Da Doo Ron Ron" and "Then He Kissed Me" for The Crystals, "Be My Baby" and "Baby, I Love You" for The Ronettes, and "Hanky Panky," an obscure B side that later became a hit when covered by Tommy James and the Shondells. Don Kirshner was another behind-the-scenes character of bubblegum, producing hits for Stipe's favorite, The Monkees. Then, when Kirshner couldn't control this made-for-TV band, he went on to assemble a band to create the music of the non-rebellious cartoon garage band The Archies. Their hits include the ultimate bubblegum song, "Sugar, Sugar," along with "Bang-Shang-A-Lang" and "Feelin' So Good (S.K.O.O.B.Y.-D.O.O.)." Another favorite of Michael's, which he mentions five times in our thirty-minute conversation, was the Hanna-Barbera live furry-costumed creation The Banana Splits, which featured Fleegle (guitar), Bingo (drums and vocals), Drooper (bass and vocals), and Snorky (keyboards). The opening theme song of their TV show, "The Tra La La Song (One Banana, Two Banana)," sticks to your soul like gum to a shoe—you just can't shake it. Al Kooper, the rock superstar who played alongside Bob Dylan at his infamous 1965 Newport Folk Festival performance, also wrote numerous bubblegum hits during this period. And before "You're the First, the Last, My Everything," Barry White—yup, Barry White—sang for The Banana Splits ("Doin' the Banana Split"). The whole Archies show was brought to you by the sweet cereal maker Kellogg's, who also distributed the cardboard records Michael used to cut from the back of his Frosted Flakes box. Beyond The Archies and The Banana Splits, he collected records by The Jackson Five and The Monkees.

Somewhat oddly, Michael doesn't recall being thrilled in the late sixties by The Beatles, The Doors, or The Byrds, bands that seem like musical soul mates to the sound he'd later create. For him, bubblegum was "a fucking great way to grow up. I mean, it put me where I am now. So I'm happy with it. I didn't have an older brother or sister who was into music. My father was a helicopter pilot in the army and a proud man. And he and my mother provided us with everything that we needed." The family moved many times during his childhood. On an army base in Germany, he remembers hearing a lot of country music. Roger Miller's "King of the Road" and Tammy Wynette's "D-I-V-O-R-C-E" were two of the few records he owned then. "I remember hearing on the radio two songs in particular that resonated with me. One of them was 'Bennie and the Jets' by Elton John. The other was 'Rock On' by David Essex. They're both amazing songs, really mysterious, odd, dark, strange. I don't know what else was happening on pop radio at that point. But if you listen to the production of those two songs, it's shocking that they ever even made it into the Top 100 . . . [and] for them to have gotten to me via whatever radio station was playing in the background of my childhood." They were huge hits and, indeed, weird songs.

Both songs were released in 1973, both were by English artists, and for both Elton and Essex it was the first time they'd hit number one. Another odd coincidence is that both begin with the words "Hey kid." Essex tells us to "rock and roll," while Elton says to "shake it loose together." Essex's song, his only hit, references pinnacle rock and roll music, including the 1958 smash "Summertime Blues" by Eddie Cochran and the 1955 Carl Perkins, and later Elvis, phenomenon "Blue Suede Shoes." While both "Rock On" and "Bennie and the Jets" pay homage to rock and roll, Elton's song, with lyrics by Bernie Taupin, pokes fun at the music biz and glam rock, which was certainly ironic and all the more humorous coming from the flamboyant singer.

The early 1970s was an odd time in rock music history. The previously focused AM radio stations with their small playlists faded in favor of new free-form stations on the recently birthed FM dial. DJs now came to work armed with the records they loved, and instead of a few musical gatekeepers there were (thankfully) multitudes. I like to think that David Essex's line "And where do we go from here?" was a prescient one. The birth of glam rock followed, with David Bowie and the New York Dolls. Then, only a few years later, the bloat of superstar rock was shed with the rise of punk. Herbie Flowers, the bass player on "Rock On," had only one year earlier performed some of the most famous bass lines in history for Lou Reed's "Walk on the Wild Side," which was produced by one of glam rock's queens, David Bowie. Reed and his former band, The Velvet Underground, unknowingly set the stage for the sounds to come, which would eventually shake the listening world of a fifteen-year-old Michael Stipe.

In the 1970s, Michael's family moved to a small town called Collinsville, outside East St. Louis, Illinois. He can pinpoint the dramatic change of his musical taste to one day in detention in 1975, when he found an issue of *Creem* magazine under his desk. The colorful Detroit rock rag was known for its quality writing by Lester Bangs, for its funny captions, for poking fun at the musicians it featured, and for coining the term "punk rock" in 1971. Michigan was home to some of the most important protopunk bands, the MC5, Iggy and the Stooges, and the early garage band ? and the Mysterians. David Bowie, Roxy Music, and the New York Dolls were all covered in the issue Michael found, "and there was an article written by Lisa Robinson about punk rock and CBGBs and a photograph of Patti Smith. And I remember that photo. And I became aware of and fascinated by whatever . . . was going on at CBGBs."

CBGB was a club in the rundown Bowery district of New York City. Its owner, Hilly Kristal, opened it to showcase country, bluegrass, and blues, hence the name CBGB. But it soon became home to burgeoning wayward musicians creating original music, such as Television, Blondie, The Ramones, and Patti Smith. Michael was fascinated with Patti Smith, a poet and singer with a passion for the nineteenth-century French poet Arthur Rimbaud, and he closely followed the happenings at CBGB from East St. Louis with a subscription to New York's *Village Voice.* "I just started quietly obsessing on and collecting everything that I could about CBGBs. It put me in a very rare position. I was one of the original punk rockers. But I was listening from this small town in the middle of the Midwest. I had never been to New York. I'd certainly never been to London or Los Angeles. . . . I bought Patti's record [*Horses*] the day that it was released in 1975 [December 13]. I was fifteen years old, and I took it home. I stayed up all night listening to it over and over and over again. But the song that resonated with me and [is my] epiphenomenal, profound, change-my-life moment was the song 'Birdland.'"

Until that day, there was truly nothing like the album *Horses.* Even the cover was something of a singular event, a photograph of Patti appearing mannish in a wrinkled white shirt with a sport coat slung over her left shoulder and a horse pin on her collar. Her skinny body and unkempt black hair read *attitude.* It was strikingly different from the way the music world usually portrayed woman. I'm specifically thinking about Carly Simon's cover for 1975's *Playing Possum*—she's on her knees, wearing knee-high black boots, black stockings, and a black camisole that barely covers her ass. Robert Mapplethorpe took Patti's photo in a Greenwich Village penthouse, and The Velvet Underground's John Cale produced the album. You can draw a line from that band's poetic chaos to Patti Smith—but still, there was nothing like her.

The song that captured and changed this bubblegum-loving boy was a nine-minute-and-fifteen-second adventure. "It's a little bit of a doo-wop song. Looking back, you realize how much she was pulling from kind of The Shirelles, The Ronettes, or Ronnie Spector, that kind of girl-group thing that I think she grew up with and that was easily moving into her music and maybe had a big influence on her." More than anything else Michael was moved by the words. "I know what the lyrics are that I latched onto and could not get out of my head. 'It's as if someone had spread butter on all the fine points of the stars because when he looked up, they started to slip.' That's the line! And that's when she goes from kind of a talking incantation into a singing thing. Within the singing there's a line, probably the second part of the lyric, a line about a little boy's face lit up with such naked joy. 'And his eyes were like two white opals, seeing everything just a little bit too clearly.' And that's when I was hooked. That was for me the dervish moment. That's when I felt transformed by rock and roll and by art and by music and by poetry and by some projection of who this woman was and what she was saying to me. She wasn't saying it to anyone else, it was just to me. I think I've been trying to rewrite those words as a lyricist . . . for most of my adult life."

Four years later, Michael finally made it to New York. "I wrote a song of my own about . . . that moment of revelation forward into finally arriving at the city that provided me with CBGB, and [the] original group of artists and writers and lyricists and musicians who came out of that scene. Arriving there . . . as a nineteen-year-old, [I looked around and realized] that New York, and where I was in my life, that this was the opportunity and the possibility that Patti Smith had sung about. This city embodied that potential . . . and it was only up to me to be able to take that and run with it. That was the year that I started R.E.M. But it was still a teenage dream. It was still this absurdly beautiful kind of naive idea of something rather than the something itself."

R.E.M. got its start in 1980 when Michael met guitarist Peter Buck while Buck was working at Wuxtry Records in Athens, Georgia. They then met musical friends Mike Mills (bass) and Bill Berry (drums) at the University of Georgia. The four of them played their first show at a birthday party that spring; R.E.M. released their debut single on a small Atlanta label called Hib-Tone in 1981. "Radio Free Europe" was named for the U.S. radio organization that targets Europe, the Middle East, and Central Asia with news. Michael's lyrics, which are tough to decipher, perhaps hint at radio as propaganda, although I was never sure of that interpretation. One thing was for sure, though—they had a raw sound bursting with personality.

Around that same time in D.C., some friends and I started a label with the intent to release our Tiny Desk Unit records. There was a local D.C. band then that was also called R.E.M., and we were about to record and release their debut album on our label. I recall sitting on the front step of the old 9:30 Club one night with their guitarist Greg Strzempka before their recording session. He told me he was worried, that he'd heard about a band from Athens with the same name. I was a good eight years older than Greg, and, frankly, felt I had a lot more wisdom than he did, so I looked him in the eye and said, "Look, there are a ton of bands out there. I wouldn't worry about these guys from Athens." Disregarding me, Greg changed his band's name to Egoslavia. Looking back, I love how wrong I was.

As we all know, R.E.M. built a big reputation. After Hib-Tone, they moved to I.R.S. Records and connected well with college radio, the only stations that would play their music. Their first album, *Murmur* (1983), was released with a rerecorded version of "Radio Free Europe," and five years later they signed with Warner Bros.

Michael achieved two seemingly unimaginable dreams. The first is that the band became as big as it did, while simultaneously maintaining its integrity. I know he is immensely grateful for the opportunity and for the talent of his bandmates. "I was maybe the least likely candidate to take a teenage dream and transform it into an adult reality." The second of these two dreams is the one that blows my mind, though. It reminds me that every singer on every stage, every song, every record can touch a heart, inspire a dream, change a life. On May 1, 2005, Michael Stipe joined his idol Patti

Smith on the stage of CBGB to sing "Ghost Dance." He tells me, "I still pinch myself. I've had a very, very, very, very extraordinary life. And I owe her as an artist for doing something for someone that she'd never met and wouldn't meet for twenty years. And we happen to like each other. She created something that radically set forth a series of dreams and aspirations of mine. . . . For that I'm completely and forever indebted to her."

PHILIP GLASS

"Some people would say, 'You know, Mr. Glass, I really tried and I've tried to listen to this piece, and I don't get it. What should I do?' And I said, 'Go listen to something else.' I said, 'You don't have to listen to it.' That's why there's all this different music around. It's for different people."

Philip Glass's compositions are some of the most important of the late twentieth century, but his music is not for everyone. Its magic often lies in its unending repetition and incessant pulse. It owes as much to Bach as it does to trance, and can be breathtakingly tearful and perpetually throbbing. Philip has written ten symphonies, hundreds of sonatas, a massive number of movie scores, and twelve tremendously groundbreaking operas. His music is serious, with a wide range of influences, everything from electronica and jazz to soundtracks and the concert music of his contemporaries. When Philip tells me the song that changed his life is Spike Jones's zany rendition of Rossini's *William Tell Overture,* I am flabbergasted. Seriously? Philip Glass likes funny things?

Philip Glass is the son of Jewish immigrants and was raised in Baltimore, or, as he would say, Ball-em-muhr. His mom, Ida, was an English teacher and librarian. His dad, Ben, was an auto mechanic turned radio repairman who opened his own shop, General Radio. "Ben himself was an interesting guy because he learned a lot of things on his own. He learned how to fix radios because he was working with the Pep Boys, who had an auto accessories line, so they started putting radios into these things, and he realized that people were going to break their radios, so he learned how to fix them. Now the same thing happened, I remember, around 1946, when television sets came out. . . . He sent away for a television do-it-yourself kit and he built one. By the time he had built one, he knew how to fix it." That sort of self-starting attitude and determination runs through Philip's own life as a steelworker, plumber, New York cabdriver, composer, and musician.

Growing up in the 1940s, Philip and his older brother, Marty, spent a lot of time working in their father's shop, which also sold records. "The records were really a kind of a distraction for the people waiting for their radios." At first they stocked only a handful, but later the records took over the store. Ben didn't know much about music at first, so he learned by listening. "The records he couldn't sell he would bring home to listen to. His idea was, well, if he couldn't sell them, there was something wrong with them, and if he listened to them, he could figure out what that was, and he wouldn't make the mistake of buying those records that didn't sell." I love this notion. It's such a logical approach to musical taste, which is usually less an intellectual choice than one of the gut. Ben soon discovered that the music he had trouble selling was predominantly modern classical. "We had Bartók, we had Stravinsky, we had all kinds of things at home, which [Ben] began to really become very attached to. And it got so that . . . if you were one of his regular customers, he would force you to buy modern music. He would say, 'Louis, take this home, listen to it, if you don't like it you can bring it back.' Well, they never brought it back, but there was a period when if you wanted to buy records of modern music, the only place in town was . . . General Radio."

At home Philip and his dad listened to those Bartók and Stravinsky records, along with other cutting-edge musicians of the forties and fifties, chamber music, and Ben's favorite composer, Schubert. As fate would have it, Philip also loved the music they couldn't sell. He also loved the classics, all released on 78s, a format that held barely five minutes of music and spun at more than twice the speed of the modern LP. Philip tells me, "Everything was 78s. . . . Many of you won't remember this, but when they did a symphony of Beethoven . . . it would take four 78 records, but there would be one side that would be empty, but the company didn't want to put an empty side, so they would put on maybe a Rossini overture . . . and for years I thought the Fifth Symphony of Beethoven ended up with the *William Tell Overture*."

That very same overture came on the radio when Philip was about eleven years old and changed his life, only this time it was hilarious. The Spike Jones version was played on pots and pans, and featured announcer Doodles Weaver narrating a very silly horse race, with puns at every turn. Philip tells me that when he heard it on the radio, "Everything came alive. . . . I mean, not only were they funny, but they were clever. . . . These were not amateurs. These were very first-class musicians who were having a good time, and that's what I liked about it." Jones also taunted Hitler with his 1942 song "Der Fuehrer's Face," where each chant of "Heil!" was followed with a rude flatulent sound, and mocked romance with his remake of "Cocktails for Two," complete with horn honking and hiccups.

Philip was a serious kid, but he also had a sense of humor about his musical choices. Aside from Spike Jones, he and Marty loved Yiddish comedy records, and since no one bought them at the store, they were allowed to take them home. Their grandparents spoke Yiddish, and they understood some of the words, but mostly they sang along with the broken, thickly accented English. When I interview Philip, he's on tour for his memoir *Words Without Music*. I try to convince him to sing one of these songs for me. Instead, he attempts to explain their brand of comedy. "There was a story about a guy who had a clothing store and he was about to die, but he called his children and said, 'Look, I have these valuables. I want you to collect them before I die.' So the kids go out and collect all this money and he gets better and they say, 'How come you got better, Dad?' He says, 'Well, with all this money coming in, there's no time for a businessman to die.'"

There was a lot of humor in the Glass family. Philip was especially close to his uncle Henry, who played drums in the Borscht Belt, the now mostly defunct summer resorts of the Catskill Mountains in upstate New York. Philip was also related to one of the most popular entertainers of the 1930s and '40s, singer, actor, and comedian Al Jolson. But despite these familial connections, Ben and Ida did not want their children to become musicians. "Years later, [when] I said I was going to go to music school, people almost fainted. It was like, What? What? We're over that. We're not doing that anymore. They thought this was . . . very déclassé. You wanted to be a doctor or a lawyer. You didn't want to be a musician and end up playing drums in a hotel like Uncle Henry. That's what they thought, and they had no reason to believe otherwise, to be truthful." I ask Philip if his parents seemed skeptical about his career choice. He responds, "Skeptical? That's a kind word. . . . At any rate, I was doing my first public concert at Queens College in a big concert hall . . . [with] three thousand seats. . . . I was invited to do a concert there and Ida Glass took the train up from Baltimore . . . and she was one of the six [people there]—but she took it very well, really. . . . She was not going to spend the night in New York, so I took her to the train station, and she said, 'Why is your hair so long?' . . . But here's the interesting thing, the next time she came to New York was only seven years later. That was 1969, and in 1976, I was at the Metropolitan Opera House with four thousand people and they had all paid for tickets."

Philip studied flute, though in his heart he always knew he wanted to be a composer—a different journey than his uncle Henry or the other musicians in his family. He eventually studied composition at Juilliard and began experimenting with harmony and rhythm, exploring possibilities never before heard in music. This was during the late fifties and into the sixties. Classical music wasn't popular, and it was difficult for him to find an audience. Even his New York artist friends, among them painters, dancers, sculptors, and writers, listened to the rock music of the day, bands like The Doors and Jefferson Airplane. Philip says, "We don't know what we like, we like what we know, and that's where we start from. And then to get out of that, for many people it's hard . . . even for composers. . . . I remember . . . the first time I heard Charles Ives—I couldn't figure it out. People who are conductors and people who are players will not play modern music, and that [might] have been true for the time of Brahms. What we're talking about is the learning curve to get from music you know to the music you like. And that's a big [leap]. . . . I discovered, for one thing, that the rate of change in the art world was about five years, and in the world of music it's about fifty. . . . If someone plays [Stravinsky's] 'The Rite of Spring,' they'll still call it a piece of modern music. It's one hundred years old. . . . Actually, it's one hundred and three years old. So our idea of modern music stops, really . . . about one hundred years ago." Philip eventually found an audience for his particular brand of modern classical. One of the reasons for his success was surprisingly simple: he made the music louder. The idea came to him following a show at the Fillmore East, a famous concert venue in the East Village that, somewhat ironically, had originally opened as a Yiddish theater in 1925. "I learned how to [create] amplified music by listening to the rock and roll players.

That technology was coming around, and we very quickly took advantage of it."

I first heard Philip Glass in 1977 while I was working at a record warehouse. At the time, my musical taste wavered between the rising punk and the spacier sounds of Hawkwind, Tangerine Dream, Kraftwerk, David Bowie, and Brian Eno. As soon as I saw Glass's album *North Star*, with its spaceship cover art, I ripped off the shrink-wrap and listened to it. The music was daunting, dramatic, unabating, and unlike anything I'd ever heard. I was attracted to his unusual use of the organ as a propelling, almost percussive instrument—the way it kept the music in motion—and he experimented with the latest crop of analog synthesizers, creating inventive textures and drones. Philip also played the ARP, a brand of instrument I would eventually play with my band Tiny Desk Unit, which led to my longtime friendship with Bill Warrell, who along with his mom, Susan, owned and curated d.c. space. It was there that I later heard and discovered new music, everyone from saxophonist Anthony Braxton, trombonist and electronic musician George Lewis, the Art Ensemble of Chicago, trumpeters Jon Hassell and Don Cherry, and other artists who were breaking rules and pushing boundaries.

Bill later organized a nonprofit called District Curators that brought great performance artists and musicians such as Laurie Anderson, George Coates, Mabou Mines, Steve Reich, and Philip Glass to various spaces around the city, most notably the Pension Building, now known as the National Building Museum. It's one of the most remarkable spaces I've ever been inside—over three hundred feet long and one hundred feet wide, with seventy-five-foot Corinthian columns. It's also where I first saw Philip Glass live. He performed with the Philip Glass Ensemble, a small, roughly eight-piece band of keyboards and woodwinds that played intense, vocals-driven, demanding music that echoed magnificently in the vast open space. It was 1983, and I was composing music for a group of friends known as Impossible Theater. I was working on a Synclavier II, an electronic instrument at the forefront of sequencing and sound manipulation, capable of creating digital looping sequences. I was no Philip Glass, but seeing that performance definitely changed the way I thought about music. In retrospect, it's likely that my use of small, slowly changing, yet repeating phrases was drawn from my love for his compositions. A few years later, I had the privilege of seeing him play a majestic organ with nearly thirty-five hundred pipes at Bill's wedding. I believe the song was "Mad Rush," a lovely, melodic piece normally played solo on piano. To say it was glorious might be cliché, but it was.

One of Philip's primary mentors was Nadia Boulanger, a composer and instructor in Paris who taught many twentieth-century American composers, including Aaron Copland, Elliott Carter, Virgil Thomson, and even Quincy Jones. Boulanger did not teach Philip composition directly, but instead provided the foundational knowledge that helped him find his own way. "If I was studying carpentry, somebody would show me how to hold the saw, how to draw a line, how to measure the board. If I didn't have that instruction and I had to make a table without knowing how to do any of those things, the food would slide off the table. . . . When I left Boulanger, I felt that she had given me a box of shiny new tools, and I knew how to use them. She had such an admiration for people who could write music that she was afraid that if she gave advice to a young composer, it might be bad advice, and she might actually ruin their career. [Those tools] became the most important part about [coming back] to New York and writing a very radical kind of music. People didn't know what it was, [but] I knew what it was. I had tremendous confidence about what I was doing. I knew what I was doing musically, [and] I knew what I was doing historically. I had a whole context for it."

At the end of our conversation, the connection between the music Philip creates and his love for Spike Jones's comedy feels clear to me—they're both mavericks, eccentric free spirits who are/were testing the boundaries of possibility. Every time I speak with Philip, I find him incredibly warm and focused. Over his career, he's experienced a fair share of ridicule, the sort that might derail a less driven, determined individual. I ask him if he finds it difficult to be thought of as "polarizing" and whether it bothers him that people deride his penchant to repeat and repeat and repeat. He looks at me with a big smile and says, "Bob, this is the oldest story in the world. Can you imagine the first people that did cave paintings and they invited their friends in and they said, 'What the hell is that?' 'What do you mean? That's the bison and that's the hunter.' 'I don't see it.' I mean, that's been going on since the beginning. Van Gogh, how many paintings did he sell in his lifetime? Zero. And his brother had an art gallery!"

I've never seen one of Philip's operas, but I've heard he peppers them with the sort of humor not found in his other music. Honestly, I'm not surprised, especially coming from a man who understands counterpoint as well as he does.

JÓNSI

It should encourage musicians everywhere that a band from a country as tiny as Iceland, singing in Icelandic over dramatic, often ambient instrumental beds, could sell a ton of records and fill arenas around the world. I marvel at this feat, and it's likely the band members of Sigur Rós do as well.

In 2014, I attend the Iceland Airwaves Music Festival and spend four days driving around the most extraordinary landscape I have ever seen. Around every curve I find a spectacular mountain of old lava, snow-covered peaks, or the most magnificent moonrise in a purplish sky at four o'clock in the afternoon. The barren terrain is beautiful. It is easy to drive for hours without seeing anything but rock, along with an occasional horse or sheep. In this landscape, I feel like I develop a greater understanding of the music of Sigur Rós. It seems obvious to me now. Their music, like their country, is full of contrast—adventurous and calm at the same time. I'm certain the landscape sets the tone for their sound, although Jónsi might not agree with me on this point.

Jón Pór Birgisson or Jon Thor Birgisson or simply Jónsi forms the center of Sigur Rós. His falsetto is at the heart of their music, and he often uses a cello bow on his guitar strings to create their signature sound. We meet at his new studio, which is housed in an old building on a quiet cobblestone street in Reykjavík. It's a wonderful space, intimate and spare, that mixes modern electronics with dark wood and dim lights.

It's likely that most music journalists question Jónsi about the impact of geography on his sound, and I'm no different; you can't help it. He answers, "You can't really know. But I think it's also a lot to do with personalities and what you're introduced to when you're growing up. I grew up in the countryside until I was twenty or something." I imagine an isolated home in a large valley like the ones I saw days earlier, but the countryside for Jónsi was a town of four thousand people just fifteen minutes outside of Reykjavík. "They call that countryside. It's probably like a suburb or something, but we kind of call it countryside." Even though his family wasn't isolated and lived in a row house alongside many other families, Jónsi was lonely growing up. "There was basically nothing around. And you had to have a car to go anywhere. . . . So, when you got to the teenage years, it was really boring."

Similar to countless other kids, Jónsi remembers listening to The Beatles when he was young, around age nine, but he listened to their music sped up, 33 1/3 albums played at 45 rpm. He says, "It was just more fun." Ironically, most all the music he makes these days is slow, though his high falsetto sometimes reminds me of a sped-up record.

His parents weren't musical and didn't play instruments, but he does remember his mom owning a Black Sabbath record. Jónsi started acoustic guitar lessons when he was nine, and "it was the worst thing in the world, my hands hurt, I had this really boring teacher, and quickly I gave that up." He had a cousin, Addi, who had a big record collection and was into metal. Jónsi would go to his house and listen to Iron Maiden. Then, when he was about thirteen years old, his father bought him a used electric guitar from a coworker. Jónsi would plug it into his stereo system and play along to Iron Maiden's "Murders in the Rue Morgue." The song, inspired by Edgar Allan Poe's 1841 short story, is eighties heavy metal with over-the-top, high-pitched guitar solos and chug-a-chug-a rhythms. He was drawn to its energy, power, and drama. I tell Jónsi I'm not surprised at all by his love for Iron Maiden's heavy metal and that it reminds me of my recent car ride through Iceland's landscape. "That's so true, actually. I kind of never thought about it like that. But it's pretty metal. . . . I can relate to it. . . . it's full of drama, really over the top."

As a teenager, Jónsi began writing music, not because he was driven to write his own songs but because he was so bad at playing other people's. He soon found that he loved it. "You just made music because you really, really, really loved it. When I think back, there wasn't even a hint of a thought like, I'll be amazingly famous. It never happened, because you were so small and isolated and nobody kind of played stuff from Iceland."

The Iceland Airwaves Music Festival is fifteen years old and lasts five days. It attracts international bands and crowds from all over the world, and a ton of Icelandic bands perform—around 150 in 2014. Another two hundred local bands wanted to play but weren't accepted. I do the math, and figure that if every band has, say, five members and there are 350 bands that apply, that's 1,750 band members in a country of roughly 300,000 people—and those are just the ones who applied to perform at the festival. That's a lot of musicians.

This passion for music making can't merely be a result of boredom or the country's dramatic landscape. So I ask Jónsi why Iceland is such a mecca for music. "There were definitely some independent radio shows that played cool music. There were really good record stores, small record stores, and also you kind of had to create something to make you feel happy. It's just dark nine months of the year. So you kind of had to be doing stuff or you would get really depressed. . . . You can't be outside, so you're just inside making music with your friends or something." Which leads us to the song that changed his life. "I never had any . . . music idol or band or musician. Nobody I really looked up to. Of course, I admired a lot of musicians and bands . . . but I never had any musician I really, really, really liked. So I was thinking about this song that changed my life [and] it's a Sigur Rós song [laughs] . . . a song called 'Fljúgðu.' I think not many people have heard it. It means 'Fly.'" It was the very first time he'd ever been in a recording studio, January 4, 1994. "We formed a band in the studio that day. We were, I remember, really pumped up, really excited. . . . [It was] the first song we had recorded, so I was really excited, and, yeah, that's kind of what started basically everything. . . . I think it was kind of like a communal center . . . where kids could go and stuff like that. But they also had a music studio where bands could go and record fairly cheap. I think it was called Fellaatullir, and we had . . . just met Gunnarsson (Ágúst Ævar Gunnarsson), our first drummer, in school."

At the time, Jónsi was about seventeen years old and commuting from the country into the city. "I met Gunnarsson and Goggi [Georg Hólm], the bass player. And they were really kind of hippies, [with] long hair and funny clothes, and I thought that was really cool. I really had a kinship with them. They were really thinking about music and art and movies and books. . . . I didn't have that many friends like that in the countryside, so I really had a strong kinship to them."

The trio took an acoustic song they'd worked up beforehand and brought it into the studio, but they still didn't think of themselves as a band. "That was kind of the first time we recorded ever, the three of us in '94. That was such a big deal in those days. . . . We started the band on that day. It was called actually Victory Rose. I remember that. My sister Sigurrós was born a week before, so we named the band Sigur Rós [which means Victory Rose], but we wanted to have English because we thought that was cooler than Icelandic. So, yeah, that was Victory Rose, then we just changed it back to Sigur Rós."

What happened in the studio that day wasn't quite what they expected. With the aid of studio effects, including reverb, delay, and distortion, the three friends found themselves creating sounds that were new and surprising. "I remember just the energy that came out, so happy and sitting on the front steps of this apartment. And then it was nighttime and [we were] drinking beer and really happy about the first song. . . . It was like a shooting star." In the days following, though, when they gathered to rehearse, the magic was no longer there. "Nothing happened: we played and played and played and really it didn't come. It didn't sound good. It didn't sound how I wanted it to be. Basically how it sounded was kind of like Smashing Pumpkins rock. We played for one year trying to simulate that atmosphere from the recording."

Over the course of that year, they began to appreciate the trickery of a recording studio. The sounds they loved were created by bands like Spiritualized, Tangerine Dream, and Brian Eno— basically, dreamy music. For a band, finding your voice is a combination of hard work and being open to possible acts of fate and magic. For Sigur Rós that magic appeared in the form of a cello bow, a large contributor to what we now think of as their emblematic sound. "Gunnarsson, the drummer, gave Goggi the cello bow for a Christmas gift. Goggi tried it on the bass but it was kind of hard. It kind of didn't work. So I picked it up and I kind of thought, That works better on a guitar. It's kind of easier to work around." They then added pedals to the guitar, delays, distortion, and re-verbs and their sound began to come together. And over the next year Jónsi's unique and high-voiced singing style emerged. "Yeah, that was something I found because I was always uncomfortable with singing. I started singing because no one else would sing. . . . Someone had to sing. So I found that if I sung high, I could control my voice better. Maybe it was because it was just so loud in the rehearsal space and we didn't have any PA and [if] I sang through some guitar amp, it was really hard to hear yourself. So maybe the high voice pierced out more and it was more audible or something. I could hear myself better. I thought I could pitch my voice better. . . . I felt really comfortable . . . in that range to sing in falsetto and I just started doing that from there."

There are many ways to approach recording. Some musicians love to plan and plot, rehearse, and then execute. Recording for them is simply a matter of documenting what they rehearsed. For Sigur Rós their strength came from exploring. They used and continue to use the studio as an instrument, not simply a recording tool. But their experimentation doesn't end there. At his studio in Reykjavík, Jónsi is working on new material, a long-awaited follow-up to his unique and, at times, joyous solo project *Go*. For this album, he's ambitiously attempting to map songs using non-linear tools of composition, including a sequencing program called Ableton Live. Music made with this software can be formed using small bits—repetitive melodies or beats, for example—and phrases can be looped and altered. It's a very different way to think about making music. Parts aren't recorded from the start of the song to the end, but viewed as modular sections that can come in and out at the touch of a button. Much of the electronic dance music you hear today is made with Ableton Live. Jónsi's new music is not thumping dance beats, though. What he plays me, still in its early stages, is filled with magic and mystery. It is also, as always, dreamy, often epic.

When I leave his studio, I walk past the Harpa Concert Hall

in Reykjavik, a stunning building of black glass that reflects the mountains, ocean, and sky. As I approach the geometric glass structure, a rainbow begins to form. At first it fills only a small portion of the sky, but soon the most spectacular full arc appears. In all my life, I've never seen both ends of a rainbow, especially not one framed between mountains and glaciers. This most remarkable view reaffirms my belief that the music of Iceland is very much related to its landscape. Perhaps it's simply part of the natives' DNA.

ÁSGEIR

"I was going to be a professional athlete. That was my goal. I started throwing javelins when I was eleven and . . . competing on a serious level at thirteen up until seventeen. I moved here [Reykjavík] because it was always between music or being an athlete and I just combined the two and found some balance in it." Finding "balance" is a bit of an understatement. By age nineteen, Ásgeir held the record for biggest-selling debut in Icelandic music history; roughly one in ten people in the country bought his album. *Dýrð í dauðaþögn* was later rerecorded in English as *In the Silence;* it's gentle and dramatic with elegant, slow builds highlighted by Ásgeir's elegiac falsetto. Not bad for a kid whose first rehearsal space was a sheep's pen. "I grew up in a few small towns and the town I always talk about, my hometown . . . [had about] forty people. And mostly—the people there are over seventy years old. . . . My street . . . [had] six houses, and in each house there was just one guy . . . no children, just seventy-year-old guys. . . . [There] were two [kids] . . . that I could kind of hang out with. They were not on my wavelength, but we could play. We'd just play like kids play—football and stuff."

When I meet Ásgeir, he is set to perform one of the many shows he will play at the Iceland Airwaves Music Festival, this one in a recording studio. He's a slender, handsome, bearded young man. Casually dressed, he wears a ski cap that folds just above his unforgettable bluish eyes. He's quiet and a bit shy, but quickly opens up. We initially met a few weeks before when he played at my desk while on his first U.S. tour. He tells me, "[I] had to play music on my own always. . . . There's a ten-kilometer drive . . . to get to a town of five hundred people, and that's where I actually spent most of my childhood from fourteen to sixteen or seventeen. And most of my friends were there, and I formed my first band there, and that's where I found three other guys that could actually play instruments and had fun doing it. After every school day we went to a garage, the drummer's garage, and we played for five hours, and we played live a few times. . . . It's kind of the best background when I think back. Being in that band was probably what formed me, because we were always just playing for the fun of it, and that's where you find yourself."

Ásgeir Trausti Einarsson was born in the summer of 1992 to a music-teaching mom and a stand-up comedian dad. "[He] was always introduced onstage as being the funniest guy in Iceland, and I always found that really interesting when I was growing up, because he really didn't seem like it when we were home. He didn't seem like a boring person, but he didn't really speak that much, he just wrote a whole lot." Between his mom, who played organ and piano, and his dad, who played with words as a poet and humorist dabbling in music, the apple didn't fall far from the tree—that is, if apples could actually grow in Iceland. In fact, all Ásgeir's siblings play, including his three older half siblings from his father's previous marriage (his dad is seventy-four) and the sister he grew up with, who picked up the violin at eight. Ásgeir started playing classical guitar at six. "It wasn't my decision to start playing classical guitar. . . . I wasn't interested in that. It was just pop music I was interested in, maybe being in a band. I thought it was cool at the time, and wanted to play . . . an electric guitar. That was the goal."

When he went to school, there were only four other students, and they were all guys with electric guitars, while Ásgeir was forced to play his nylon-stringed one with perfectly seated posture, the instrument situated between his legs—not exactly a rock star pose. "Between every classical guitar lesson . . . I used to go outside with my friends and just play Nirvana records . . . really loud on the fields, like the open fields. I guess what grabbed me the first time was 'Smells Like Teen Spirit' . . . but as I kind of thought about it more, I started not liking [it] . . . because I knew that [the band] didn't like playing it, and I would listen to it so often that it kind of ruined it for me. But 'Milk It' is one of their songs that I can't stop listening [to], it will always be . . . it's always in the back of my mind. . . . Musically that song has a lot to offer. It's powerful, the beat, I'm all about thinking about songs when I'm writing. . . . I think firstly about the beat and how everything is structured from that, and Dave Grohl [is] one of my favorite drummers—this is just so much him—and then he tightens it all together. ['Milk It'] connects to me in that way, in the rhythmical sense. I don't know if it connects to me in the lyrical sense much, but it's more about this deep-down rebellious structure of a song and [it's] powerful."

Ásgeir's friend Júlíus (Júlíus Aðalsteinn Róbertsson), now the guitarist in his band, turned him on to Nirvana. "The first time I met him he came up to me in a Kurt Cobain T-shirt and I just asked who the fuck this is? And he told me, and then we started listening to it and we started collecting albums and it sort of became an obsession . . . and I must say that I haven't really felt that kind of an obsession with anything since, it kind of was the beginning of everything." At the time, there were only fifteen kids living in their town, where they would blast Nirvana from his boom box. But during the summer, when the town was flooded with young campers, Ásgeir and his friends shared their passion with everyone they met. "We used to go up to strangers—talking to new people about how fucking great this band is. Like, 'Have you heard this band?'" I tell him that I recently had a face-to-face interview with Dave Grohl, and his eyes nearly pop. It's clear he still possesses a deep affection for Nirvana, even though he's now an international star. After all, at only twenty-three years old, he isn't far removed from his teenage obsession.

Ásgeir is a wonderfully accomplished guitarist. His melodies are thoughtful and his fingerpicking intricate. You can tell he spent his teen years alone with his instrument, and while most young, aspiring musicians play songs by the artists they love, Ásgeir didn't—well, except for Nirvana's. "When I was not practicing classical guitar, I would just play . . . my own songs, and so I started really early. . . . I always felt that writing songs was what kept me in music and just wanting to do it. And that was the only thing I kind of had—that was my biggest interest in terms of music. [I] just wanted to write my own. . . . But with Nirvana, I wanted to learn their songs because I wanted to try to play them in practices, so we did that a few times. 'Milk It' is one of the songs . . . I can always listen to again and again and again."

Ásgeir's influences—metal and grunge, and particularly his love for Nirvana—are almost impossible to identify when you listen to the quiet, wistful sounds of his first major release, *Dýrð í dauðaþögn* (or *In the Silence*). "The other guitarist in my band listened a lot to Metallica and Slayer and some more hardcore. And the drummer listened to more old rock, like The Monkees, The Smiths, and stuff like that—and the bassist listened to Icelandic folk music, so it was all over the place. Grunge, metal, yeah. We recorded an album when I was thirteen, just on our own. I listened to it a few weeks ago. It didn't sound that good." Influences take many forms, though, and for Ásgeir it became more about emotional expression than about the explosive volume you hear on an album like *In Utero,* the one that contains "Milk It" and also "Heart-Shaped Box," which I saw Ásgeir cover in the spring of 2014 at WXPN in Philadelphia. He and his bandmate Júlíus sat on stools as they performed, each with an acoustic guitar. Ásgeir's voice held a quiver where Cobain's bore a rasp, and when the song burst into the chorus—"Hey! Wait! I got a new complaint, forever in debt to your priceless advice"—Ásgeir and Júlíus harmonized sweetly, powerfully. I'm so used to hearing Cobain's venom erupt that their version, with its clearly enunciated lyrics and delicate vocals, elevated the meaning, for me, of an already significant song.

I believe artists do their greatest work when they play to their strengths, and singing loud and ballsy isn't what Ásgeir does best. He tried when he was growing up. "I was all about trying to sing with my throat and yelling something, but my voice is too fragile. After just a few minutes of singing like that, I'm just done." Singing at all and projecting volume, even without the screaming, with his fragile voice, was tough at first. "When I started playing with a band, I could sing like two or three songs, and then my voice would just be done, and I couldn't get anything out. . . . The first concert we did, I got through five or six songs, and then I just felt that I couldn't do any more. Because I didn't even talk, I don't talk that much now. . . . I moved here [Reykjavik] when I was sixteen . . . and I didn't speak to anyone for four years and I never asked questions. I just got through it somehow, just said like, 'Fuck it, I don't need anybody. I just need myself.' . . . When I had some time off I just went home and played guitar, and when I had to go to school I just went to school and I didn't use my voice in any way."

Nirvana wasn't Ásgeir's only influence; he was also inspired by fellow Icelander Jónsi, whom I'd spoken with the day before. "I used to look up to him. I always found it fascinating [how he uses] the voice as an instrument, more as telling a story. So early on I started to build songs from my voice . . . harmonies, and stuff like that. And the high-pitched thing comes both from [him] and my brother, actually; my brother has the same range." Harmony has always been central to Ásgeir's music, even when he first began playing with his band. "When I was younger . . . the other guitarist and me, we would spend half of a band practice writing a lyric to a song—and sometimes we would think a little bit about it, but usually it was more about getting the harmony. We used to harmonize everything because we were two singers. And so it could be about a dragon, it could be about a girlfriend, it could be about whatever." Still, they always sang in Icelandic. The idea of a more universal sound or singing in a language with more potential listeners didn't enter their mind then, even though Ásgeir learned to speak English in elementary school.

Ásgeir's guitar style was inspired by Kelly Joe Phelps, an American slide guitar player with a passion for jazz and Delta blues, and by Johnny Cash. "I had heard his songs before, but when I saw [*Walk the Line*] with Joaquin Phoenix, I really fell in love, just started really listening to it and got really interested—and just thinking [about] that kind of a structure when I was writing a song." He also found inspiration in Icelandic folk artists like KK (pronounced "Cow Cow"). "He's an old fellow now, but he used to make some great folk like bluegrass, country records, and is a really good folk artist. His name is Kristján Kristjánsson, also known as KK, and he's like a household name that everybody in Iceland knows, and is really respected here." Kristján Kristjánsson was actually born in Minnesota and at times makes music that would fit nicely beside the work of Johnny Cash and Bob Dylan. However, many of his songs possess a gentle lilt that's more Icelandic than American—and I can definitely hear Ásgeir's attraction. "I heard his songs when I was just six, then I tried out writing Icelandic lyrics in my songs."

———

When I see Ásgeir perform in the Harpa Concert Hall, his second show of the festival, he sings entirely in Icelandic, a decision he and his band come to mere minutes before the show. Even though I know they originally conceived and recorded their album in their native language, it's still odd for me, as I've never heard it this way. But it's also a thrill to watch the crowd lip-synch the lyrics in their own language. When he performed at my desk in D.C., the songs were as I'd come to love them: in English. It was the band's idea to rerecord the album, and Ásgeir enlisted the help of American songwriter John Grant, who was living in Reykjavík at the time. To my ears, the songs sound natural, but not for Ásgeir. "I do feel it's more intimate and natural in Icelandic, and I feel that *that* album is *the* album. . . . I feel like we could have done a much better job . . . [and] taken a lot more time. . . . I don't regret it. It was just a time we went through—[and] I had no idea what was going on. It was so much change in my life, and this idea came up and . . . nobody knew what was going to happen."

Like many talented songwriters before him, Ásgeir envisions the melody first when he sits down to write, while the words often remain gibberish to start. It's not a new technique: famously, when Paul McCartney wrote "Yesterday," he originally sang the title as "scrambled eggs." Ásgeir tells me, "I feel the main thing for many songs is that you want to get the flow of the words into your singing, you know? And as I'm writing a song and as I'm singing the melody, I'm writing, I always put words into it. . . . Not words that have to make sense . . . that's where you really get the right flow and the magical feel that the song and the lyric come together." Cobain expressed a similar idea, and said his lyrics were "just garble, just garbage that would just spew out of me. A lot of times when I write lyrics it's just at the last second, 'cause I'm really lazy." I wouldn't call Ásgeir's lyrics lazy or last second (or Cobain's, for that matter), but it's true they shared the same approach to songwriting—they listened to the music, then reacted viscerally. For Cobain, his initial words often became final, while for Ásgeir they're merely a starting point until he finds the flow and builds dramatic moments.

These days, Ásgeir struggles with one basic question: what language to write and sing in for his next album. "I always want to keep Icelandic in there. It's just a different thing. But I don't want to say good-bye to the English lyrics and singing in English, because we have been getting more popular outside of Iceland . . . and I don't want to give up somehow, you know?" Ásgeir is an agile talent who knows how to connect with an audience. He somehow found a balance between tossing javelins and playing music, so I'm confident he'll successfully navigate the language barrier as well, crafting songs that work for all audiences, and continue turning his gibberish into beauty and telling tales that are universal in his own inimitable style.

HOZIER

As soon as Andrew Hozier-Byrne started to sing, I knew he was a star. What I didn't foresee was the vast number of young screaming girls that would fill his concerts merely one year later. Hozier is tall and charismatic, a handsome Irish-born songwriter and talented guitar player with one hell of a voice. The twenty-four-year-old sang unadorned and unamplified when we hosted him for a Tiny Desk Concert, and the vibe felt familiar—it was the sort of deep, resonating tone I'd heard from powerful singers like Adele, The Avett Brothers, The Tallest Man on Earth, and Miguel when they played at my desk. I know a truly gifted voice when I hear one—it's shiver inducing, bone chilling. Hozier's Tiny Desk Concert, in May

Hozier performing to a screaming crowd at the Lincoln Theatre in Washington, D.C.

2014, preceded the release of his debut album by four months. I was already in love with a number of songs from his first EP, including "Take Me to Church." By the end of that year, that very song had turned him into a big name, perhaps somewhat sparked by its powerful music video depicting a love story between two men in an intolerant country. As I write this, the anti-homophobic video has more than a quarter of a billion views on YouTube.

Hozier grew up on the east coast of Ireland. "I lived in a place called Newcastle, County Wicklow, which is this very small village. It's at least an hour from Dublin's city center. Now, there were small towns around me, and as you get closer to Dublin, those towns get bigger and bigger, but yeah, it was a fairly quiet kind of upbringing." Quiet in the rural sense, but his family home was far from it. Before Andrew was born, his dad was a drummer in a blues band, and the family record collection was filled with rocking blues music. That vinyl, CD, and cassette collection was quite the lifesaver during Andrew's adolescent and teen years, especially since his Internet connection, when there was one, worked at a glacial pace.

Hozier speaks to the significance of his dad's records, and I find myself wondering about the nature of digital music collections and how their influence compares with their physical counterpart. In some ways, I cherish the idea of discovering a vinyl album, with its beautiful artwork, and falling in love with something tangible, tactile—but I grew up that way. When my son was a teenager, he was free to search my thousand-plus album collection, but was more likely to share my iTunes library and discover music digitally. Yet so many of the conversations I've had for this book revolved around a parent's vinyl or physical collection. I suppose it plays into the nurture part of my theory about music discovery—that what you love is part nurture (family and friends) and part nature (what you're naturally attracted to), and I don't think that will ever change. What *will* change as the latest generation grows into adulthood with fewer physical remnants of their musical loves is the act of discovery. It will likely be informed much less by parental curation and personal stories than by happenstance—swiping through YouTube videos, listening to Internet radio, or whatever the unimaginable future versions of video and audio distribution may be. In the end, though less tangible and, one could argue, less personal, the act of online discovery is not that different from sifting through record bins or hearing a random tune on the radio. So while I may romanticize the traditional method of discovering music, I won't assert that one is better or more authentic than the other, they're just different.

For Hozier, his dad's collection and passion for music became a blueprint for his musical career. It mapped out the style he loves and channels as an artist. "It would've been a lot of Chicago blues, so a lot of Texas blues, too, so Muddy Waters, Howlin' Wolf, John Lee Hooker. It would've been Stevie Ray Vaughan in there and then soul music, things like Otis Redding, and Sam and Dave, James Brown, Nina Simone as well. Some of my earliest memories are kind of seeing him [my dad] more when he was playing, and with musicians in the house. By the time I was a teenager, I felt just like it was music I'd heard before, but you don't know where, you don't know how. So I had a fascination with blues music and the roots of African American music, too, and then just going backwards from there, back to Delta blues and gospel, and stuff like that."

In the 1960s, when Andrew's dad was drumming, Dublin had a thriving blues scene. During our conversation, Hozier mentions Rory Gallagher, a fiery guitar player I recall seeing with his band Taste at a Baltimore arena in 1969. Gallagher sold millions of records and is the most famous of the Irish blues-rock musicians. "He's a big Irish hero," says Hozier.

Among his dad's collection, there were cassettes and mixtapes he had compiled so his band could learn traditional blues songs, and Hozier spent a lot of time with those as well. But it wasn't always easy for him to identify the artists on those homemade tapes. He knew Muddy Waters and Son House, and recognized the high voice of Skip James. "For me these were kind of almost distant mysteries, in a way, because it was before I had access online to information about these people, and so for Skip James [it] was just that voice, that kind of real haunting . . . very particular style. He sings in almost like a falsetto, but it doesn't sound like he's singing properly in his head. He moves a lot in this kinda modal thing from major to minor. So when you listen to 'Hard Time Killing Floor Blues' and 'Cypress Grove,' for me it was something that creeped me out in the best way possible. I remember being a teenager and buying Skip James collections."

A father with a passion for the blues certainly explains this Irishman's love for the historically American genre, but the connection between the Irish and the blues goes deeper than a father and son: it dates back generations. We think of the blues as African American in origin, a sort of fusion between traditional African music and European folk, and its familiar call-and-response style is one remnant of its African origins. Other enslaved people shaped this musical form, though—and some were Irish indentured servants, and political prisoners, who worked the sugarcane fields in the West Indies and America alongside enslaved Africans. Additionally, both Irish and African cultures were built on oral traditions, and though independent of one another, they tended toward music composed in minor keys telling stories of oppression. I'm a firm believer that there is something more than environment that shapes our musical being, that it resonates deep within us just as it did for those early folk and blues musicians, the creators of the genre. It's nature/nurture again. And so Hozier's love for the blues is about more than his dad's history as a musician. His connection to those classic inflections goes deeper than a simple aural affinity—and each subsequent generation pushes the form a notch. For instance, Rory Gallagher's electric blues is clearly reminiscent of American blues, but its volume and ferocity set it apart from the traditional form.

For Hozier, another American artist helped define his personal brand of the blues. "I was teaching myself how to play guitar at the time. I was in a band singing soul covers at the age of fifteen with some older guys who were about eighteen. I was a vocalist, but that kind of spurred me to pick up a guitar." He learned to play by ear, first by listening to John Lee Hooker and Muddy Waters, and later took lessons from a fellow named Kieran Murphy. "He gave me my first slide and showed me an open chord, and then for me that was just it. I was listening to Robert Johnson. I was listening to slide player Bukka White, anything I could, and then third fret, fifth fret, seventh fret, twelfth fret. For me the thing that really changed it, though, was discovering Tom Waits. . . . My cousin Oisín Murphy played for me 'Step Right Up' from *Small Change,* and all he said was 'That's a skinny white dude.' I was like, 'That's what? That's insane.' "

Hozier and I are backstage at the 2015 Newport Folk Festival. He stops talking and launches into a spot-on impression of Tom Waits's deep, graveled voice. "Step right up," he sings and then tells me, "I was amazed by it, and . . . [that] led to me, with a dial-up Internet connection, trying to find anything I could on Tom Waits." So he'd listen to samples available from online retailers. "I was hearing thirty seconds of *Alice* or hearing thirty seconds of something off *The Black Rider* and then try and download him singing. I think the first thing was 'Cold Cold Ground' from *Big Time* and I think at that stage I just fell in love with him, and for the next two or three years I was obsessed with his catalog of songs."

That catalog is huge. Tom Waits has been making his distinct style of music since his debut album, *Closing Time,* in 1973. In that time, he's recorded more than twenty albums, all filled with theatrics, poetry, storytelling, and noisemaking. He's an iconic artist with a relatively small but dedicated fan base—and for one budding fifteen-year-old songwriter and guitarist in Ireland, he changed everything. "It definitely was my starting point on writing songs, because I think a lot of his songs were the first ones I learned to play on guitar. I'd say not my first education in music, but my first education in the construct of songs. For me, his songs changed what a songwriter could be. It was just populated with characters, and sometimes it paints a picture of—I don't know—a very sad, empty land that these people populate. All the characters in the songs just fascinated me." Hozier rattles off the lyrics to Waits's "Cold Cold Ground," then says, "Yeah, it's just his lyrics, like 'Call the cops on the Breedloves / Bring a Bible and a rope / And a whole box of rebel / And a bar of soap / Make a pile of trunk tires / And burn 'em all down / Bring a dollar with you baby / In the cold cold ground.' For me there was such a sad loneliness to the song. There's one line, I think, and it goes, 'Beware of my temper / And the dog that I've found / [Break all the windows in the /] Cold cold ground' . . . I don't know what it was about—I was just so attracted to this man. There was ugliness to it, there was ugliness to his voice and ugliness to the way he held himself, but it was such a brilliant ugliness. . . . I was enthralled by it. As a teenager when you feel like shit as well, you want that one thing that is yours and kind of captures your own feeling of awfulness. That was Tom Waits for me. It was like this thing that I had that just consumed me, and it was looking at the way he handled ugly things in a beautiful way."

As a singer-songwriter, Hozier is less known for his lyrics than for the power of his hooks, which is a shame, because his words are brilliant. Blues lyrics are often simple, straight to the point, even when wrapped in metaphor. Hozier's are more reminiscent of Tom Waits's, though; the stanzas are often long and bursting with potent cinematic imagery. His hooks swirl through sometimes complicated song structures, and his lyrics wrap around a chorus of complex emotions. Take, for example, "Work Song," from his debut album. The rhythm feels straight from a field of toiling workers, but the lyrics seem more romantic, and—after speaking with Hozier about his love for Waits—strike me as somewhat inspired by "Cold Cold Ground":

When my time comes around
Lay me gently in the cold dark earth
No grave can hold my body down
I'll crawl home to her

There's a lyrical form in Ireland called an aisling (pronounced *ashling*) that dates back to the poetry of the late seventeenth century. For me, "Work Song" qualifies as part of that tradition. Traditionally, in these poems and songs, the female form symbolized Ireland, and the artist's description of her represented a greater sentiment about the land itself. "A lot of Irish folk songs were written about women," says Hozier, "but they're deliberately representative of Ireland because it was illegal for a long, long time to write songs about loving Ireland, like, nationalistic songs were banned outright." Here are some more lyrics from "Work Song":

And I was burnin' up a fever
I didn't care much how long I lived
But I swear I thought I dreamed her

Throughout our conversation, music from the various stages at Newport blares in the background, and I'm reminded of his performance here exactly one year ago. "This is one of the first festivals I did in America . . . [and] one of the first performances in America. That was the first time that I ever felt like the music was connecting so far from home . . . [and] an audience was listening and wanted to hear the songs." The Newport Folk Festival is steeped in tradition, in African American gospel, blues, and many other folk forms. It's not a coincidence that this audience understood this

Irishman's tunes when he first played for them, and then even more so in 2015. They're a different audience than the screaming fans at his D.C. show, and that's partly how he's advanced the genre—like the lyrics, his music works on many levels and spans categories of listeners. In the tradition of Rory Gallagher, who electrified Irish blues and found a young audience for an old music, Hozier has made a traditional sound his own with hooks that sink deep, history their anchor.

REGINA CARTER

It is accurate to describe Regina Carter as a jazz violinist. Yet as I write the words, I'm listening to her play "Honky Tonkin'," a yearning version of Hank Williams's classic, from her 2014 album *Southern Comfort*. This expressive and resourceful musician's most recent record weaves southern family history between her bow hairs. Long ago, her grandfather was an Alabama coal miner, and she always wanted to play the sort of music he might have heard. It's a concept that works, even when she stretches to contemporary country and covers pioneers like Gram Parsons, specifically "Hickory Wind." She manages to connect disparate styles, eras, and genres. It's why I keep an ear open to any new Regina Carter

Regina Carter performing old songs of the Deep South, inspired by her father, at The Birchmere in Alexandria, Virginia.

project. For this MacArthur Fellow's music turns on a moment: she might play a swinging version of a Duke Ellington tune and then bring you to tears with an adaptation of Ennio Morricone's score for *Cinema Paradiso*. She's also the first African American to play the famed Il Cannone Guarnerius violin, once played by Italian virtuoso Niccolò Paganini. At the same time, she's hooked on the sounds and soul of Detroit, her hometown. It makes for a magical combination of musical traits.

Regina Carter was born in 1966. There's musical talent in her family, but not her immediate one. "My grandmother, my maternal grandmother, actually graduated from Morris Brown with a degree in piano pedagogy in 1915. And she was in our house a lot and played, so there was always some kind of live music going on." It's the spring of 2014, and we are backstage a few hours before her sold-out show at The Birchmere concert hall in Alexandria, Virginia. Her face shines with a bright smile as she leans in and tells me the story of how she came to music at age two, during her brother's piano lesson. "I walked up to the piano one day when my brother's teacher was there and started playing a piece he'd been practicing. And they were all shocked. And [the teacher] said, 'Who showed her how to play that?' They were like, 'No, we didn't even know she could play.' And so she tested me and said, 'Yeah, she's got a musical ability.' So I started piano lessons with a woman named Anna Love in Detroit. She was trying to teach me the conventional way of reading notes. I would go in and I would take her my pieces that I had composed. [She's two and three years old writing music!] I would draw these fake things that looked like dinosaur eggs, but that would be my composition, and I'd play this whole thing for her. And she actually kept them, and when I graduated high school she sent them to my mother. She made a book out of them."

Impressive as this was, reading and writing music wasn't Regina's core strength; hearing music and playing it was. She began playing violin in public school in Detroit, studying the Suzuki method. When she was four years old her teacher sent her home with a stack of classical albums. "We'd take records home and . . . we were told [to] put the record on and go to sleep because you . . . internalize it." Mind you, this was Detroit in the early seventies, the absolute hotbed for the best American pop music, maybe the best pop music anywhere—Motown. Her brother and sisters listened to The Supremes, The Temptations, Stevie Wonder, and The Beatles, but Regina had more exotic interests. "Detroit was a very culturally rich, culturally mixed, rich city." There was an array of diverse communities in the area, including Greek, Polish, Mexican, and the largest population of Assyrian-Chaldean Christians in the U.S., so, according to Regina, "you had an opportunity to go into these neighborhoods and just eat there, shop, whatever, and you hear all these sounds." The Detroit jazz scene was a hotbed of talent, too, but she wouldn't discover the music that would become hers until a bit later in life.

Regina learned many classical works during those early years, and often went to the symphony with her mother on weekends. There was one song that especially moved her as a child. "I think the first time I had a piece really touch me, because for me it was just fun, but the first time I think was . . . 'The Swan.'" The piece, composed by Camille Saint-Saëns in the late nineteenth century, is part of a larger work titled *The Carnival of the Animals*, where instruments represent the movement and sounds of wild creatures. "I remember just listening to it over and over and over. It stirred something really deep in me."

All the while, Regina was surrounded by the music of American pop culture. Her brother DJed small house parties in the room below hers, but she felt there was a disconnect between the music she played and the music of the time. She didn't see how pop music was something she could perform on her instrument, even with all the strings that can be heard in Motown and other radio hits of the period.

Then, in ninth-grade Spanish class, she met a new friend named Carla Cook, who became Regina's link to a type of music fairly unknown to her: jazz. "She would come to school and talk about Eddie Jefferson every day or Miles Davis. . . . I had never heard of these people. She brought me some records. She brought me a Jean-Luc Ponty record and a Noel Pointer record and a Stéphane Grappelli record." All three made music on the violin. For young Regina, the music they produced on the instrument she loved was unimaginable. Grappelli is the granddaddy of the jazz violin, whose swinging music from the 1930s with guitarist Django Reinhardt is alive and influential to this day. In his early days, violinist Ponty straddled the line between classical orchestral music and nightclub jazz. Carla Cook played upright bass, and they began making music together. "We would try those tunes, like there was one Jean-Luc Ponty tune called 'Renaissance.' It was only four notes, really, on the bass. I mean, not to say it was an involved piece, but it was easier for us to do as a duo together. Then we both also loved Stéphane Grappelli . . . [and Carla] wrote a piece called 'Potter à Regina.' And it was in a Grappelli style, [so] we played that. And we went to a music, art, and science high school. It was a special high school in Detroit. Everyone was so creative . . . writing music and playing."

I often wonder about the role fate plays in the life of an artist, and ask Regina if she feels her life in music was somehow predetermined. "I think about [that] sometimes. I think, well, I do believe that it was my road. I feel that I'm really lucky to have been born when I was born, because even if my parents didn't pay for the music lessons early on, I got it in school. I had music. I had strings in school. We'd play on the little xylophones. We'd sing in class. . . . And so I had that opportunity even if I hadn't been able to afford the lessons early on." Through her friend Carla and the rich culture of Detroit, sixteen-year-old Regina saw the world's master jazz violinist Stéphane Grappelli perform on a nearby hotel rooftop. This was her first concert outside the classical world. "Oh, it was amazing. . . . I was like, This is it. I found my thing. This is what I've got to do. Finally, I don't have to have someone tell me, 'One more time. No, it has to be played like this.'"

Regina also fell in love with the music of Noel Pointer, a contemporary American jazz violinist about eight years her senior. He, too, was classically trained but had found a way to tap into pop music; he played in the Love Unlimited Orchestra and the Apollo Theater Orchestra, as well as with the Dance Theatre of Harlem. Regina hung a Noel Pointer poster on her closet door, and would spin his albums on her Panasonic portable record player. One day, Pointer came to play at a club called Baker's Keyboard Lounge, about a mile from where she lived. Regina's mom took her and her violin-playing friends to the show. It was an inspired performance, not at all uncommon at Baker's, the world's oldest operating jazz club. "Noel was playing at Baker's and he played through the hairs on two of his bows, so I went home and got one of my bows so he could finish the gig. And I got everyone's signature in the band and I never had the bow re-haired. It was just in my room." Pointer died from a stroke at only thirty-nine years old. Years later, Regina played a tribute for him with some of his band members. She describes Pointer, Grappelli, and Ponty as her green lights, her signposts, the way she knew she was heading in the right direction and expanding her vocabulary on the violin.

Throughout our talk, I'm sure Regina will choose Noel Pointer's now classic 1977 cut "Night Song," or his classic remake of Stevie Wonder's "Superwoman," as the song that changed her life, but she throws me a curve. "I heard this tune and it was so funky, but it had these string arrangements that were amazing. . . . I was standing in the mirror and I learned all the string lines." It was "Lovin' Is Really My Game," by a band not well known to me but pivotal for Regina—Brainstorm, a Detroit funk band. She used to pretend she was onstage performing while she listened to their records. At that point she was about sixteen, and played an electric-blue violin like Jean-Luc Ponty. She owned a wah-wah pedal but still needed an amp, so her dad took her to Wonderland, a nearby music store. "I'm paying for it and I'm getting ready to leave and this guy goes, 'So you play violin?' I said, 'Yeah.' He goes, 'You any good?' I said, 'Yep.' I was very sure of myself back then. He goes, 'You ever hear of a group called Brainstorm?' I was like, 'Yes!' He goes, 'Well, I'm the co-leader of that group.' Can you imagine? He's working at this music store. I played for him and then he said, 'Do you want to do a gig with us?' So I was over the moon." The band was about to go on tour with The Jacksons. "My mother was like, 'No. No. You are not going, no.' They begged her. I was like, 'Mom! You don't get it. This is my time. If I wait, by the time I get to be twenty I'm going to be too old.' I really thought that. I just thought twenty was old."

For this tour, Mom won and Regina stayed home. Eventually, though, she toured with the band, but only on weekends and if her grades were good. "I would do all the little string parts just myself. I would take parts and make stuff up, and it was so much fun." Their music was a bold departure from "The Swan" and from all the classical music she had spent so much time studying. But all of it became Regina Carter—from those songs her grandfather knew in Alabama to the music that put Noel Pointer's bow in her bedroom and Paganini's violin in her hands.

"I knew I wanted to be a professional musician, but . . . my mom wanted me to be in a symphony orchestra so I could have the pension, health insurance, blah, blah. And I always would sit in the audience and watch the symphony and say, No, I want to be the soloist in front of the symphony, I don't want to be in it. I'm a leader. It's just my nature, I have to be the boss."

And these days, she is.

ASAF AVIDAN

I clearly recall driving home one icy winter evening and hearing a voice like no other. Before I leave work each day, I load my phone with songs from that day's submissions, a playlist titled *Today*. I just hit shuffle and drive. That night, as I made my way up North Capitol Street, with the beautiful domed basilica of Catholic University on my right, an over-the-top-incredible voice came through my speakers. I was stunned by this woman's vocal prowess—she sounded a bit like Janis Joplin. I couldn't wait for the next red light so I could search for her name. When I looked, my screen read: ASAF AVIDAN. I had no idea who she was. At the next light I quickly googled the name and found a picture of a handsome, skinny, bearded man and thought, That can't be right.

A mesmerizing set from Asaf Avidan at the 9:30 Club in Washington, D.C.

When I got home, I discovered a fact that any music lover in Israel could have told me—Asaf Avidan is a beautiful, famous, thirty-something Israeli singer. I was completely blown away; the voice and the bearded face didn't connect for me. Imagine hearing Janis Joplin or Nina Simone and discovering it was a guy. The song that floored me was the title track from *Different Pulses,* his first solo album, released in Israel in 2012, soon afterward in Europe. I received my copy in 2014, though it's never been formally distributed here. In fact, until 2015's *Gold Shadow,* Avidan had never released a record in the States.

Avidan is best known as the driving force behind the band Asaf Avidan & the Mojos. *The Reckoning,* their debut, from 2008, is one of the biggest-selling Israeli independent albums ever released. It's a bluesy folk record comprised of songs of heartache sung in his amazing voice. The band produced two more successful albums, *Poor Boy/Lucky Man,* in 2009, and *Through the Gale,* in 2010. Here's where it gets even weirder. In 2011, a young Berlin-based DJ with the stage name Wankelmut took the audio files of "Reckoning Song" and, with the aid of the program Ableton Live—and without Avidan's permission—added steady, pulsing drums and effects processing to the original vocal and acoustic guitar track. He uploaded his remix to SoundCloud and later to YouTube, calling it "One Day/Reckoning Song," and the thing went viral. On YouTube the number of views totals nearly two hundred million—and that's in spite of Avidan's request for Wankelmut to take it down.

As fate would have it, only weeks after I first heard "Different Pulses" in my car, Asaf Avidan came to North America, just him and his guitar, a one-man band on a twelve-city tour. One of his concerts was a few blocks from NPR. I asked him if he would play a Tiny Desk Concert, and he didn't disappoint. In fact, he stunned quite a few colleagues, casual listeners, and music geeks.

—

Avidan never aspired to be a musician. As a kid he had his "own kind of imaginary world," Dungeons & Dragons. Born in Israel, he moved to Jamaica at a young age with his diplomat parents and two brothers. He was around seven at the time and somewhat of a loner. The role-playing game allowed him to create characters and lose himself in fantasy. He has an early music memory from those days, though: the time his dad gave him a pair of large headphones and played Pink Floyd's *The Wall* on their turntable. Avidan was captivated by the sheer theatrics of this epic 1979 double LP filled with songs of isolation. He remembers the beautiful gatefold art and illustrations, but what really stayed with him were Roger Waters's fragile vocals. "It was an honest vulnerability that I love. Maybe that's what I like about most of the vocalists that I like, that they are not trying to sing beautifully."

Years later, when Avidan was twelve and his family was back in Israel, he discovered his passion for rock. He was at his friend Tal's place when he heard a cassette tape of Nirvana's *Nevermind*. "Remember how you used to press play and you had that hiss and you wait until, like, a couple of seconds? I didn't have the patience, so I fast-forwarded . . . and then it was like the tenth second of the song ['Smells Like Teen Spirit']. And my friend said, 'No, no, no, no. You have to listen to it.' Because it starts with that guitarist and then the drums kick in. And I remember that—that start—changed everything for me. That's when I realized what rock and roll is. It was the first honest thing I've ever heard. I was like twelve years old. It sounded [like] the only real thing I've ever heard in my life. It had that vulnerability that I loved. It felt like somebody in genuine pain who could understand me and could give voice to what I was going through. So that was the defining moment . . . what got me into music, but I didn't become a musician until much later in my life."

Growing up, Avidan heard a lot of blues from his dad and began to explore the roots of the rock music he loved. As he dug deeper, he discovered more "honest vulnerability." From Led Zeppelin he learned about John Lee Hooker, a black American bluesman known for his guitar-driven rhythms and for talking the blues. "Boogie Chillen" was one of those great John Lee Hooker songs.

In the NPR studio with me, Avidan is like a kid chatting about his musical quests. He tells me that he went on a sort of archaeological dig back then with the blues, starting with white kids playing the blues, then discovering their black roots. He has a look of revelation on his face as he says, "It's almost like, that's the coffee beans, you know the rest is just the water." He's not dismissing the Led Zeppelins and Janis Joplins of the world. These artists are all part of what he sees as a natural musical progression, the "living language" that Tom Manoff wrote about in *Music: A Living Language*. It's the idea that music is continuous—it inspires and influences what follows it, forming a never-ending cycle. Artists like Bob Dylan and Leonard Cohen, who inspired many, were influenced by those who came before them. Then Avidan chokes up a bit as he recalls a Leonard Cohen quote that for him defines the music he loves: "'We must never lament casually, and we must always do it with a sense of honor and beauty.' I get goose bumps just saying that. And that is exactly music to me. And it can define any music that I like. It can define *The Wall* and it can define Muddy Waters: 'Never lament casually.'" He leans forward and tells me the one song that changed him forever: Leonard Cohen's "Famous Blue Raincoat," from his brilliant third album, *Songs of Love and Hate,* released in 1971.

"Famous Blue Raincoat" is structured as a letter from the singer to another man, an old friend who had an affair with the singer's lover. It almost reads as a thank-you note, an outpouring of emotion written long after the affair has ended. Avidan explains its effect: "I can almost feel the surgeon's saw cutting his rib cage and just pouring it out there. His wife slept with his friend and he forgives him." And then he quotes, "'I guess that I miss you. I guess I forgive you. I'm glad you stood in my way.' And then there's—and I get goose bumps as well, but when he says that line, that one line that is the essence—'And thanks for the trouble you took from her eyes. I thought it was there for good, so I never tried.' I mean, that is just, wow!" It *is* the killer moment of this song. Cohen not only forgives but thanks his old friend, recognizing that he was able to do something that Cohen couldn't—take the pain and sadness from her eyes. "Famous Blue Raincoat" is truly a triumph of thought and pen.

Avidan discovered most of Cohen's canon through his ex-girlfriend Natalie. She was his first real love, and the one who eventually inspired him to write and sing. Most of the songs he wrote then can be heard on his first album with the Mojos. He was with Natalie from the age of nineteen to twenty-six, and Leonard Cohen was their music, their glue, their melancholy. They found their way through all of his music while on a journey to find a particular song that she had heard once with the word "Eskimo" in it. It was pre-Internet as we know it, and they figured the best way to find the song was to buy every one Cohen ever recorded. The song was "One of Us Cannot Be Wrong" and it was on the Canadian singer's debut album from 1967, which also contains one of his most famous songs, "Suzanne."

Avidan most admires the sense of tradition in Cohen's music. His song forms are familiar and combine a variety of genres. You can hear flamenco in his guitar styling, his love for the spiritual in his yearning, and the blues in his pain. After Avidan and Natalie parted ways, Avidan tried to find his own voice and write his own songs. "It was, in the most cheesy but most profound way, it was my way of not having to pay for a shrink." The experience went beyond writing words about his breakup. He found value in vocalizing and regurgitating, in hearing himself sing. "You let it out and then you can start chewing it back in and digest it better. And then it goes out again, and it's a form of understanding yourself and releasing—and that's also the essence of the blues." He also discovered the commonality between the music he loved and the music he made: honesty. That is key for him, what ties it all together. "They are messages to somebody you are trying to tell somebody about, and that person, somebody, broke your heart."

One of the great ironies of Leonard Cohen's career is that despite his deep, alluring voice and avid fan base, he never sold many records. His fame grew as other artists covered his work. The most famous instance is "Hallelujah," a song he released in 1984. One of the first to cover it was John Cale, a founding member of the seminal band The Velvet Underground. Cale's version is just voice and piano; it was recorded for a tribute album called *I'm Your Fan*, a title that plays on Cohen's "I'm Your Man." Cohen wrote something like eighty verses to "Hallelujah," and the lyrics vary between recordings. Before he covered it, Cale asked Cohen for the lyrics and received fifteen faxed pages. He ended up using what he considered the "cheeky verses." Cale's version helped shape Jeff Buckley's a few years later—one of the most inspired cover songs ever recorded. Buckley, the son of one of Cohen's peers, Tim Buckley, made the song his own; his voice soars, the guitar sears, and the feeling, while somber, is also uplifting, more so than the original. His 1994 album, *Grace*, which contains "Hallelujah," is one of rock's most brilliant albums, but he never knew how the world came, over the years, to embrace it: Jeff Buckley drowned in 1997.

One of the great ironies of Avidan's career, like Cohen's, is that it took another artist's version of his song to make him a worldwide name. (Remember Wankelmut?) Avidan is still young and his career yet to be defined, but I think this fact speaks to the universal nature of his music—passionate, honest, and vulnerable. It's the compelling force behind whichever version of "Reckoning Song" you come to love. His lyrics are sung with fervor:

One day, baby, we'll be old
Oh baby, we'll be old
And think of all the stories that we could have told

I find that same lyrical truth at the heart of Cohen's "Hallelujah" and "Famous Blue Raincoat," and his declaration "Never lament casually" certainly defines the music of Asaf Avidan. It's no wonder versions of their songs are embraced the world over.

VALERIE JUNE

When I listen to the music of Valerie June, I hear an old southern blues woman (and sometimes a man) tell tales of a weary life. I first saw this stunning, dreadlocked woman perform at my desk on a hot summer day in 2013. The voice full of experience from such a young, fresh face was enchanting, and her songs of rural Tennessee flatlands, cotton fields, and fortune-tellers feel like they're from another time altogether. The first song she sang that day opens her album *Pushin' Against a Stone;* it's called "Workin' Woman Blues":

> I ain't fit to be no mother
> I ain't fit to be no wife

Valerie June performs a set of timeless and original tunes at the Newport Folk Festival in 2014.

I've been working like a man y'all
I've been working all my life

Valerie June Hockett was born in 1982, in western Tennessee. She is the oldest of five children, and grew up in the cities of Jackson and Humboldt. Her dad was a music promoter for gospel, blues, and R&B shows, and worked with artists like Bobby Womack and the young Prince. His profession was a blessing and a curse. Valerie tells me that for a long time it soured her mother's attitude toward music. "When I was growing up, she stopped listening to music because promoting is very difficult, and you can lose a lot of money. . . . He would put all his money . . . it's like gambling . . . into bringing in a great artist, and then if it rained or something, then they lost money. So she wasn't listening. She was like, 'Aw, man, that racket. There's that racket.' She's not like that now. She loves listening to music. But at that time, I think she kind of shut down to music."

Valerie remembers living in a nice little house when she was young, but then the promoting business fell apart and her dad, who was also in construction, "lost his shirt." "We had to move to the other side of town, and it was not such a nice house. We got broken into all the time, and there were, like, rats in there and stuff. They had this dream, because he builds houses and he has a company of construction, that they would buy land, and that they would build their dream house. My mom was into drawing and architecture, so she was drawing the house and everything, and then he had an architect he was working with, so they got the plans made. Finally, they found the land. We moved out there, and they built . . . a massive garage big enough for his eighteen-wheeler trucks, and his dozers and tractors. . . . They made it into an apartment. And the kids were upstairs, and downstairs was their area. And so that's where I lived, in a garage for most of my life. And what happened, it burnt down. When I was fourteen, fifteen, it burnt down. We came home, and we lost everything. It was gone. Baby pictures, clothes, everything. Everything. Nothing was saved. So we stayed in a motel . . . until he got another . . . job, and he got the money for it up front so that he could purchase [another] house . . . which was finally a real house. And it's very nice. It's a country home, big enough for a family of seven people. And I was excited because I was embarrassed to live in a garage. All those years in school, I was just like, I don't want anybody to know where I live. But now I wish I lived in the garage because I could turn up my amp, and I could get crazy in there, man. Nobody would care."

Valerie received her first guitar as a gift from her grandfather when she was fifteen. She promised him she'd learn to play and was inspired to sing when she heard bluegrass artist Alison Krauss cover Keith Whitley. "She sang, 'When You Say Nothing at All.' Her voice was so crystal clear, and it was so beautiful, and I was like, Oh my God, that voice is like glass. It seems so delicate and fragile, but so beautiful and clear at the same time. . . . When I heard her voice, I was like, I want to sing. I just want to sing." Even though this song inspired her, it's not the one that changed her life.

In her late teens Valerie left home to live with her future (now former) husband, guitarist Michael Joyner. Valerie and Michael's Memphis band was called Bella Sun. After they parted ways, she took the time to really learn to play the guitar and banjo. She calls her style "organic moonshine roots music" that blend of gospel, blues, country, and folk that I first heard in "Workin' Woman Blues." Soon her mournful sound, with its deep, heartfelt southern roots, attracted the attention of MTV, which featured her in the online series $5 Cover; the series follows Memphis musicians as they try to do what they love and also pay the rent. Valerie sang "The No Draws Blues," a song about liberation. It's a song her mother doesn't much like, because of lines like these:

I don't wear no draws
I just want to be free

No panty hose down to my toes
And no thongs they do me wrong

Valerie doesn't write many songs about her vision for the world, but this one, with its crude humor and honesty, surely lays bare her philosophy.

When Valerie tells me about the song that truly changed her life, inspiring her to write music, we are sitting in an old historic fort on the grounds of the 2014 Newport Folk Festival. I don't see this one coming. She heard it back in that garage at around fourteen years old. "We had a classic rock station down in Jackson. It was a guilty pleasure. . . . 'Imagine,' by John Lennon [came on]. And the beautiful story, and the lyrics, and that made me start to study his life. I was curious. Who is this person? I wasn't really into The Beatles. I wasn't really into that. I didn't know names of musicians and stuff. I was kind of a little bit aware, but not so much. . . . It was the lyrics . . . the vision of living in the world like that. I mean, and to sing it. I thought about the time that he was singing it in the sixties and seventies, and that stuff, and how the world was changing, and people were trying to become more open in a lot of ways, and with racism, trying to overcome that here in America, and I just thought it was really magical and beautiful, that song. And the soft sweetness of his voice, and I was like, I want to live in that world that he just created. . . . I think if a song can make you want to get inside it, then it's probably gonna be a really great song."

John Lennon wrote "Imagine" in one swift session on his Steinway in May 1971, eleven years before Valerie June was born. He recorded it at his home studio in Tittenhurst Park, England, and finished it in New York City. The lyrics were inspired by Yoko Ono's poem "Cloud Piece." It's remarkable to think that this song never reached number one on Billboard's chart; three was its highest position, though it was Lennon's best-selling single. It's also hard to imagine that "Imagine," now revered, was beaten out by Cher's "Gypsys, Tramps & Thieves" and Isaac Hayes's "Theme from *Shaft*." In that same year, fellow Beatles members George Harrison and Paul McCartney both hit number one, with "My Sweet Lord" and "Uncle Albert/Admiral Halsey," respectively. Over time, though, I think it's become clear that "Imagine" resonated much deeper than those other tunes. It's been covered by over 150 artists, including Elton John, Stevie Wonder, CeeLo Green, and Queen, who performed it at the Wembley Arena on December 9, 1980, the day after Lennon was murdered.

Interesting things happen to pop songs when they are played as frequently as "Imagine." Despite becoming an anthem or classic, they're often dissociated from their original meaning. It's easy to think of this song as simply a dream for world peace, but if you listen to what Lennon is really saying—imagine a world without heaven, hell, religion, material possessions, greed, or hunger; a world of sharing—it's revolutionary. And it pissed off a lot of people, especially his line "no religion too." It was a subversive pop number wrapped in a lovely piano ballad—and the wrapping made it digestible worldwide. This, of course, includes the classic rock stations that continue to play it constantly, just as they did eighteen years ago when it first caught the ear of a young girl in Tennessee. It's impossible to know whether Valerie will ever write lyrics that show us her vision of the world in this way. It's not the kind of song she writes, even if it is the kind that resonates with her. And though she's now in her early thirties, approximately the same age as Lennon when he wrote "Imagine," she hasn't recorded at the breakneck pace that he and his peers did during the 1960s— sometimes releasing three albums a year. And her career is still young.

Before 2010, Valerie produced three solo albums, all "bedroom recordings." Then she started a Kickstarter campaign to record a proper album and raised fifteen thousand dollars in sixty days. Soon

L.A. producer Kevin Augunas, renowned for his skill with vintage recording gear, heard her music and flew to Memphis. He asked her who she'd like to record with, and she named Dan Auerbach of The Black Keys, whom Augunas had worked with in the past. Valerie and Auerbach cowrote a number of the songs on *Pushin' Against a Stone,* he plays guitar on eight of them, and they coproduced it with Augunas. The album's vintage tone perfectly highlights her songs and sound. And when I hear the fiddle and banjo backing the beautiful refrain of "Somebody to Love," I sense a glimmer of the dreaming vision she so admired about John Lennon.

Are you watching the moon risin'
In the darkest of night
Battered and broken
'Cause you know it ain't right
. . .
And I'll be somebody
I'll be somebody
Somebody to love

Valerie is now learning to play piano. Maybe one day she'll write a song we'll want to get "inside of." I trust it will be a really great one.

CONOR OBERST

"There was always a guitar sitting on the couch, and so it wasn't a big stretch to just pick it up one day—and then right away my dad was like, 'Do you want to learn a chord?' And showed me how to play an E chord. . . . I can remember being so little—he had a big, beautiful, dreadnought-sized Martin guitar—and I can remember trying to get my arm over the top of it to get to the strings and . . . how hard it was physically to do it."

I'd say Conor Oberst is a pretty fortunate fellow. He grew up with loving and supportive parents. His mother, Nancy, was a lifelong educator, a schoolteacher and principal, and his father, Matthew,

Conor Oberst and big band, including members of Dawes, perform songs from *Upside Down Mountain* at the Newport Folk Festival in 2014.

played cover tunes like "Maneater" in his band while working full-time as information manager at Mutual of Omaha, where Conor grew up. "It's sort of an oldish part of Omaha. Nice brick houses, but they're not too big and the lots are pretty close together, so I wouldn't say you're right on top of your neighbors, but they're right there. . . . It was a pretty idyllic place to grow up, really. I spent a lot of time out playing with all the neighbor kids . . . capture the flag and running around, riding our bikes everywhere."

From an early age, Conor was passionate about writing, and one of his teachers, Miss Allen, encouraged him. "I started to become interested in words first. I remember, I would have been in third grade. They give you these little creative writing assignments . . . and I wrote some kind of poem or a story. I don't even remember what it was exactly. But I remember my teacher having to call my parents because she didn't quite believe that I had written it without help, you know? And they were like, 'Well, I'm pretty sure he did it by himself.' . . . It was funny because was I going to be in trouble, and then instead of being in trouble, [Miss Allen] lavished me with praise and let me do more. . . . She was a great teacher, figured out that I was interested in words and language."

The music around the house was a good mix of literate song-writers. "I would say my early exposure to music was a pretty even split between what my brothers listened to and what my parents listened to. . . . Fortunately my parents had pretty good taste. . . . There's definitely a lot of Simon and Garfunkel, a lot of Fleetwood Mac, Jackson Browne, Joni Mitchell, Neil Young, all that kind of stuff, and then my brothers—it was kind of *120 Minutes* era of, like, alternative music, R.E.M., Smiths, Cure, all that great stuff in the eighties, so that was sort of where my musical journey started."

Conor recalls one particular car ride when he was a child, the first time he heard Don McLean's "American Pie" on the radio. "[It] was one of the first songs that really caught my ear in a deep way, just hearing it on an oldies radio station and asking my mom to stay in the car. I wanted to keep the radio on until the song was over, which, it's a long song." It clocks in at eight minutes, thirty-three seconds, and to this day it is the longest song to hit number one on *Billboard*. More important, it is a song that got people talking. Those eight and a half minutes tell a history of America from the late 1950s to the late 1960s, all related in an oblique and metaphorical way that begins with the death of three promising young rock and rollers—Buddy Holly, Ritchie Valens, and J. P. Richardson, best known as the Big Bopper, who all perished in a small-engine plane crash on February 3, 1959. Conor first heard the song around the same time *La Bamba* was released, in 1987. The film was about Ritchie Valens's eight-month music career, which ended with his death at seventeen. Conor loved *La Bamba* and was inspired by Don McLean's classic: "And I remember my dad explaining to me what the song was about, or at least 'the day the music died' part . . . and it made a really strange, deep impact on me, the fact that you could be singing indirectly about an event, I guess, just alluding to something, that idea was very new to my seven-year-old brain. . . . And I think in a strange way, it set me on a path to wanting to do that somehow."

Music played a significant role in Conor's childhood home. His dad kept a number of guitars in their basement, along with a piano—his brother played guitar as well—and then there was the family hi-fi. Conor also spent a lot of time with his own music. "I had a little boom box in my room and I would say most of my listening was tapes that had been dubbed onto blank cassettes that I played endlessly." He recorded music from his parents' collection and from friends and neighbors. "There were a lot of kids in our neighborhood. A little later on my next-door neighbor had a band, and me and my next oldest brother would sneak over and watch their band practice. . . . [I] met a lot of friends I still have, actually, from those days."

About a year following his class with Miss Allen, Conor picked up the guitar. "[At] ten or eleven I started playing guitar and pretty much immediately—I mean, I don't know if you'd call them songs, because I don't think a lot of them were completed ideas—but pretty much immediately wanted to combine those two interests of the language and the words with being able to, even very clumsily, strum two chords back and forth. . . . To me, that was much more exciting than learning scales. I think it's part of the reason I'm still not that great of a guitar player, because I never had particular interest in that. It was sort of a means to an end. I got better over the years just through playing, but I was never one to sit in the basement with the guitar magazine and the tablature and figure out 'Smoke on the Water.' I gravitated much more to the poetry side of it, and the melody. I've always really loved a good hook, a melodic vocal hook, and I guess singing was of more interest than guitar in that sense."

Conor's biggest role models then were his musician friends, like Ted Stevens, and other local songwriters, "the biggest ones being this guy Simon Joyner, who is still a hero of mine, and Tim Kasher, who is of course [in] Cursive and [the] Good Life. He's five or six years older than me. He's about my oldest brother [Matt]'s age, and they actually played music together in high school. So Justin [Conor's next oldest brother] and I were young enough that we started to become obsessed with Tim as fans, because we would go see his bands play." Between Tim's group Slowdown Virginia and Ted Stevens's band Lullaby for the Working Class, Conor found a path to his own music. "Tim and Ted were both songwriters who I really admired, but they were also close enough to have access to—I could talk to them. I was kind of a little kid tagging along, but they were always sweet to me. And then Ted was the first person who heard me playing a song I had written on my porch, probably on his way out of band practice at the neighbors' house, and stopped and was like, 'Will you play that for me? Will you start at the beginning?' And I was, of course, beside myself with nerves, but I got through the song and he was like, 'Wow, do you have any more?' And I was like, 'I got this other one.'" Right there on the porch Ted made Conor an offer. "[He said,] 'Maybe I'll come over and record you,' and I was just like, 'What? That seems insane.' And sure enough, he did it, and that ended up being the first little cassette tape that I sold at the local record store." The cassette was called *Water*. On it you can hear a thirteen-year-old, prepubescent Conor play deeply felt tunes without enough skill on voice or guitar to execute what was clearly in his head. I don't know if you have embarrassing memories of singing around that age, but I do (and so do most Jewish men, because at thirteen our parents forced us to sing a portion of the Torah in Hebrew in front of our relatives and friends at our bar mitzvahs). It takes a brave kid to put his or her musical dream out into the world—and Conor was a talented lyricist even back then. From *Water*'s opening song, "You Should Be in Sweden," it's clear you're listening to the words of a mature thirteen-year-old. The imagery reflects his age:

I saw you at the subway the other day
You were drinking hot chocolate
I thought about asking you for a sip
But on second thought I didn't want to burn my tongue

Conor tells me about those early attempts: "I sang in a really strange, affected accent, almost because I liked the way that Tim [Kasher] sang, but Tim was trying to sing like these English singers, like Morrissey and Robert Smith. . . . I think for any singer it takes them a while to find their true voice. . . . A lot of times you're imitating someone you like, or you're just singing in sort of an intentionally strange way that makes it easier for you to hear yourself." Conor was a fan of Robert Smith's band, too. In fact, the first cassette he owned that wasn't dubbed was The Cure's *Standing on a Beach*. "Man, I love that tape. I listened to that so much because it was the kind of extended long tape, so it had all the A sides of all the singles, and then had their kind of weird, moody B sides on the back. . . . I don't even know how they made tapes that long, but yeah, I memorized every second."

Conor started playing solo shows around age thirteen. It was just him and his guitar at the local coffee shop. "I had played a couple of shows, and then I remember—[I'm] about to play my little set—and someone being like, 'Hey, Simon's here. He's in the back.' And just being like, Oh my God. Here goes nothing." Simon Joyner was a local music hero in Omaha. There's something encouraging about being a big fish in a small pond, about beginning your musical career in a place where you can make a splash early on. I'll never forget the first time I was ever onstage. It was with Tiny Desk Unit, and I was twenty-six years old—twice Conor's age—and playing my ARP Odyssey synthesizer. Around 1979, there were probably a few hundred active music fans in D.C. interested in live, original shows, and very few clubs in which to play. D.C. may be considered a big town, but back then its music community was more akin to Conor's experience in Omaha. That night my friends made it possible for me to get through what became an unnerving near disaster of a show. I was pumped with adrenaline, smashing my keyboard too hard, and within a few songs, I had broken the instrument so it would play only one note. I was forced to turn it upside down midshow, take a hex wrench to the bolts, and unstick the wires that were shorting out the keyboard. I was sweating profusely the entire time, but finished the repair and the show—and haven't found it scary to be onstage since. I figure, if I can get through that, I can get through anything.

In high school, Conor formed his first band, Commander Venus, and then his idol Tim Kasher joined. "And so then all the sudden, I'm in a band with my hero. . . . I feel like the local music scene and being able to meet Simon Joyner after worshipping his records and have him say, 'Do you want to play a show together?' . . . those little things, when you're that age, put so much wind in your sails and make you kind of believe anything is possible."

I first met Conor in the winter of 2005 at the 9:30 Club. I'd just fallen in love with two albums he simultaneously released with his band Bright Eyes, *I'm Wide Awake, It's Morning* and *Digital Ash in a Digital Urn*. I knew little about him then but was immediately taken by his songwriting, the vast scope of his music. *I'm Wide Awake* is the more acoustic side of his sound, and *Digital Ash* the more electronic. At the time, I wanted to do something special with him, beyond featuring his music on *All Songs Considered*. I have a long history with the 9:30 Club and know the owner, Seth Hurwitz. He allowed NPR to host a live audio webcast of Bright Eyes from his club—so just four days following the release of their albums, Conor and his band were performing before an audience that far exceeded their expectations.

The song that first drew me in was the opening track of *I'm Wide Awake, It's Morning*, "At the Bottom of Everything." Like Don McLean's "American Pie," this one opens referencing a plane crash. Conor begins by telling us a story—with no backing music, almost off the cuff—about a female passenger, a bit of a lost soul, who is "high above the largest ocean on planet earth" on her way to her fiancé. She feels bored and despondent, and is seated next to a man, thinking about starting a conversation, when:

Suddenly there was this huge mechanical failure and one of the
    engines gave out
And they started just falling, thirty thousand feet
And the pilot's on the microphone and he's saying
"I'm sorry, I'm sorry, oh my God, I'm sorry"
And apologizing and she looks at the man and she says
"Where are we going?" and he looks at her and he says
"We're going to a party, it's a birthday party

It's your birthday party, happy birthday, darling
We love you very, very, very, very, very, very, very much."
And then, uh, he starts humming this little tune and, uh, it kind of
    goes like this . . ."

Then Conor launches into the song that won my heart. Like all music, the lyrics and meaning are open to interpretation. My take-away: it's about making the most of life's every moment. And like "American Pie," it focuses on an America adrift, straying from its dream, becoming cynical, rote, and losing its innocence.

Conor put it this way:

We must blend into the choir
Sing as static with the whole
We must memorize nine numbers
And deny we have a soul
And in this endless race for property
And privilege to be one
We must run, we must run, we must run

Don McLean put it this way:

Oh, and there we were all in one place
A generation lost in space
With no time left to start again
So come on, Jack be nimble, Jack be quick
Jack Flash sat on a candlestick
'Cause fire is the devil's only friend

"There's so much imagery in ['American Pie']. It's, I think, still one of the greatest songs ever written." It's clear that Conor has always been driven by words. I can't help seeing the parallel be-tween the song that changed him as a seven-year-old boy and the stories his songs tell today—and wonder about the path he might have chosen had it not come on the radio that day. Conor tells me that hearing "American Pie" was an "awakening." That it opened his mind to possibility, to "the way you can put words and imagery together that becomes greater than the sum of its parts. I can't venture to say exactly what he was getting at, but to me it seems like the ultimate song of loss of innocence, and, obviously, you can think about the innocence of early rock and roll, and losing these three very talented people in a plane crash, but it seems even wider than that. To me, it sounds like he's singing about all of America, or his youth, or maybe the idealism of a time that we have to let go of at some point. But again, it's like, he shows it, he doesn't tell it—and I think that that's a basic rule of writing. I think it's one that really holds true and that I try to stick to in everything I write, as much as you can."

What a lesson to pull from a song—"show it, don't tell it." It's a manner of composition more akin to that of novelists, or even photographers and painters. In a sense, that's what both of these songs do—tell a story about individuals but also one about the world at large, and because they show and don't tell, they're open to interpretation from their audience. Songs like these fire my imagination. I get to connect to them in my own way. It's likely why Don McLean never explained the meaning behind his epic tale. Listeners can continue to engage with it, and its meaning will change and grow as they do. It's the reason I've rarely embraced music videos. For me, it's like seeing a movie adaptation of a beloved book—it forever colors the thing I love with someone else's interpretation, leaving less room for imagination and inspiration. Perhaps imagination is something most people tend to lose as they grow older, but for artists, it is something to hold tightly to and to build on. I, for one, am thrilled that young Conor wrapped his small arms around that big guitar, and that his family, friends, and Miss Allen were there—and that Don McLean inspired him to imagine what a song could be.

COURTNEY BARNETT

I'm at the 9:30 Club for a second night of sold-out shows by the brilliant twenty-seven-year-old Australian singer-guitarist-songwriter Courtney Barnett. I've wound my way toward the front, a few feet from the stage. I'm with my son, who's in his early twenties. As I survey the room, I notice an unusual trend for a rock show: parents attending with their children. A gray-haired man, roughly my age, stands in front of me with his daughter, roughly my son's age. A few feet to my right, another father and daughter, and when I stepped outside before the show began, there was another parent, this time a mother with her teenage daughter. In a crowd of mostly twenty-somethings, the scenario repeats itself, though there are

A blistering set from Courtney Barnett at the Black Cat in Washington, D.C., 2014.

plenty of older folks sans children, too. Over the past few years, I've seen Courtney five times and never noticed anything interesting about her fan base until now. Perhaps it's because she finally released her first official album this year, 2015. I'm not alone in thinking *Sometimes I Sit and Think, and Sometimes I Just Sit* is the standout album of the year.

Courtney Barnett grew up in the north-coastal suburbs of Sydney, near the Pacific Ocean. As a teenager, she and her family moved to Tasmania, an island south of Australia's mainland. These days she lives in Melbourne. From our conversation, it seems her mom and dad had little influence on her musically: her dad loved jazz and her mom classical. "There were a couple of Abba records [in the house]. But I kind of just found all my music through my older brother. And . . . lots of people at school listened to kind of trashy radio, hit music." Her brother Blake was four years older and they were close. "We had bedrooms across the hall from each other. And he pretty much had music going all the time. And so I could just sit in my room and listen to it. And we had a neighbor, two neighbors, Nick and Josh, who made mixtapes for us." Nick Williamson and Josh Madden were friends with Blake in particular. It was the mid-nineties, and even though most people were burning "mixtapes" on CDs, Nick and Josh's mixes were lovingly crafted cassettes, which was great, because the Barnetts didn't own a CD player. "That's kind of all we had . . . so we kind of listened to what they gave us. And it was like Nirvana and Hendrix and Red Hot Chili Peppers and Guns N' Roses and all that kind of stuff. It was good, because otherwise, it would have just been Abba."

Sometime around 1997, when Courtney was about ten years old, Blake and those mixtape neighbors started playing guitar. "And I started copying them. And they'd teach me songs. . . . Then when I finally started getting lessons, my guitar teacher was like, 'Hey, check out *The White Album* and *Grace* by Jeff Buckley.' . . . So it was another level of discovery." Courtney is left-handed, and she first learned to play on a right-handed guitar, upside down—perhaps one of the reasons she was attracted to Jimi Hendrix, who also played upside down and lefty. She later began proper lessons and now plays a left-handed guitar.

As teenagers, Blake and Courtney spent hours in his bedroom listening to music, eventually on compact discs. Courtney recalls her first CD purchase: Nirvana's *Nevermind*. "I started buying CDs every week. I'd go to the CD shop after school and spend my pocket money. . . . I liked *Rolling Stone* magazine. . . . I just got obsessed." Devouring and making music became the focus of her high school years. She wrote poems and simple lyrics, but her real passion for songwriting came from an unlikely source—an English assignment. "When I was in grade ten, so sixteen, my English teacher set a class one day to pick apart this song called 'To Her Door,' by Paul Kelly. And so we had to go through the lyrics and figure out what every word meant and why he used this word instead of that word. . . . And I think that was a bit of a moment, because I'd kind of been writing poetry and playing guitar . . . but I think it just hit a different level . . . learning what little parts of the songs were, which you might otherwise just brush off."

Paul Kelly is a legend in Australia, almost to the level Dylan is here. He was born in 1955, and wasn't a young artist when Courtney first heard him. "To Her Door" tells the story of a young man's failed relationship with his wife.

> They got married early, never had no money
> Then when he got laid off they really hit the skids
> He started up his drinking, then they started fighting
> He took it pretty badly, she took both the kids
> She said, "I'm not standing by, to watch you slowly die
> So watch me walking out the door"
> She said, "Shove it, Jack, I'm walking out your fucking door"

What's most beautiful about this song is the way the story is told. Each line reveals a key detail, and is full of sadness, bitterness, and hope. Verse two takes place sometime later:

She went to her brother's, got a little bar work
He went to the Buttery, he stayed about a year
Then he wrote a letter, he said I want to see you
She thought he sounded better, she sent him up the fare
He was riding through the cane in the pouring rain
On Olympic to her door

A hot country-flared guitar solo follows that is so full of hope it makes the listener feel certain its ending will be a happy one. And that's what makes this song brilliant—the way Paul Kelly chooses to end it. The third and final verse starts with a series of unanswered questions:

Did they have a future? Would he know his children?
Could he make a picture and get them all to fit?

Those questions, especially the line "Could he make a picture and get them all to fit?," make my eyes water every time I hear them. This moment showed Courtney how a story can develop inside a song, something she now does better than anyone, as far as I'm concerned. In 2013, when I first discovered her music, "Avant Gardener" drew me in. It contains some of the best lyrics I've heard in rock, and struck me the way Bob Dylan's "Like a Rolling Stone" once did, with phrases that seemed rambling and focused at precisely the same time. Courtney's song is a true story told in a stream-of-consciousness style. She relates an attempt to both order her life and distract her mind by turning her weedy yard into a garden, only to be sent into anaphylactic shock.

My hands are shaky
My knees are weak
I can't seem to stand
On my own two feet
I'm breathing but I'm wheezing
Feel like I'm emphyseming

On the surface, "Avant Gardener" simply tells the tale of good intentions gone awry, but it's a deeper metaphor—one's fear of failing as a justification for laziness. The line at the top of the song is telling and drips with sarcasm.

I sleep in late
Another day
Oh what a wonder
Oh what a waste

And as she's in the ambulance unable to breathe she sings this line, one that questions the relevance of her life and talent:

The paramedic thinks I'm clever 'cause I play guitar
I think she's clever 'cause she stops people dying

I saw Courtney play this and so many others on three different occasions the week she launched her second self-released EP, *How to Carve a Carrot into a Rose*. Twice she played with a band, once solo, and each song was jam-packed with playful rhymes like this from "History Eraser":

I found an Ezra Pound
And made a bet that if I found
A cigarette, I'd drop it all and marry you

Or this from "Lance Jr.," a song on her first EP, *I've Got a Friend Called Emily Ferris*:

> I masturbated to the songs you wrote
> Resuscitated all of my hopes
> It felt wrong but it didn't take too long
> Much appreciated are your songs.

A few years before, when I saw Courtney play in New York City as part of the CMJ Music Marathon, her shows were a mixed bag. I heard a brilliant lyricist and stylized vocalist pull off two- and three-chord tunes. Her guitar playing was good, not stellar, and her band merely okay—their talent not quite equal to the power of her words. Just one year later, everything had come together. The band was hot, and serving the songs with a rock-solid foundation of drums and bass, and sometimes they added a guitarist, which gave Courtney the freedom to keep her rhythm guitar crunchy and in step. They were on their way to becoming a great rock and roll band. In 2015, she returned to tour the U.S., and NPR Music presented her new album at South by Southwest. By then she and the band were on fire. Their new songs were still basic rock, but more dynamic, and the words popped. "Elevator Operator" is about an encounter on an elevator between a young daydreamer heading to the roof and an aging beauty who believes this daydreamer is about to kill himself:

> Don't jump, little boy, don't jump off that roof
> You've got your whole life ahead of you, you're still in your youth
> I'd give anything to have skin like you

The track's bouncy, straight-beat chorus provides a nice contrast to the stuttered feel of the verse. Courtney and I talk about her growth as a writer and musician and she chalks it up to a song she feels may have changed her even more than Paul Kelly's, one by the Chicago band Wilco: "'Handshake Drugs' would be the one that stood out. That song always sticks out for me just because . . . [the] kind of moment that I had with it . . . started a bit of a snowball of change. I remember when I first heard Wilco . . . that was like a year or so after I released my first EP. It just kind of stood out as something different. And it was, again, like a bit of a life-changing musical moment for me. And it's just kind of dreamy. Like you disappear into it . . . and then . . . it just falls apart in the guitar at the end. It's incredible." "Handshake Drugs" is a six-minute-plus meditation by singer Jeff Tweedy on his addiction to painkillers, which he started taking to treat acute migraines.

> Saxophones started blowing me down
> I was buried in sound
> And the taxicabs were driving me around
> To the handshake drugs I bought downtown

The music shifts in tone and mood, from gentle strumming to a steadfast beat, only to end in a dissonant, mind-bending guitar solo, a new approach for Tweedy. Unlike the lilting, languid solos you get from bands like The Grateful Dead or the blistering, bluesy sound of Led Zeppelin, this solo is less about melody than about tone, at once droney and frenetic. Stylistically, it sounds more like Lou Reed with The Velvet Underground, a band whose influence can easily be heard in both Wilco's "Handshake Drugs" and in Courtney Barnett's music in general. It's a propulsive sound cut with electric punctuation. Courtney is enamored with the shifts in that song and says it continues to change her. You can hear some of this evolution on her new album. Many of the songs don't end as they began; they're more complex than her earlier work. "I feel like I'd kind of written the first EP songs, and then I discovered this band. . . . I'm sure everything that comes into your life changes it in some way. It feels like a lot of those songs that I'd done on the first EP were kind of like they knew what was coming, if that makes sense, because I was trying to write . . . really simple, repetitive, one-chord, two-chord songs and find the kind of contrasting moments. But since hearing Wilco's song there's that shift . . . [and] the dynamics in the actual music, in the playing, has [become] a pretty big thing for me. From then on, going into studios and making more music and just being really aware of how powerful that actually is, on top of the song itself, and the lyrics, and the music. Starting super quiet [with] beautiful piano and then crunching into something huge and ugly but beautiful."

One example of the artistic shift Courtney refers to is her seven-minute song "Small Poppies." It goes from lulling to cutthroat. "Kim's Caravan" is another one that's more ambitious than the two- and three-chord songs I'm used to hearing from her. But the transformation has truly taken shape at her live shows, in which her trio CB3, with Bones Sloane's intense thrashing bass and Dave Mudie's hard-snapping beats, takes the audience on a journey, expanding the dynamics and accentuating the structural and tonal shifts in her songs. There's no reinvention going on here, purely an awakening to her own musical approach—a timeless structure with great lyrics. Wilco has the same appeal.

Tweedy sometimes plays music with his son, a multigenerational collaboration with wide appeal. Their sound is both familiar and expansive. As I watch Courtney at the 9:30 Club, with my son at my side, surrounded by families who have come to share her music, I think about her growth as a songwriter and have this vision: It's 2035. Courtney is forty-seven, the same age Tweedy is now. The sons and daughters who were here with their parents in 2015 attend her show with their own children, and tell them about the night they saw her when her career had only just begun.

POKEY LAFARGE

Pokey LaFarge is from another time. His jolly, bluesy music, his singing megaphone tones, his sharp, loose suits and classy hats and slicked-down hair—every bone in his body is touched by a reverence for the past and a passion for the present. He's not a throwback. He's an original with deep admiration for the origins of greatness. "I am from the cornfields of Illinois where there ain't a damned thing around, and I had to learn myself, which I did from Kerouac and Twain and Steinbeck, that there's a huge world out there."

Pokey plays music steeped in early-twentieth-century Americana. It's somewhat country and somewhat blues, with a touch of western swing, and he owns it all. On the surface it may seem like a novelty.

Pokey LaFarge exudes joy while performing lovable tunes at the Black Cat in Washington, D.C., 2014.

It's not; it's his own musical stew. "I didn't have music in the family, that's the thing. I didn't have instruments around. I was born creative. I was born interested. I was born curious. I should say, I was always looking for different ways to express myself. And, thankfully, I discovered an outlet. I was already way into literature. That was my first means of expressing myself, writing, but as I started writing, I started listening to music and getting into music through The Beatles and classic rock stuff. And then as a history buff from my dad's side, I was exposed to World War II history, Civil War history . . . was way into baseball, and was always interested in the roots of things and where things come from. Maybe that's human nature, but I took it to another level. Like, I really wanted specificity, where everything comes from, the names, the dates, everything. I'm a future biographer in that way, about everything. Baseball players or sports or musicians . . . I think that does say a lot about you."

Pokey LaFarge was born Andrew Heissler. His mom nicknamed him Pokey as a kid because he was always dragging his heels when it was time to hurry. And "LaFarge" just felt right. His uncle on his mother's side was a ragtime banjo player who took him to his first bluegrass festival around the age of thirteen. Pokey was already interested in that sort of music, and spent a lot of time reading liner notes and copying CDs he found at the local library. At a time when most teens were listening to Nirvana or Puff Daddy, Pokey received a mandolin from his maternal grandfather. It was 1997, and he was fourteen. "I had some guidance from my grandparents, my mom's father and my dad's father." His grandfather saw something in him as a young boy that Pokey didn't. "I don't know what he saw in me, because I sure as hell was a confused kid." The mandolin was primarily considered a bluegrass instrument; its main proponent, Bill Monroe, the father of bluegrass, had passed away a year earlier.

I'm sitting with Pokey LaFarge at the 2014 Newport Folk Festival, a place that seems made for him. The festival grounds are located on a large historic site, Fort Adams, which was active during five wars: the Mexican-American War, the Civil War, and the Spanish-American War, along with World Wars I and II. We're tucked away in a cavernous back room while a band of country musicians works out its tunes behind us. Pokey is a serious, philosophical young man, somewhat different from the fun-loving fellow you see on-stage. As a teenager, he traveled around the country, busking his way from city to city. It's the philosopher in him that looks off in the distance as he says, "Is it all meant to be? What have I been given and what have I taken? Because I realized at an early age that you create your own world. No one, in my opinion, knows what life is all about or where we go when we die, and I felt like, at an early age—and maybe it's all the philosophy and the existential poetry I was reading at a young age, and maybe I was screwed up and I led myself astray, I don't know—but I feel [drawn to] that whole idea where you can create your own reality. You have to go out, and you have to grab life by the balls, and so that's kind of what I did." Pokey hitchhiked to the West Coast at age seventeen and then, eventually, east to Asheville, North Carolina, where he met drummer Ryan Koenig and bassist Joey Glynn. Later, they formed the South City Three, along with guitarist Adam Hoskins, who joined in 2009. These days they've added Chloe Feoranzo on clarinet and TJ Muller on cornet, bringing some 1920s and 1930s jazz flair to their sound. As a group, they've traveled five continents and played more than 250 shows.

Many artists have touched the life of Pokey LaFarge. Of the ones he spoke about with me, all are American, male, and all (except one) would have been filed in the "Country" bin back in my record store days. Pokey's favorite is a soulful singer from southern Arkansas named Lefty Frizzell. Frizzell recorded the first version of "The Long Black Veil," a classic tune about a man falsely accused of murder, who could clear his name and escape execution but refuses to reveal his whereabouts at the time of the crime—he was in the arms of his best friend's wife. Pokey proudly tells me about Lefty: "He's the only guy to have four songs on the Top 10 of the country charts at the same time. Lefty is arguably the most influential country singer of all time in terms of his style. George Jones says it, Merle Haggard says it." Pokey's passion is clear. I ask him what it was about Lefty that grabbed hold of him when most kids were listening to pop. He says, "That style, the complete original style, the raw emotion that comes into his voice. That's what I can't explain." I press him for specifics. "Lefty was the first country singer to take, say, like, 'Waiting for a Train.' He wouldn't say, 'Waiting for a train,' he'd go, 'Way-ah-ay-tin' for a tray-ay-ayn.' No one did that, and that was him, and he would just hang on to the—like Merle said, he would hang on to this phrase until, like, 'How'd he do that and have the breath to come in?' It's just so wilting. Listen to Randy Travis, listen to Keith Whitley. Listen to George Jones. Listen to all these modern country singers and that's where [it] comes from."

With all this talk of country music, I ask him if he can nail it down to one song, or moment. I'm sure it will be a Jimmie Rodgers tune, or maybe Lefty's big hit "Saginaw, Michigan." Pokey throws me a curve, though. "If I had to say the greatest recording, there's . . . Louis Armstrong's version of 'St. James Infirmary.' I believe it was Peanuts Hucko on clarinet and Trummy Young on trombone, and I can't remember the bass player, or the pianist, or the drummer. Anyway, there's this version where they start out, 'Oo, oo,' like this four-part harmony." Pokey does his best impression of the various parts of the great jazz band, including Armstrong's remarkably expressive trumpet. "That, to me, might be my favorite recording of music of all time." "St. James Infirmary" is a great American folk song whose origins, like most others in the genre, can be traced to an even older folk song. "The Unfortunate Rake" is a sixteenth-century English ballad and the template of this story about a young person cut down in his prime from his morally wayward ways—mostly gambling, overimbibing, and sexual promiscuity, which sometimes led to syphilis. As Louis Armstrong sang so sweetly and sadly:

I went down to St. James Infirmary,
Saw my baby there,
Stretched out on a long white table,
So cold, so sweet, so bare.
Let her go, let her go, God bless her,
Wherever she may be,
She can look this wide world over,
But she'll never find a sweet man like me.

It's easy to categorize Armstrong and his New Orleans–flavored, Chicago-tinged music as jazz, but these divisions frustrate Pokey and send him on a thoughtful rant. He wishes we could strip away the genres and judge music by listening to it—look beyond current trends and see only great music. "That song, yeah, it's jazz because it's got horns, but that's the thing. Just because it's got horns, it's not fucking jazz. Just because it doesn't have a fiddle, it's not country. You know? People need to tweak their heads like this. Like yeah, it's jazz, but this is archaic. I mean, this goes back to caveman times, a song like that." Timelessness, that's what connects Pokey to his musical passions, and to all his discoveries at the public library growing up in the cornfields of Illinois. For the music he loves, there are no filters between thought and expression. He hears it in Lefty Frizzell's enunciation, Bill Monroe's melodies, and Louis Armstrong's yearning trumpet. "The most inspiring things I've found with music are the things that you can't quite classify. The people that invented things on their own that we now call rock and roll and . . . country, and things that we've mislabeled by calling it country and rock and roll because we had no other name, or because we are so eager to put a name on it. That's the thing I'm inspired by, raw, natural, organic expression. That's why I like

German beer: [it has] three ingredients. [And] I like organic local food. It's like, raw music!"

Whether Pokey makes his mark on the music world in the manner of his heroes, contributing to the American canon, remains to be seen. He's just thirty-one and still stretching his boundaries. He tells me his music might get a little darker, creepier, and that they might flesh out their sound with a full drum kit (which he has since done) and more vocal accompaniment. "I want to be rooted . . . [and] I definitely want to be honest with who I am, but I also want to be honest to the other part of me. That's the part that keeps me going forward . . . the searcher, the person who is constantly evolving and changing. . . . I want to be modern, I want to be relevant, I want to be progressive. It's an interesting position that I'm in, Bob, because for the traditional musicians, I'm progressive. . . . I'm writing all my own tunes, [and] the arrangements are very different . . . but . . . to people who are very much modern musicians and don't know much about where the music has come from, they may chuck it off as somewhat novelty. I also want people to take me seriously, because I do think that it's bigger than me now. I need to be ultimately saying things for the overall good and trying to encourage people and make this world a better place. So, if they don't take me seriously, then it sort of distorts my message." Of all the artists I know, digging through the roots of American music and attempting to unearth a new way to express and represent what defines it, Pokey LaFarge is the one most likely to succeed, and as with Louis Armstrong, I trust that the ensuing music will be timeless.

KATE TEMPEST

"He not busy being born is busy dying." This line, from Bob Dylan's "It's Alright, Ma (I'm Only Bleeding)," are also the words that changed the life of a young Kate Tempest, inspiring her to become a stunning poet, playwright, and songwriter. "It's such an incredible lyric. It's like the perfect—the perfect lyric—and it's just so rich. . . . I began my relationship with Bob Dylan through listening to him with my dad, [but] this was the first song that I heard under my own steam and in my own right, and understood on my own terms. . . . This is like my moment of [saying about] Bob Dylan: Okay, you're mine now. You know, you're not just something that belongs to a previous generation, this is like, okay, I get this."

The intense and spellbinding Kate Tempest at U Street Music Hall in Washington, D.C., 2015.

Kate Tempest, born in 1985 as Kate Calvert, is a white rapper from London. Her performance at SXSW in 2015 was many things—riveting, chilling, uplifting, and simply the best thing I witnessed in the nearly one hundred performances I saw that week. She perched high above the crowd at Latitude 30, the microphone pressed to her lips, and her electronic band ceased playing for a moment while she talked about the state of the world and the disgraceful way humans treat one another. The audience's collective jaw dropped as she pleaded, "More empathy, less greed, more empathy, less greed," and the slow repetition, a powerful call to action, brought me and the roomful of newfound fans to tears.

Kate's desire to pick up a guitar and play was partially sparked by those early days with her dad, listening to him talk about what Dylan's music meant to him and why it was beautiful. At the time, the songs were over thirty years old, and Kate was about twelve. Her brother listened to Oasis and Nirvana. "I remember sneaking into his room and rewinding all the swear words on the Nirvana tape. You know, the things you're just like fascinated for. I didn't really connect with rock music, or I didn't really connect with it in the same way. I don't know why." Then, at around age eleven, she became obsessed with Michael Jackson. "I absolutely lived and breathed for him. I used to watch the *Moonwalker* videotape every day, every single day." And then she discovered hip-hop. "Hip-hop was just everywhere, it was all around. It was a dominant cultural music of force. My next-door neighbor, and on the street where I lived, loads of the girls, they were a bit older than me, and they were, like, doing . . . dance routines to American rap artists, and then realizing what a rapper is, and what lyrics are. Wu-Tang was the first that really—I think I must have been thirteen or something. . . . [I] always listened to lyrics first, that was ever since forever. It's really interesting when I hang out with other musicians and they haven't even heard the lyric, they've just heard the bass line or, like, the drum."

Kate didn't do well academically, though she did have a primary-school teacher who inspired her to read books and poetry. Instead of studying, she hung out with her friends, a group of rappers, graffiti artists, and writers. "We used to sit around in the park and just get stoned all day. . . . I really enjoyed the company of people who were maybe a little bit older, and I just fell into this community of people who were mostly male and really into hip-hop. . . . My kind of access point was through these guys, who were kind of like older brothers to me. . . . It was hardly, like, a secret, you know—it's, like, the biggest kind of underground movement, and the biggest kind of cultural movement, of my generation, and the generation before, even. . . . When I was about fourteen, I had a job in a record store, in kind of a hip-hop record shop—I was absolutely living and breathing for rappers and rap music. I saw Mos Def around that age. And I was too young to get into the concert. . . . I was outside with my friend [and] we were, like, rapping to the bouncer until he let us in." Inspired, Kate started making music after that with her drummer friend Gia, in his bedroom. They still work together. In fact, he accompanied her when she played her Tiny Desk Concert.

In 2001, when she was fifteen, Kate went to the Essential Festival in Hackney, London, and saw many of the artists she loved, yet had never imagined she'd be able to experience live. "We saw like Biz Markie, Gang Starr, and, like, DUB Sound Systems. . . . I saw Jeru the Damaja, you know, like all these kinds of names that I didn't ever think would ever come to life for me . . . because I couldn't work out how to see them in England, and then suddenly here they all were in this kind of dreamy weekend in the distant past. I can only kind of connect with the feeling of astonishment, but I can't really remember what happened."

By age sixteen, she was performing at the open mic at a small hip-hop club in London, and she'd changed her name from Calvert to Tempest, in part inspired by Shakespeare and her own whirlwind lyricism. She started touring with her band Sound of Rum, a spare but potent hip-hop trio with one guitar, a drum kit, and Kate's words front and center. "So Low" is a great example of her writing from 2011:

Obsessed with the carnivalesque and the grotesque
Then I stand onstage and talk the truth like I know best

At the time, Kate was also devouring the words of famous writers, reading Sophocles, Freud, *The Odyssey* (a favorite of her dad's), and attending poetry slams and slamming her own poetry. Her passion for music fed her passion for writing. Then, about five years ago, she had a moment: "I managed to get tickets to see RZA, when he was touring as Bobby Digital. I'm watching the concert, and Bobby Digital, you know, it's the kind of party thing. And I had never really been a kind of party hip-hop lover. . . . I want it to be deep, and I want it to mean something. So I was watching the Bobby Digital show—he's kind of pouring out liquor for everyone in the front row—and it's all really good and fun, but it gets to the end of the show, and he walks offstage. And I'm . . . screaming at him for 'Twelve Jewelz.' I was screaming at him like, 'RZA!' I'm at the front, you know, 'Play "Twelve Jewelz."'" He comes back out and he's like, 'What?' Like, he sees me in the front. There's this like white girl asking me for 'Twelve Jewelz,' he's really confused. And so then he came back out and he did it a cappella, the whole verse, straight into my face. He held my hand for a couple of bars. You know, and he just leant down off the edge of the stage—I used to rap that verse to myself on the way home from school. And he was just rapping it to me at this club. It still fills me with tingles just to think about, you know. Because Wu-Tang, they're like gods—I mean, they're just men, they're humans, but that was the moment of like, Okay, the power of lyrics . . . the power of words."

———

When I saw Kate Tempest perform at SXSW, I was certain she was staring straight into my eyes. Yet, at the same time, it's likely every audience member there felt the same. She has a rare gift, a talent for forming community among strangers. What she *wants* from a performance, she *gives* in her performance. "When I started rapping it was in kind of ciphers, or small groups of people. You're talking to people, it's always been live. It's always been about kind of connection and communication. And then doing the spoken word stuff, it's the same thing, you're directly communicating with whoever you're talking to. And then, for me, what I've learned through all these years of performing and working around—the most important people in the room are the people in the audience. This is what it's all for. This is why anybody does anything—it's for this energy, this gathering of people in the room. And if you're telling a story, the most important part of any story is the people that are hearing it. That's why it will live."

Kate Tempest seems selfless. Her music isn't about ego, it's about the people who gather to hear it. "I have huge respect for the people.... In other cultures and in other times, the artist had a role in the community. It wasn't about this kind of ego-driven pursuit of glory, or this kind of art in a vacuum. . . . It's about my place within this thing. This isn't about me, this is about us in the room. And if I can have some access point into all these people's hearts and minds, then I need to . . . at least return that . . . [to] be there in the moment and let them know it's real." In 2014 Kate released *Everybody Down*, produced by Dan Carey. The album's twelve songs are more like chapters in the story of three characters, Becky, Pete, and Harry, their life in the city, and their love in a time of adversity. The words to "Lonely Daze" provide a sense of Kate's storytelling style:

Becky is a young woman
Heart full of earth
Eyes full of mornings

Spent without sleeping
Grew up in a city where it's hard to be heard
And nothing really has much meaning

Carey's production punches hard but also provides melody under Kate's speak-singing. She breaks into melodic singing for the chorus, one filled with questions:

But will it be this way forever?
These are lonely days
What if she could be the one that makes it better?
He looks away, can't hold her gaze
But will it be this way forever?

In a successful musical collaboration, the strengths of each individual enhance the collective. *Everybody Down,* which was nominated for the 2014 Mercury Prize, is one of those magical collaborations. Kate's words unfold along with Dan's textures and rhythms, and his sounds shift and change as her stories develop.

In the years leading up to this release, Kate was often recognized for her writing. She won the Ted Hughes Award, a UK poetry prize, in 2013 for her spoken-word piece *Brand New Ancients,* which imagined everyday Londoners as ancient gods. Every ten years, the Poetry Book Society names twenty remarkable poets from Ireland and the UK as Next Generation Poets; she was one of the honorees in 2014. I could go on, but after I spoke with Kate Tempest, it's clear she doesn't focus on the past. Her time is right now. "What happens is that you start making music when you're young, and I didn't know the kind of person that I was [then], let alone the kind of artist that I was. So for many years, I was battle rapping, I was arrogant . . . and then as I grew older and as I grew into myself, I understood who I was as a woman. And it's important to say 'as a woman,' because in hip-hop, the trope for a woman, the path for a woman . . . was not necessarily where I was at, and who I am. . . . The one amazing thing about hip-hop . . . that it's taught me is: be real, be who you are, know what you're saying, know where you are, and know where you're from. . . . I'm twenty-nine now. I've been through a whole lot in life. I've lost people, I've found people, I've loved, you know, it's all the stuff that's happened. When I stand in a room full of human beings, I feel them. I want them to know that I feel them, it's important for me. And, like, five, six, seven years ago, that wasn't necessarily where I was at. I just wanted to do my thing. Now I feel ready to be me, to be Kate. It's maybe worth saying—it's kind of awkward that you are expected as a musician, as a woman musician . . . to kind of have your moment at eighteen. To go out there and . . . have your thing, this kind of cool, sexy, young pop star. In other careers, if you're a carpenter, you're not expected to know your trade . . . until you're well into your career, your age. It's a strange thing that we have these kind of dispensable artists, you want that kind of young, youthful, rock and roll energy, but you don't have the wisdom yet to carry your talent. I don't know. It's been a journey, that's what I'm saying."

What seems a constant for Kate, despite her self-admitted youthful arrogance, is her passion for words, especially for those that show compassion. When she asked RZA to sing "Twelve Jewelz," she wanted to hear a song that begins with a plea for life.

As long as you got mentally dead people
Who are living in a mental death
Meaning living in a mental grave
You need somebody to dig that grave up and bring them back to life

These words are not unlike Dylan's: "He not busy being born is busy dying."

It's the kind of maturity not often seen in rock or hip-hop, both genres of music often made by confused, unsure youth, sometimes bent on self-destruction or self-loathing or simply self-promotion. The words that sent Kate Tempest on her path resonated with her even as a preteen. I believe it's in her heart to care, that it always has been—and I look forward to wherever she sees fit to take us from here. "More empathy, less greed."

IAN MACKAYE

I don't expect a musical conversation with Washington, D.C., punk legend Ian MacKaye to begin with *country* legend Floyd Cramer. The brash sounds Ian made with the Teen Idles as a bassist, then in Minor Threat as frontman and lyricist, and later as guitarist and singer in his best-known band, Fugazi, seem the opposite of Cramer's smooth country piano. But Floyd Cramer's 1960s hit "Last Date" was the soundtrack to this boy's life when he was four years old. "My parents had a Grundig, like a fold-up phonograph. We had that single and I would play it over and over, and just lay my head next to the speaker and listen to it. . . . I was obsessed with that song." Ian's mom played the piano and kept a baby grand in the house. While she was pregnant with him, she played it constantly with her belly up to the keyboard. "It's all vibration for me," he says.

I meet Ian at the Dischord house in the summer of 2014. The house serves as the archive for Dischord Records, an independent label he began with his friend Jeff Nelson in 1980. We spend hours together talking, much of it a guided tour through filing cabinets of posters, concert cassettes, and record art. It's more than impressive. It's a massive labor of love. "These are all Fugazi photos here, early D.C. punk stuff photos. Early fanzines, these are all the interviews that Mark Andersen did for the *Dance of Days* book. I spent a year digitizing the tapes. These are all Fugazi tour posters in acid-free tubes. These are Dischord singles, my personal collection of all the early stuff. This is random stuff, this floor stuff. You see, there's a database for everything. These are the Fugazi live shows. This is my workstation when I'm doing transfer stuff. I just think if I die, someone's got to figure this out. I'm trying to make it easier."

As we wade through the semiorganized tornado of 45s, LPs, DAT tapes, and hard drives, he finds a box of cassettes. "These are all tapes of—my grandmother was a journalist, she wrote an advice column called 'Can This Marriage Be Saved?' for *Ladies' Home Journal*. She wrote for thirty years. It was one of the first advice columns. Dorothy Cameron Disney was her pen name. At some point she started recording her interviews, and I have so many of these cassettes. These are just people talking about their relationships in the late sixties, early seventies. These are my mother's tapes. My mother also recorded. These are just tapes around the house. There's a pretty interesting one here. It's Mom and Amanda, my sister Amanda, driving around in a car the day Reagan got shot." His mass of tapes, all stored in a single room, ranges from the historic (every live Fugazi show) to the mundane (his grandmother calling the hotel front desk to ask whether they have Coke in the vending machine). His mom was a bit of an archivist, too. "When she died, she left maybe three filing cabinets of journals and correspondence very carefully organized."

I don't have the mass of material Ian does, but I do have boxes of rehearsal tapes from Tiny Desk Unit and numerous posters. In fact, I recently sorted through my stash of seventies and eighties memorabilia and came across two copies of a poster from February 3, 1979, an event I hosted with my then apartment-mate, David Howcroft.

The day I meet Ian, I bring the extra copy as a gift. The show was intended as a benefit to stop the sale of Georgetown University's radio station. WGTB was the pinnacle of free-form radio in Washington and to this date, in my opinion, the best music station D.C. ever had. It was also a thorn in the side of Reverend Timothy Healy, the president of Georgetown University. The Jesuit priest was sick of the station's left-wing politics and the many off-campus kids that ran its free-form airwaves. Healy called it "the great animal that doesn't belong in the zoo." Many of us, myself included, attempted to raise awareness and enough money to keep this crazy animal alive. Sadly, a few days before our fund-raiser, Father Healy shut down WGTB. It was the end of an era, and one of the saddest days of my life—but it turned out to be the spark that lit a burgeoning music scene. At least a thousand mostly angry, lost souls showed up to our benefit concert for a station that no longer existed. One of those kids was sixteen-year-old Ian MacKaye, and that show—hosted by David and me—changed his life.

When I arrive at the house, I hide the tissue-wrapped print on a chair. After my hour-long tour, and before we sit to talk about his song choice, I hand him the thirty-five-year-old poster. "Oh, wow, I totally remember this. Wow, that's amazing. Yes, my first show. Fucking awesome, I love this. I remember this poster. Wow, Rollins is going to freak out." Rollins is Henry Rollins, a former bully who became Ian's skateboard buddy and later another D.C. punk legend, first with his local band State of Alert, and then in Los Angeles with Black Flag and the Rollins Band. He's a wordsmith, actor, journalist, and activist. Ian and Henry skated together when Ian was eleven. "It was the alley behind Beecher Street. . . . We were building a ramp and Henry, just riding down the other alley, saw us and he came back up and we're like, 'Oh, that fucking dick.' He's like, 'Hey, can I ride your ramp?' Skateboarding brought us together. Then we just started hanging out and we listened to Cheap Trick. I'm sure he's the one that brought Ted Nugent to the mix. It was really *Double Live Gonzo!* era. That was the record. That was the one. I first saw Nugent cussing from the stage, spitting, just take no prisoners, jumping around in a loincloth. Then, part of my adherence to skateboarding was really looking for something to belong to, like an underground kind of thing. I always loved rock and roll, I was obsessed with rock and roll, like Woodstock and all that, but it just seemed impossible growing up here to ever do such a thing."

That show on Georgetown's campus was a pivotal moment for Ian MacKaye. "I saw . . . a room filled with deviants, and that's exactly what [I'd] been looking for my whole life." When The Cramps stomped onstage, the wild-eyed singer Lux Interior gripped the mic, snarled at us all, and said, "Some people wonder if this is a concert or a dance. Let me tell you, the concert just ended!" The place went insane. The punk-infused rockabilly sent people into a frenzy. Kids crawled through windows to get inside the overcrowded venue, and danced on tables that collapsed under their weight. They screamed and shook, and my God, it was so much fun! It was the start of a new day and the inception of a new wave of music, and all those kids, like Ian, finally found somewhere they belonged. "That was a hugely, hugely important show. Within a month . . . we started talking about the band. I had a terrible guitar. I bought it at a yard sale for ten dollars; each string was like an inch off the neck. I learned how to play 'Smoke on the Water' on one string, right? I can figure that part out, but I couldn't learn the relationship between the other strings. I had no idea what a chord would be on a guitar at that point. Mark [Sullivan] was the singer and Geordie [Grindle] played guitar and Jeff [Nelson], who played timpani, [said], 'I'll play drums,' so I said, 'Okay, I'll play bass.'" The band was The Slinkees. They played only one show before their singer headed off to college. Then Nathan Strejcek came along and The Teen Idles were born, followed quickly by Dischord Records. (That Georgetown show made an impact on me, too: not long after, I quit my job running the record warehouse, bought my ARP Odyssey synthesizer, and found my bandmate Michael Barron.)

In those days, the nightclubs hosting shows earned their primary revenue from alcohol sales and weren't about to admit underage kids—so DIY spaces were born, where bands could play for an audience of all ages. It was about music, not money. In the early days of the 9:30 Club, Dody DiSanto, who managed the club, and her husband, Jon Bowers, who owned it, did something revolutionary: they allowed, even encouraged, underage kids to come to their shows. They marked their hands with big black X's like the scene in Los Angeles, so they wouldn't be served anything more than soda. They also hosted special nights—three bands for three bucks—so kids could afford music and form a community, which inspired in them the courage to create, form bands, establish fan-zines, and take social action against injustice. It was also a damn lot of fun. We began to see possibilities in the idea of playing music and to understand that being a passive listener wasn't our only option. D.C. was on fire with bands, some of them punk, like the Bad Brains, others more art-based, like the Urban Verbs and our own Tiny Desk Unit.

Ian MacKaye was a young man with a creed: no drugs, alcohol, or casual sex. Those principles helped birth the "straight edge" movement, rejecting everything from drugs to eating animals. Straight Edge coalesced around his song of the same name, first performed by The Teen Idles, later by Minor Threat. It was a unifying centerpiece for many in the "harDCore" scene. "As a teenager I felt the only revolutionary act that was being offered . . . was self-destruction. You could either go to college or you could just become a drug addict or something. I had [a] friend who started smoking dope when he was eleven and another friend who started [at] twelve, thirteen, and they'd say, 'Let's get some grain alcohol.' I never drank or used drugs. I just never did."

Ian and I led parallel lives, though our paths didn't cross much. There was an age gap: he was sixteen and I was twenty-six, which seemed like a big difference then. I'd already experienced three years of punk by 1979, while it was still new and invigorating for him. I grew to want more out of music than a fiery and fierce experience, and sought texture and adventure. Ian and I spent a long time talking about our differing tastes. I lean toward a more imaginative side, often involving a façade, characters, theatrical storytelling, and poetry—think Bowie, Eno, The Velvet Underground, and Patti Smith. Ian's tastes are more direct—fuck the façade, hit the heart and muscle, and no corporate machinery: "There's so much music to study, and if it's got a machine behind it, pushing it, then I'd rather find the music that [came] to the surface on its own account."

Ian's inspiration came, in part, from records he received from his sister Kate and his buddy Bert Queiroz. It was the music of the late seventies: the Sex Pistols, The Ramones, Tuff Darts, Generation X, The Dead Boys, and The Clash. He found it puzzling at first. The shout-singing style was alien, the lyrics strange. They weren't about the usual boy-girl stuff or rock and roll but about self-empowerment, and they expressed outrage at the cookie-cutter system of education and culture. "It's something that really resonated with me because I grew up in the sixties. I was born in '62,' and I was totally fascinated by youth revolution culture. My family . . . [was] an activist kind of family, not super activist, but we were involved with an extremely activist church, St. Stephen's Incarnation, which is a super-liberation theology joint up on Sixteenth Street. There was a lot of civil rights stuff and women's rights and gay rights. . . . St. Stephen's facilitated a gay marriage in 1974. That's how we were rolling."

It makes sense, then, that the song that made the biggest impact on Ian MacKaye was "Bodies," by the Sex Pistols. Its main character, Pauline, is based on a mentally unstable woman the band knew. She was raped in an institution and had multiple abortions. The song itself is about the horror of abortion and the tragedy of taking a life. "That was a really pivotal song," says Ian. "It scrambled my brain. It lured me in."

She was a no one who killed her baby
She sent her letters from the country
She was an animal
She was a bloody disgrace

"[Johnny Rotten's] delivery was so intense. It has a deep rock bass to it, like the guitars on it, but then the lyrics and the atmosphere . . . [are] so deep and dark. I think it's the first time I heard cussing on a record, so shocking. Yeah, and then it just made me rethink everything. Really, ultimately, it led me to discover the counterculture, and that's all I ever wanted to do. That's what I wanted to be."

The Sex Pistols amped up conventional rock, not only in volume but in speed and snarl. Early incarnations of the band started in 1975 with guitarist Steve Jones and drummer Paul Cook and then bassist Glen Matlock. But it caught fire with the addition of John Lydon, a green-, sometimes orange-haired nineteen-year-old, who was discovered while wearing a Pink Floyd T-shirt held together with safety pins, with the words I HATE written above the band's logo. He was nicknamed Johnny Rotten. Their shows were mayhem and their fashion, supplied by manager Malcolm McLaren and his Sex boutique, helped define the look of punk. Poverty and a lack of hope in decaying Great Britain were punk's main catalysts, and the do-it-yourself mentality that defined its sound probably its greatest influence on fans and later generations. The Sex Pistols' first single, "Anarchy in the U.K.," was released in the fall of '76. It wasn't the first punk single, but it *was* the first anthemic punk record. It was a call to arms and spit in the face of the tedious music the industry had cranked out for too long. Ironically, the single was released on a major label, EMI, but the band was quickly axed after an incident of profanity on the Thames Television *Today* show. They then signed to A&M, which also quickly dropped them. The Sex Pistols only had one real album, *Never Mind the Bollocks, Here's the Sex Pistols*. It was released in the fall of that year, also on a major label, Virgin in the UK and Warner Bros. in the U.S., and its final, sneering cut took aim at the band's first label:

I do not need the pressure (EMI)
I can't stand those useless fools (EMI)

To understand the mind-set of a teenager in love with music before punk, you have to remember that rock was predominantly focused on superstars in the mid-seventies; music was selected and released by a few gatekeepers. It was a real detriment to creativity. The only way to those gatekeepers was to record an album at the studio rate of three hundred dollars an hour. Punk tore down the wall and empowered even nonmusicians to pick up a guitar and play. That's what happened to Ian MacKaye, and his band's success was on their own terms. They owned the music; he owned the label and distribution and set the price. These days, with advances in digital technology, anyone's bedroom can be a recording studio—and that level of artistic independence might not have happened without the example of punk, without brave kids who imagined a future on their own terms. Ian MacKaye is one of many, but he's the one who put my town on the map and helped make music about community, not commodity. And for that, I thank you, Ian.

LUCINDA WILLIAMS

Lucinda Williams was ten years old and living in Louisiana when she first dreamed of becoming a songwriter. "I didn't think of myself as a singer, really, so I decided that I [would] learn how to write songs." I'm thrilled she did, because nearly forty years into her recording career, I can fill my day listening to her tales of heartbreak and frustration, death and God, love and home, sex and pain. Lucinda has made her mark on both rock and country, though it's fair to say her slow ride to notoriety had something to do with her rock being so country, and her country rocking so hard. It's a sound that helped launch a genre in the early nineties: Americana.

Because she had a poet for a father, a piano-playing mother, and

A captivating set from Lucinda Williams, including a song she cowrote with her father, Miller Williams, at the Lincoln Theatre in Washington, D.C.

a troubled childhood, Lucinda's desire to write songs seems a mix of nature and nurture. "It wasn't a real stable kind of environment. My mother suffered from severe mental illness, and she was in and out of psychiatric hospitals the whole time I was growing up. I really bonded with my dad, and we had a real close relationship. . . . He was like my rock."

There was plenty of music around the house, though. Her mom loved show tunes, Erroll Garner—if you think of the best piano version of "Misty" you've ever heard, it was probably played by Garner—and Nat King Cole's "Ramblin' Rose." In the late fifties and early sixties this was popular music. These days, parents are just as likely as their children to love quirky indie bands. When Lucinda was growing up, most of them gravitated to music that was wholesome, safe, and romantic. In this kind of pop music, sex was only alluded to and everyone's dream came true, while musicals tended to tackle the more difficult issues of the day. *South Pacific,* a smash hit by Richard Rodgers and Oscar Hammerstein that Lucinda loved as an eight-year-old, focused on issues of racism as experienced by a mixed family, even though songs like "Happy Talk" were remarkably catchy. "I loved anything with a really good melody. . . . I remember that song [from *South Pacific*], 'I'm gonna wash that man right out of my hair, I'm gonna wash that—' So it was just all these musical influences coming around, just seeping in." Hearing her sing these words during our chat at NPR reminds me of one of her early tunes. She released "Change the Locks" in 1988, and it is one hell of a breakup song:

> I changed the tracks underneath the train
> So you can't find me again
> And you can't trace my path,
> And you can't hear my laugh

The lyrics are perhaps more cutting than the ones Mitzi Gaynor sang in *South Pacific* about washing that man out of her hair, but

I can see how the "seeping" Lucinda refers to could have turned to seething, and then inspiration.

From her dad, Lucinda learned about the blues. "He would bring albums home in the sixties of Mississippi John Hurt, Lightnin' Hopkins, and I remember hearing a lot of the Columbia releases of Bessie Smith recordings and *Live at the Apollo Theater.* I remember that album . . . was a collection of different artists. A lot of them more obscure . . . like Butterbeans and Susie, you know? And it was early stuff from the early days of the Apollo Theater. Songs like 'I Want a Hot Dog for My Roll.' I made the leap from Mississippi John Hurt to Robert Johnson. He was like what The Doors were to rock music . . . his stuff was a lot edgier. Mississippi John Hurt was more like folk, like country blues."

Lucinda dug into the music she loved the way many of us who were born in the fifties did. If she heard a Led Zeppelin song, she would search for its origins and discover Muddy Waters singing "You Need Love," which you can clearly hear in "Whole Lotta Love." From there she'd learn about Willie Dixon, the songwriter behind "You Need Love" and a significant player in the Chicago blues sound that influenced great rock bands like The Rolling Stones. For Lucinda, the more obscure the better. Her personal identity was completely wrapped up in her taste, and she liked her music "raw, soulful, and sexy." She later picked up the guitar, following many failed attempts at the piano—she didn't like her teacher and became discouraged. "I remember feeling real frustrated, 'cause I would sit at the piano and kind of try to learn it by myself. . . . My mother's music books would be there and I just remember thinking, God, I wish I knew how to read music, and I could just sit here and play. . . . I was just searching for something to . . . play, so I could sing songs. I wanted to pick up the guitar because I had musical genes in me from my mother, and it was the easiest instrument for me to learn and it's portable. I knew I already wanted to be like Joan Baez."

One day, William Harrison, a novelist friend of her father's, visited and left his guitar behind. "It just had this big crack in it or something—and I picked it up, and just kind of started fooling around with it, and eventually my dad bought me a Silvertone guitar from Sears. . . . I decided at that time of my life that's what I wanted to do." Lucinda began guitar lessons in 1965, when she was twelve. As I've discussed in this book, it was a time, thanks in large part to the success of The Beatles and the new wave of English bands, when a large proportion of the teenage population bought guitars. My life runs somewhat parallel to Lucinda's. I also tried to learn the guitar around this time and was discouraged by my teacher. For Lucinda, though, the instrument was her gateway, and she became obsessed with learning to fingerpick along with songs like Elizabeth Cotten's "Freight Train." To this day, she can't play with a flat pick.

Later that same year, Lucinda heard the music that redefined her life. "I remember . . . a student of my dad's came over to the house, excitingly waving this album in the air, and it was Bob Dylan's *Highway 61 Revisited*. You know, he's going, 'You've gotta hear this album.' . . . My dad was like, 'Yeah, okay, whatever,' and they went into a room to talk. . . . I immediately put it on the turntable and I was completely changed from that moment on." Bob Dylan released his iconic—and for many people life-changing—album fifty years ago. Its title was taken from the famed highway that connects the musical South, from St. Louis and Memphis to Mississippi and New Orleans (it also stretches far north, to Dylan's home state of Minnesota). The songs featured took you on a similar journey through American blues, only they were newly framed for a fresh, more literate generation. This was also Dylan's electric album, recorded both before and after his historically controversial set at the 1965 Newport Folk Festival. He'd previously released four acoustic albums; his fifth was a mix—side A electric, side B acoustic. In writing and recording the lead-off track for his sixth, *Highway 61 Revisited,* he was revitalized, excited about making music again. It was a transcendent, eye-opening album and still feels that way a half century later. The lyrics are some of the most puzzling and thought provoking ever written, from the very first line of the opening track, "Like a Rolling Stone":

Once upon a time you dressed so fine
You threw the bums a dime in your prime, didn't you?
People'd call, say, "Beware doll, you're bound to fall"
You thought they were all kiddin' you

The language continues to thrill throughout the album, until the eleven-minute album closer "Desolation Row," a potent mix of the grotesque and surreal with its vivid, fresh imagery taken from science, the circus, the Bible, poets, and popular film:

Einstein, disguised as Robin Hood
With his memories in a trunk
Passed this way an hour ago
With his friend, a jealous monk

For twelve-year-old kids like me and Lucinda, Dylan was a puzzle to unlock, endlessly fascinating. "All of a sudden here's something that [brings together] the two worlds that I was from— that I was exposed to—the literary . . . [and] the folk music world of Woody Guthrie and Pete Seeger and all the traditional sounds . . . and it blew my mind. . . . Of course, I didn't understand all the songs. When I was fifteen and sixteen—by then, of course, I was completely, madly in love with Bob Dylan—I decided, I want to learn how to write songs like that. I set the bar really high from the beginning."

There was also a long-running debate around Lucinda's house as to whether Dylan was a poet or a songwriter. "I remember my dad would have his creative writing students . . . over . . . and they'd get into these long-winded debates about whether Bob Dylan was a songwriter or poet. And my dad was really adamant about it. He says, 'No, he's not a poet. He's a songwriter.' You know? There was a difference. And they'd go, 'Yeah, but he's different, he's a poet.' My dad would go, 'No, he's not. He's a songwriter.' I was never sure what I thought about that, but I tell you, as soon as I sat down with one of my dad's poems and tried to turn it into a song, then I knew the difference." Before this conversation, I always thought Dylan was a poet—his words stood on their own—but after speaking to Lucinda about her father's poetry, I see it from their perspective.

With a dozen albums, three Grammy awards, and fifteen nominations across her thirty-five-year recording career, Lucinda knows songwriting. And her dad, Miller Williams, with twenty-five books and several awards, knew a thing or two about poetry. He even read at President Clinton's second inauguration. Lucinda recalls how her dad was constantly thinking about his writing. "I have images . . . in my mind of him. You know, he always carried some three-by-five index cards in his pocket with a pen, and he would take out a card and scribble something down and put it back. He would kind of like mumble when he was thinking of a line—I could see his mouth moving . . . his mind was just always going like that. . . . Regardless of how much chaos was going on in the house, he was always writing. He could just kind of shut all that out."

In 2014, Lucinda released a double album, quite the feat for an artist who's been known to make her fans wait four, six, eight years for new material. The hour and forty-three minutes of new music on *Where the Spirit Meets the Bone* opens with their father-daughter collaboration. The song "Compassion" is where the album gets its title, and it's based on one of her father's poems. From the experience, Lucinda will tell you this: you can't take a poem and sing it. Even for a songwriter as gifted as her, it was a struggle to turn her dad's words into a song.

Here's the poem:

Have compassion for everyone you meet,
even if they don't want it. What seems conceit,
bad manners, or cynicism is always a sign
of things no ears have heard, no eyes have seen.
You do not know what wars are going on
down there where the spirit meets the bone.

—MILLER WILLIAMS

Lucinda had to first break it down into lyrics, and then find a rhythm and pattern that would lay nicely on a melody (she loves a good melody). And all these elements—melody, words, fingerpicking—have to fit together in a way that pleases the ear. She broke the ideas down. This verse deals with her dad's notion of conceit:

Have compassion for everyone you meet
Even if they don't want it
What seems conceit
Is always a sign
Always a sign
Always a sign

And then bad manners:

For those you encounter
Have compassion
Even if they don't want it
What seems bad manners
Is always a sign
Always a sign
Always a sign

By breaking it down and adding repeating phrases, the words became singable, musical. Then the refrain, "always a sign," rings beautifully and builds on the line—so potent in the poem and un-forgettable in the song—"Down there, where the spirit meets the bone." Her raspy voice conveys yearning. She's no Joan Baez, but her confidence comes straight from Dylan. All the while, her light fingerpicking sets the tone. Lucinda tells me her dad was thrilled with the song. "It's kind of a nice thing to, all these years later . . . collaborate with someone you are so close with. It's kind of my trib-ute to him." Fifty years after she picked up a guitar, and almost as many since she first heard Dylan's *Highway 61 Revisited,* Lucinda agrees with her dad: Dylan was a songwriter, not a poet. "You can't just throw a melody on the poem." Sadly, Miller Williams passed in the winter of 2015.

Lucinda Williams is a confident songwriter with a poetic heart, but when she began to sing she knew she could never be another Joan Baez. Dylan's music gave her the confidence. "Bob Dylan wasn't a great singer, and everybody used to criticize his voice all the time. So I remember thinking, Well, if I can learn to write like that, or be as good as he is, I won't have to be a great singer." What Dylan does and what Lucinda and so many other greats have learned to do is embrace expression. It seems a given now, but if you think back to before the mid-sixties, you'll be hard-pressed to name a pop singer who couldn't really sing.

Lucinda couldn't pick one particular song that changed her life from *Highway 61 Revisited.* The album was everything and it changed everything.

JOSH RITTER

If you don't know the music of Josh Ritter, than you're missing some remarkable storytelling. I'm thinking of 2010's "The Curse," which tells the tale of a mummy who awakens and falls in love with the female archaeologist who discovered him. As the song unfolds she grows old and the mummy lives to see her passing. It's a beautiful love story told in waltz time. Recently, Josh sang about his own love and loss when his marriage to singer Dawn Landes ended after a few short years; a new romance soon blossomed with author Haley Tanner. These days he uses his heartbreak and joy to simply sing the truth. At Washington's Lincoln Theatre, I see firsthand how his songs connect with an audience. Early in "New Lover" the sentiment is sweet:

> I don't know who you're with these days, might be with someone new
> And if you are, I hope he treats you like a lover ought to do.

But he is setting us up for the following:

I hope you've got a lover now, hope you've got somebody who
Can give you what you need like I couldn't seem to do.
But if you're sad and you are lonesome and you've got nobody true,
I'd be lying if I said that didn't make me happy too.

I'm sure anyone in the crowd who has ever lost a love can connect to the last line, a sort of universal middle finger to the past. The night I see Josh play, it has a thousand people on their feet cheering.

Josh Ritter grew up in the city of Moscow, in northern Idaho. His parents were neuroscientists who studied functions of the brain, such as how it regulates appetite. In 1986, when he was around ten, he had his first life-changing musical experience. It still informs his songwriting to this day. While in England on a family trip, his dad bought a CD player, new technology at the time, for his and his wife's anniversary. Along with the player, he bought a copy of The Beatles' *Sgt. Pepper's Lonely Hearts Club Band*. Josh recalls the album's sweet and anniversary-appropriate opening line: "It was twenty years ago today," even though "Lucy in the Sky with Diamonds" was the song that captured his young imagination.

Josh is wide-eyed as he tells this story in his dressing room, especially when he recites the line "Plasticine porters with looking glass ties." He tells me about its effect on him. "All this amazing imagery that didn't feel like a song, the imagery was something more akin to a novel. I don't think I've ever heard something that felt quite that strange. It was fantastic." A similar sort of imaginative, intense imagery, not always found in songwriting, has come to define Josh's style. A good example of his storytelling quality can be found in "Kathleen," from 2003. The opening line alone slays me: "All the other girls here are stars—you are the Northern Lights." The song continues with his desire to drive Kathleen home and to share a moment together. It ends like this:

So crawl up your trellis and quietly back into your room
And I'll coast down the length of your drive by the light of the moon
And the next time we meet's a new kind of hello
Both our hearts have a secret only both of us know

In the world of pop and folk, fanciful storytelling doesn't happen enough. It doesn't surprise me that similarly fantastical descriptions of people and places populate Josh's 2011 novel *Bright's Passage*. The story is set in France during World War I and stars Henry Bright, a new father whose wife has recently died in childbirth. While he is fleeing a raging wildfire and a trio of avengers, he encounters an angel in the form of a horse. I did say it was fantastical.

Josh had spent much of his childhood learning classical music on the violin. "I'd been playing violin for so long. I really hated it. It was like scratching an itch but not feeling the satisfaction . . . of it." He wanted a guitar. His parents were nervous; they thought if he owned a guitar, he'd quit the violin. When he was about sixteen, he visited the Kmart in Moscow, Idaho, and bought a cheap, shiny guitar. It turned out his parents were right. "It felt like there was something deeper there and the guitar was like an instant thing."

Josh was exposed to a lot more than The Beatles in his family home. One day after moving to Australia with his parents, not long after he'd acquired his guitar, the bored eleventh grader found a record player at the bottom of a closet, along with a stack of albums. There was harpsichord music played by Wanda Landowska, the somewhat baroque British folk sounds of Pentangle, a soundtrack showing the languid, romantic side of Ennio Morricone, Muppet tunes, and finally Bob Dylan's 1969 release *Nashville Skyline*. The opening track, "Girl from the North Country," a duet between Dylan and Johnny Cash, is the song that forever changed the way

Josh heard music. "When I heard that song it made me realize what all the other songs up to that point that I'd been interested in [were] about. It was like a dog who watches tons of cars pass and then one day decides to chase one, you know what I mean? It was that feeling: I don't know what this is, but I'm gonna go for it."

"Girl from the North Country" was like a spike to his brain. Afterward, he began writing music. "There was absolutely nothing that meant anything to me besides that guitar at that time. Like, not the guitar itself, but, like, the actual freedom to write songs, which was what I was doing. I would write. I would find a chord that I didn't know and I would write a song around it, so I could practice it. And I would write and write and write. And that was all I cared about."

Nashville Skyline, the album that so inspired Josh, was a new Dylan for us all. I was sixteen when it was released, about the same age Ritter was when he first heard it many years later. Dylan's newly expressed love for country music and complete immersion in its style surprised his fans. Even for folk music, this was a stretch. Until then, the trend leaned more toward the kind of folk coming from England than from the heart of America. But Dylan was on a new path. You can hear his more playful, romantic, and happier side in his duet with Cash. Ritter talks about its effect on him. "They messed up and . . . nothing was being done to their voices. They weren't really harmonizing. They were just singing a song. And not so well that you couldn't sing it if you wanted to jump in. And it got me. . . . The words really touched me. I mean the song [is] about leaving, and I didn't have a girlfriend or anything, but there was girls that I liked. . . . The idea that I would go away and . . . someone [would] remember you just seemed like a really intensely romantic thing. . . . [The song] just felt very important. Those lyrics, it just seems like they were just living, breathing, and had never been written. . . . That was so attractive."

So if you're travelin' in the north country fair
Where the winds hit heavy on the borderline
Remember me to one who lives there
She once was a true love of mine.

Unlike *Sgt. Pepper* or Paul Simon's *Graceland,* another album
young Josh was obsessed with, *Nashville Skyline* felt accessible—
just a few guitars and a voice. You didn't have to learn anything
special, you didn't have to go to school for it. Afterward, he would
go to the public library and listen to old blues albums. And when he
heard Mississippi John Hurt, he realized, "Bob Dylan wasn't playing two guitars at once. He was just playing one and he was fingerpicking. . . . [It showed me] that I could play it and I could learn how
to fingerpick. It was a really big song."

By the time Josh was thirty years old, he was employing the same
sort of amazing, rapid-fire imagery that defined Dylan's style. The
depth of his songs necessitates and rewards repeated listening, and
his 2007 release, *The Historical Conquests of Josh Ritter,* opens with
just such a track, "To the Dogs or Whoever":

The stain of the sepia the butcher Crimea
Through the wreck of a brass band I thought I could see her
In a cakewalk she came through the dead and the lame
Just a little bird floating on a hurricane

I think even Dylan would admire lines this good. Josh's com-
plexity and the layers of his imagery are underappreciated. Does the
stain of sepia refer to the early days of photography, which is how
the Crimean War was captured? And does the cakewalk line refer to
the popular dance done on southern slave plantations in the nineteenth century, and to another horror—our own Civil War? Josh says

a lot, in a Dylan-esque way, about American culture and humanity in this song.

While working on his 2013 album, *The Beast in Its Tracks,* following his divorce, he found his songs were coming out bitter and hateful.

"I was writing for a person. . . . [Then] I started realizing that that's not who I wanted to write for. I wanted to write for people who had this thing, who had gone through an experience like a broken heart . . . and then I thought, well . . . if that's who I'm singing for, then . . . it doesn't have to be about me anymore, it could be about this universal experience."

These days, with seven albums behind him, Josh still thinks about Dylan's storytelling format while writing his own music. "When I'm working on a song and it gets too complicated and the rhymes are getting forced . . . I think about a song like 'Girl from the North Country' and realize that my relationship with that song has no relationship to how hard it got worked on. I always like the simple songs, but there's so much strangeness that goes into making them simple." I think what Josh finds so inspiring about "Girl from the North Country" is also what makes it so perfect—a complicated emotion simply expressed. Here's how Dylan put it:

Please see if her hair hangs long
If it rolls and flows all down her breast
Please see for me if her hair's hanging long
For that's the way I remember her best.

Josh wrote the following lines about finding love for the first time in a long time:

And any more, it'd stretch the rhyme
So let me leave this where I started, I'm

Just happy for the first time
In a long time

As with Dylan on *Nashville Skyline*, *The Beast in Its Tracks* shows us a happier, more playful Josh Ritter—and a more poignant one as well.

CHRIS THILE

When you see Chris Thile onstage, you see a performer whose mind and body are constantly engaged, always cranked to ten. Whether he's playing with Yo-Yo Ma, Stuart Duncan, and Edgar Meyer, mixing mandolin with cello, violin, and bass; or creating progressive classical and bluegrass with the Punch Brothers; or reuniting with his childhood friends in Nickel Creek, he always pushes himself, his fellow players, and the very boundaries of music.

Even when he was five, there was nothing casual about Chris Thile's relationship to music. "I can remember having this really physical reaction to music that I felt sounded like music . . . I'd already heard. . . . As a little kid, if my parents would put on some-

Chris Thile and the Punch Brothers performing a Tiny Desk Concert on his thirty-fourth birthday, 2015.

thing, and . . . it didn't set itself apart in some way, I would get fairly angry with them and their selection." Chris wanted music to be fresh, to do something it hadn't done before. This idea is at the heart of what he does now to bluegrass with Nickel Creek and to progressive classical with the Punch Brothers (and to other genres in his numerous other musical excursions).

Chris's path to becoming a world-class, groundbreaking mandolin player feels, in many ways, eerily preordained. He was, in part, motivated by his folk-music-loving parents, Scott and Kathy, who would take him to sessions at That Pizza Place in Carlsbad, California, at a young age. One player at those pizza sessions made a lasting impression on him: a guitar and mandolin player named John Moore. Chris describes him as a "super magnetic, charismatic guy." He was tall and funny and a great musician. "I absolutely decided when I was two, [and] I kept telling my parents, 'I want to do that.' . . . The same way that I also wanted to be the quarterback, and . . . the pitcher. I want to be that guy in the center of shit." Chris's dad was a musician and would host jam sessions with his friend Joey Latimer. "I was five, and we went over to Joey Latimer's house for dinner. He and his then wife, Elaine . . . had a little daughter, Erin. . . . Erin and me and my little brother John were all playing, [but] then I saw he had a mandolin just hanging on the wall like a decoration, this old Delta mandolin . . . and I jumped up and down. THAT! I was like, This mandolin is here. Oh my God. . . . He got it down, and I just sat in the middle of the living room just kind of like strumming the thing the rest of the night." Later on, John Moore became Chris's teacher.

I'm at the Newport Folk Festival with Chris Thile. We're sitting in the Nickel Creek tour bus. Sara Watkins is warming up her voice. The group's highly anticipated performance is about one hour away. Nickel Creek—Chris with siblings Sara and Sean Watkins—are on their twenty-fifth-anniversary reunion tour. I haven't mentioned this yet, but Chris is thirty-three. Do the math. Nickel Creek formed when he and Sara were eight; Sean was the elder at twelve. They met through John Moore, while both Chris and Sean were his students. Nickel Creek began at That Pizza Place, eventually moved to bluegrass festivals, and released their first album when Chris and Sara were twelve. Ten years later, they won a Grammy for *This Side*.

Beyond the folk music, there was classical as well. Chris's dad was a piano technician, and his parents would take him to recitals. At the time, he didn't connect to the music at all. In fact, he made fun of it. When he was about seven, "I would do these smart-alecky impersonations of these flourishy arpeggio things, but like nonsense . . . I had closed ears." Chris's ears stayed closed to classical for a long time. His parents also played pop for him, their generation's version, but he was much more interested in American folk tunes and instrumental music, everything from the brilliant banjo player Béla Fleck to astonishing composer and bassist Edgar Meyer. They also showed him The Beatles. "My parents thought it was probably for the best if I heard a Beatles record." Oddly, they didn't own any Beatles records, so they went to the local library and checked out the 1965 album *Rubber Soul*—a great choice, I might add. The album shows the band's more introspective side and marks the beginning of their experimentation with different instrumentation and more complex vocal harmonies. "I listened to *Rubber Soul* and it blew my mind, particularly the harmonies, because for the first time, I was hearing layered vocals. [They] weren't just in three straight parallel [lines], which is what bluegrass is. There's that high lonesome chorus—it's beautiful—but all the parts move the same way. And . . . The Beatles, weirdly, introduced me to counterpoint. [If] you think about a song like—" Chris breaks into a rendition of "You Won't See Me," doing his best impression of both McCartney's lead and the high Lennon/Harrison harmonies. "Like 'When I call you up' and all of a sudden you've got that *whoo, la la la, ooh*. . . . That line right there . . . is so classically Beatles. I think that paved the way for me. I started listening to that."

Chris was around ten years old then, and though he found The Beatles inspiring, he does not identify any of their music as life changing—and he doesn't pick any of the folk he loved, either. The music that had the greatest impact on Chris is the same he closed his ears to as a child—classical, specifically Bach, in a 1955 performance by Canadian pianist Glenn Gould. In some ways his choice seems inevitable. He comes from a family with great passion for the piano. "My grandma Celia, who's my mom's mom, was a piano teacher. Very good pianist. . . . Then my grandpa Bob also taught piano. He taught composition at Illinois and was kind of an avantgarde composer." And like Chris's father, he was a piano technician. "His second wife, so my stepgrandma, Sal, sat me down: 'Have you been listening to Bach?' 'No, I'm not really that—' 'You should listen to Bach.'" For a long time, Chris's issue with classical was that it didn't grab his body. "I think rhythm has always been the way out of myself—rhythm grabs me. You see a room full of people, and if the rhythm is strong, the rhythm is good, people—despite themselves—start moving. It actually takes them out of themselves. Anyway, that never happened to me with classical music."

I often think about the way music relates to the body: the head, the heart, the ass, the feet. While I tend to gravitate toward music of the head and the heart, the songs that have the greatest impact on me connect with the rest as well. Like Chris, I've always considered classical to be of the head and heart. Disco might be an example of music that relates to the bottom half alone. Perhaps Chris puts it best: "I can't fully enjoy a piece of music if it's leaving my mind hanging. If it's only the body, I get bored. If it's only the head, then I'm restless. Then I can't focus. And because the whole world is clamoring after your attention, you need that thing that transports you out. Then you can exist in this never-never land of just listening to this song, and time doesn't even pass."

That day Chris's stepgrandma Sal, Sally Shallenberg, played Gould's famous first recording of Bach's *Goldberg Variations* for him. "And I'm all set to kind of get something that strikes me as being pretty and neat, but not life changing . . . just not my thing. So Gould plays the [aria]; I'm like, This is really nice, and I can actually hear what it is and it's beautiful. But then he kicks into the first variation. And pounds the grooves so hard, and this music that's so beautiful. He pounds the grooves so relentlessly in a folk or rock [way]. I mean he—go and listen to this!"

The *Goldberg Variations* were written by Johann Sebastian Bach and published in 1741. They consist of an aria and thirty variations. Johann Gottlieb Goldberg is believed to be the first person to perform the piece, which was named for him. The works were performed on harpsichord and written to help ease the insomnia of a Count Kaiserling. Glenn Gould recorded two versions of the *Goldberg Variations*; the first, the one Chris's grandma played for him, is from 1955. He made another recording in 1981. "The first recording is amazing and it's a barn burner, he takes it so fast. But his second recording of it, he sits there and it basically just—" Chris sings the first variation to me as recorded in 1981. "You could head-bang to it, it's so incredible." And counterpoint, what first captured Chris when he heard the Beatles harmonize, is essential to these Bach scores. "So all of a sudden with Bach's—the elegance of his contrapuntal thought—his perfection of contrapuntal thought. The searingly alive thinking [was] framed in a physical context by Gould for me. You can present music that holds up to any amount of analysis that also engages and subsequently disarms the body so that you can live inside of this piece of music with your entire being engaged for its duration. And to me, that absolutely changed my life."

Chris's childhood belief that music needed to set itself apart, be unique in some way, feel and express something new, continues to drive him. Bach and Glenn Gould helped him find his way. I've watched his current band the Punch Brothers take rather heady music and flesh it out with foot-stomping rhythms. I've also found myself moving at his concerts to rather quirky melodies with constantly changing structures all held together with a beat—sometimes angular, but one that jells. The two-year-old who wished for something new is now thirty-four years old and making it happen. As Chris says, "To relate to music in a new way, to know that the mind, soul, body, heart can all be fully engaged, that is the ideal."

LEON BRIDGES

"The first time I heard Sam Cooke was in the *Malcolm X* film. I was with my father. And I remember [him] . . . telling me the story of Sam Cooke, and I was actually really intrigued as a kid, but none of that carried over to make me want to write the music that I am writing today."

So what caused Leon Bridges, a twenty-six-year-old black man from Fort Worth, Texas, to channel the spirit of Sam Cooke? I am fascinated by the story he tells, not only by his varied influences but by—given how late his musical career began—how quickly he became amazing. I first meet Leon after inviting him to play a Tiny Desk Concert, and later learn it was one of his life dreams. He per-

Leon Bridges seemingly from a time long ago at WXPN's World Café during Public Radio's NON-COMMvention, 2015.

forms with a strong big band, a hot guitar, snapping rhythms, and a growling sax that perfectly punctuates his sweet, mellifluous voice. It's a voice anyone can love, a universal sound, and by that I mean classic and classy. And he always looks sharp, whether he's busking on the streets of Dallas in a suit and tie or performing onstage in his large-brimmed hat. The clothes may seem a gimmick until you meet him. He's sincere, warm, and a bit shy, and his style reflects his gracious manner.

Many Leon Bridges fans first discovered him in 2014, with his song "Lisa Sawyer." It's a slow story song about his mom and her baptism that is closer in style to doo-wop than standard R&B. "I remember as a kid, my mother and father—they were separated when I was very young—and I lived with my mother, and I would go to my father's on the weekends and in the summer. But my mom, she was a big fan of Donnie McClurkin and Anita Baker, and so I would hear that in the house. And when I was at my father's, he would play Curtis Mayfield, and when we were in the car he would play Stevie Wonder, but none of that really made me want to pursue soul music."

Born in 1989, Leon was a child of the nineties and loved the popular R&B he saw in videos and heard on the radio. "I listened to whatever came on . . . but I loved guys like Ginuwine and Usher, and 112, Dru Hill, Silk. I was like ten years old when I first heard Ginuwine, and I remember being at a friend's house and the music video had [come] on. . . . I was just kind of drawn in from there. . . . Ginuwine . . . started around mid-nineties, and he was almost a pioneer in what he did, because prior to that you had a lot of R&B music, but [he] . . . was very smooth, and just a lot of great melodies and good phrasing. I don't even know how to explain what I was feeling. It was just the way he sang . . . [it] really spoke to me."

For Leon, one of the most striking things about Ginuwine's music was its rhythm. It sparked his love of dance, specifically the hip-hop variety. He shared a room with his brother and they'd often practice routines. Ginuwine's "Tribute to a Woman" was a particular favorite. "We'd just sit out on the porch turning the CD player on and go at it all day." For a long time, dance was his passion. In fact, he didn't pursue singing or music at school, he studied dance, at Tarrant County College in Fort Worth. "The love for dance started at a very young age. You know, seeing guys like Ginuwine and Usher in their music videos . . . I'd watch and try to imitate. . . . When I got to college, I wanted to take it a little further, so I started learning jazz dance and ballet and African and modern."

Leon had begun to find his voice in high school, though it was a slow discovery. "I would sing to the radio and I thought that I couldn't sing, because I didn't know that . . . [a] lot of those songs . . . [weren't] in my range. . . . But in high school—I don't know what made me realize that I could—where I got confidence, but me and my buddies, we would just walk around the hallways and we would sing some Usher songs. And on the way to school, walking to school, we'd sing. . . . I still wasn't all the way confident, but I knew I had a little something."

When he comes to our office, Leon and I spend a lot of time talking about the music he loves. I especially want to see his reaction when I play Cooke's "Bring It on Home to Me." He's sitting across from me in our studio, listening on his headphones, and I can see the distance in his eyes. Remember, he first discovered Cooke's music with his father, who told him that Cooke was his mother's favorite singer, and about the artist's tragic death. Leon tells me he was around fifteen years old and, after that day, used to visit his local Barnes & Noble to listen to Sam Cooke. He still wasn't inspired, though, which is highly surprising if you've heard Leon's music.

For that, we have to fast-forward another four or five years to when he began writing songs, more in a neo-soul vein than an R&B one. One of them was "Lisa Sawyer." As soon as he played it for his friend Brian Winchester, Brian asked him if Cooke was an influence, but at twenty years old, Leon still didn't feel close to Cooke's music. "He asked me [if] I felt bad as a singer and songwriter that I didn't know my roots. . . . So I . . . went on Pandora and YouTube and the first song I heard—the first song I searched—was 'Bring It on Home.' And after listening to Sam Cooke, I was seeing some similarities as far as some of the runs that I was doing." The runs he refers to, those up and down inflections in his melodies, the way he stretches his phrases, and the timeless quality of his sound, are what likely struck his friend that day. It's definitely what moved me and countless others the first time we heard Leon Bridges. He tells me, "I saw how soul music was created by black people. . . . Not to say that we're the only ones entitled to it, but I saw the music, black music of today, and I saw that . . . nobody was really carrying it on. . . . So I felt that as a young black man, I needed to go back to the roots and to where it all started. . . . Not to say I wanted to be the next Sam Cooke or the next anything. . . . It's just a sound that I fell in love with, and wanted to make it for myself."

Once Leon tells me this, I figure, the story ends there. That's the song and the artist that changed his life—except it isn't. *Wanting* to do something and *doing* it require entirely different levels of commitment. When Leon was twenty, he wasn't pursuing music, didn't even own an instrument. Now, at twenty-seven, he's a star. So what happened? It turns out a trip to his local coffee shop pushed him in the right direction. "I remember hanging out at Starbucks, and . . . these older guys . . . would sit around and play Crosby, Stills and Nash songs. And I was just so in love with music, I would go hang out . . . and I tried to, like, sing and harmonize with them. I didn't even know the songs, but . . . they were like, 'Hey, man, you sound good. You should buy a guitar one day.' . . . One of the songs that they would play was 'Just a Song Before I Go' by Crosby, Stills and Nash. I mean, that was like one of the . . . songs that made me go out and buy a guitar."

Of all the music we talk about during our conversation—from

classics like Roy C's "Shotgun Wedding" and Arthur Alexander's "Keep Her Guessing" to Sam Cooke—it turns out that a two-minute soft-rock tune from 1977, penned by Graham Nash, inspired Leon Bridges to buy a guitar and become serious about pursuing his dream. I am stunned. The connection between these two artists isn't obvious. True, Graham Nash's band The Hollies covered Arthur Alexander's "You Better Move On" in the mid-sixties, on their first album, but their version was more inspired by Buddy Holly and the harmonies of The Everly Brothers. I think it was, at least in part, the harmonies that hooked Leon. It was also the time and the place.

We can grow up surrounded by amazing songs, as Leon was, but inspiration often occurs at the moment we're most receptive to change, when we're likely to take action. I believe Leon says it best: "It was special for me because I was very hungry to play and learn and sing. . . . The fact that these guys just kind of opened the door and let me hang out with them . . . It was just great . . . hearing those harmonies. It was kind of a new world for me, because I didn't really know anything about that style of music. It was just cool to sit there and hang out and really enjoy life."

At the time, Leon didn't have the money to simply run out and buy a guitar, but it happened soon enough. After that, he started playing open mics and focused on writing his own music. Then one day, at a bar called the Boiled Owl Tavern in Fort Worth, he met Austin Jenkins, the man who helped define his sound. "I was wearing my high-waist Wrangler denim, and his girlfriend came up to me and was like, 'Hey, you got to meet my boyfriend. He likes to wear Wranglers.' . . . That was the first time we met, and we sat and talked about music. He said he was a musician. I told him I was a musician, but he never said what band he played in. . . . He saw me a week later [when] I was playing solo at this little club called Magnolia Motor Lounge. . . . After I got done playing he came up to me, and he's like, 'Man, we got to record some songs.' . . . After he left, the bartender was like, 'You know that's Austin Jenkins from

White Denim, right?' And I was like, 'Who is White Denim?' And so I went and looked them up on Spotify."

White Denim is a rock band from Austin that first appeared on the scene in 2008. Austin Jenkins turned the somewhat psychedelic rocking trio into a quartet when he joined in 2010. "It's funny, when I first met him, I mean, I wouldn't have guessed that he even played this music. I thought he was, like, a country singer. But there was something about him, like, I knew that when he approached me that it was something special. I knew that he could definitely get on down on some soul music for sure. And so we sat down at his crib, and I just played out all my songs, you know, [on] acoustic guitar, and we recorded it on his little phone. . . . He sent back some GarageBand arrangements, and I . . . was seeing my vision really come to life. . . . When I decided to go down this path, it was just me on guitar, and I'm no guitar player. . . . I didn't really see a future—this is what made me happy, but I didn't see it really going anywhere."

Austin Jenkins and his bandmate Josh Block were setting up a recording studio, where musicians could record live using old gear before a live audience. Their studio is called Niles City Sound, and that's where Leon Bridges recorded his debut, ten tracks in four days. It's a raw, simple sound, similar to the one that defined the greats of soul music—everyone from Sam Cooke and Jackie Wilson to Otis Redding—and has now helped this young artist in the twenty-first century create one of the standout albums of the year.

SHARON VAN ETTEN

I'm in the sanctuary of St. David's Episcopal Church in Austin, during the 2010 South by Southwest (SXSW) music festival. On any other day, I might hear a powerful sermon from that pulpit, but tonight Sharon Van Etten pours her heart out. Hiding her small frame is a large red Gibson hollow-bodied guitar. She's plainly dressed—jeans, striped top, a black sweater—and her voice is heaven. My friend and *All Songs Considered* cohost, Robin Hilton, sits beside me, weeping. Unbeknownst to me, Robin passes a note to fellow work buddy Stephen Thompson. It reads: I CAN'T RECALL HEARING ANY-THING MORE BEAUTIFUL IN ALL MY LIFE.

For me, SXSW is a giant taste test, a musical feast. I search for bands I like, take notes, then move on to the next surprise. For one week in Austin, I see bits and pieces of about one hundred performances. My mission: to discover who I want to spend time with during the upcoming year and who I don't. At this show, I make a note to listen to more Sharon Van Etten and see her again. As any fan of our show knows, we've closely followed Sharon's rise. We've played her music on *All Songs Considered,* invited her to perform a Tiny Desk Concert, and covered each of her four albums, along with many live performances. But SXSW and the show at St. David's was a turning point.

Four years later, this thirty-three-year-old New Jersey girl commands a large stage with her heartfelt tunes. As a songwriter, she's grown immensely, and her arrangements have transformed from stark and guitar based to fully fleshed out, with expanded instrumentation and magnificent harmonies. Her latest songs exude confidence—they're bold yet still intimate, because her honest lyrics remain at their center.

Sharon's love of music and her desire to sing go way back. As a child, around fifth grade, she bought Whitney Houston's "I Wanna Dance with Somebody (Who Loves Me)" on cassette. A few years later, she was listening to Elastica (repeatedly) on her Walkman, a present from Santa. It was the model that flipped automatically between sides of the cassette. She also had a boom box with a microphone, so she could sing along to her favorites. Her tendency toward harmony also dates back to her childhood, spent listening to the oldies station 99.9 FM with her parents Stephen and Janice in New Jersey. Before her sold-out 9:30 Club performance in June of 2014, Sharon tells me that station "was good for sing-along stuff because [they were playing] a lot of doo-wop music at the time, and we liked The Everly Brothers and Lesley Gore and The Mamas and the Papas, and The Four Seasons. I especially liked the male-centric doo-wop. . . . I always sang the harmony because the melodies were either too low or too high for me. . . . My mom's a huge Beatles fan, Stones, and Neil Young, and my dad was a rocker guy, so The Kinks and the Stones, and Jethro Tull . . . and Dylan and all that."

Sharon's first concert was at the Garden State Arts Center in the early nineties—Aimee Mann opened for The Kinks. She recalls liking The Kinks' hits "Lola" and "Apeman," but also remembers Aimee Mann singing "That's Just What You Are" on the TV show *Melrose Place.* "I fell into choir when I was in sixth grade with my older sister, Jess. [It was] called The Mini Singers. . . . Then when we moved from that elementary school to where I ended up going to school, they had [a] more . . . serious choir called The Madrigals." In high school, during the mid- to late nineties, her musical tastes were quite mixed. "Well, PJ Harvey for sure, Liz Phair, Sonic Youth, and Pavement. But I also did musicals and stuff . . . so I was a very confused kid. I had Nine Inch Nails' *Pretty Hate Machine* that my brother gave me. I was in *Camelot* as the background chorus and then in a couple that I . . . wasn't very psyched about, and then I got to do *West Side Story,* which was my favorite. . . . I was Anybody's, the girl that wanted to be part of the gang. And I had, like, the Jersey accent down and everything."

This Jersey girl with a passion for music later moved to Tennessee, where she studied recording at Middle Tennessee State University. She dropped out after a year but found other ways to learn about music. She and her friend Stephanie worked at a coffeehouse called the Red Rose, "and it turned into, like, a venue and record store and screen-printing studio in the years that I worked there. It kept growing as a community. So we had a lot of shows there, and I learned a lot about music through the people that passed through, but for the most part, it was very male dominated." At the time she was in an intense, controlling, abusive relationship. She was learning to play and write music on acoustic guitar, though her boyfriend disapproved of her dream. He didn't think she was good enough to play in public, so she hid her music, sneaking out to play open mics.

One night, in her friend Stephanie's red Volvo, she heard PJ Harvey's *Rid of Me*—and was never the same afterward. "I remember I was late coming home, and I think my boyfriend at the time was probably worried about me, but I didn't care. . . . I just asked [Stephanie] if we could listen to the album again just sitting in the car chain-smoking after we got off work, and I just had never heard anything like that before. . . . [PJ] could sound like so many things, from . . . defiant [and] sad to . . . angry . . . [and] tough, and never did I feel bad for her." The title track was the killer cut for Sharon, with a soft chug to pull you along and the words sucked you in:

Tie yourself to me
No one else
No, you're not rid of me
Hmm, you're not rid of me

Halfway through this four-and-a-half-minute gem, Harvey's guitar erupts and her voice curdles with the lines

Till you say, don't you wish you never never met her?
Don't you, don't you wish you never never met her?

For Sharon, this rocker of a tune was completely unexpected coming from a woman with a guitar. "Yeah, it was just sort of a different side than I had seen, because the other female singers I listen to that I still respect, like Juliana Hatfield or Tori Amos, they're kind of tough, but they're, like, pretty, too. Like, there's a sweetness about them, even though it might be tongue-in-cheek. . . . I just thought PJ was more of a badass, and much more cathartic to sing than a Juliana Hatfield song." After that night, Sharon bought an electric guitar and no longer felt bad about writing music, and soon—in the middle of the night—left her abusive relationship. After spending six years in Tennessee, she moved back to her parents' house, lived in their basement, and focused on writing and recording.

During her time in New Jersey, Sharon saw a lot of shows in

New York City. One night she went to the Bowery Ballroom, on the Lower East Side, to watch Celebration. She didn't know the opening act, Kyp Malone, best known for his work with the New York band TV on the Radio, but recognized him as the brother of a high school friend. She talked to him after the show and gave him one of her homemade CDs. He loved it. This moment was responsible for getting Sharon's career off the ground. He helped her book shows around the city, and when he guest-DJed *All Songs Considered* with Robin Hilton, in November 2009, he chose to play Sharon's song "Tornado." That was the beginning of our love affair with her music. It is also why Robin, Stephen, and I went to see her play in that Austin church at SXSW one year later.

Kyp Malone had known Sharon for about four years then and for a long time witnessed her, as he puts it, "silencing rooms in drunken bars." Sharon's first official album, *Because I Was in Love*, was released in 2009. Its strength lies in its simplicity, harmony, and intimate lyrics. "Tornado" is one of the many songs that confront the abusive relationship she ran from in Tennessee. Sharon is a destructive force in this song, out of control with another man because of her past experience.

I'm a tornado. You are the dust.
You're all around and you're inside.
You are the nature.
I'm the roar that comes from you.

She titled her next record *epic*. The small letter *e* reflects the fact that for her it was an epic change, even though she admits it might not be in the grand scheme of things or in the PJ Harvey sense of the word. Sharon's confidence strengthens with each album. Her convictions are more forceful, as is the sound—and so are her words. This is from a song called "Your Love Is Killing Me," from her 2014 release, *Are We There*:

Break my legs so I won't walk to you.
Cut my tongue so I can't talk to you.
Burn my skin so I can't feel you.
Stab my eyes so I can't see
When our minds become diseased.

While talking about PJ Harvey, Sharon tells me, "I think in general people absorb all of their influences, but as another female, I think that she embraces the tough side of her influences, which not enough women do." Years after fleeing Tennessee, and now thankful for the music those tumultuous years inspired, Sharon is writing with a toughness that I'm sure would make PJ Harvey proud, and she's doing it in her own intimate style. I trust some budding songwriter somewhere is listening to a Sharon Van Etten song on Spotify through a tiny Bluetooth speaker—cranked and distorted—and will one day tell a story about how their bravery came from a Jersey girl with a passionate voice and a guitar, played on repeat.

FANTASTIC NEGRITO

He is a man who beat the odds. Fantastic Negrito rose above the nearly seven thousand submissions to our Tiny Desk Concert contest and won our hearts—but at the time, I knew little about the real odds he'd beaten in his personal life.

In late 2014, I helped concoct a contest, a chance for some great unknown to play at my desk. At this point, over four hundred artists have played behind my desk as part of a series we launched in 2008, Tiny Desk Concerts. The name is a bit of an inside joke that refers to my band from the late seventies. It's an intimate series in which a solo artist or band squeezes behind my working desk at NPR and performs a few songs. The shelves seen in the background of the now relatively well-known series are filled with CDs I need

Fantastic Negrito's Tiny Desk Concert as our contest winner in 2015.

to hear, memorabilia of mine and the other NPR Music staffers, and little trinkets the bands leave behind. It's been a turning point for many baby artists that now have substantial careers: Hozier, Macklemore, Passion Pit, The Civil Wars, Edward Sharpe and the Magnetic Zeros, and The Tallest Man on Earth, to name a few. Because of this and the numerous already famous folk who have graced the office, like Adele, Tom Jones, T-Pain, The Avett Brothers, Yo-Yo Ma, The National, Phoenix, The Decemberists, and Wilco, it's a coveted place to be and a bucket list moment for many artists, especially up-and-coming acts. For our Tiny Desk Contest, we asked folks to film one original song behind a desk of their choosing.

We received entries from all fifty states, filmed at desks everywhere, on mountains, in deep snow, in the ocean, in swimming pools, in warehouses, and, in the case of Fantastic Negrito, in a freight elevator in Oakland. What stood out for me were his spirit, his conviction, and his soul. The song "Lost in a Crowd" was a turning point for Fantastic Negrito, an attempt to move away from obsessively writing about his own life to empathizing with the struggle of others. In this case, he saw a cashier in a grocery store and was struck by the man's face: he looked distraught, tired, and overworked. The singer ran to the parking lot and wrote these words:

Feelings of rage
Broken bones
Lost in a crowd
Now you're on your own
This is your life
Now you're grown
There's no tomorrow
It's here, it's on

When we chose Fantastic Negrito as our contest winner, I did some digging to uncover his story. I was stunned.

Xavier Dphrepaulezz grew up in a family of fourteen siblings in rural Massachusetts. His father was Somalian and loved music, but was also a conservative Muslim. "Yeah, my dad was the one that was always playing music. We had, like, an old Victrola-looking thing. It was an antique. He was big into jazz and Harry Belafonte—and played the Boston Pops and Louis Armstrong. That is a record right there. Louis Armstrong, the 'St. Louis Blues.' There's something about that record; when I heard it as a six-year-old, it just blew my mind. Louis Armstrong was one where I really noticed music. There was something about that riff. I couldn't get it out of my head. It didn't make me wanna be a musician, I just thought it was amazing. That was my favorite song when I was five and six." In 1979, when Xavier was eleven, his family moved to Oakland, and that's when he started getting in trouble. "At twelve, I ran away and I never came back." He lived in foster and group homes, "but I spent probably the first couple years just living in abandoned cars, and I ran with these kids who are still my best friends."

In high school his love of music led to a passion for performance. "We did this talent show, like, dancing to 'When Doves Cry,' and we were doing, like, this whole Prince routine. We loved Prince. I mean he was the hero, and we won the talent show. Yeah, I'm a self-confessed exhibitionist. I need it. Something [about] being up there, and people, they loved me. It's the attention. And I just loved the applause and it felt great; you know, growing up in a big family, you kinda miss the attention. . . . And I thought, Man, I could do this—but I was a terrible singer, I don't know how to do anything. I don't have any talent. And so . . . I looked up, what did Prince do? It's like, wow, he taught himself how to play all these instruments. Well, I'm gonna do that. So then, I remember, I just went out and I snuck into the jazz room at Berkeley High. The teacher of the incredibly talented jazz music program was Mr. Hamilton. I used to stand out in the hall and listen to Joshua Redman and Jubu Smith play, these two amazing players [who] were in the Berkeley High

Jazz Band at the same time. I was terrible, and Mr. Hamilton caught me in the room playing once and let me know how awful I was. So, I'd go up to Cal-Berkeley. I'd kinda sneak in. I'd stand upright and act like I was a student and I'd get into those practice rooms and I'd just keep messing around and I remember the moment I figured out do-re-mi-fa-so-la-ti-do, and I was like, Oh, shit. And I thought I figured it out in every key, da, da, da, da, da, so I'd sit there and I'd do that for hours, man, and it kept me off the street at that time and it was keeping me out of trouble. And it just started making sense. I could put those two together and it was a chord, then, I think, [within] the first six months I'd written a song. I remember the song, it was called 'Have Faith in Time'. "

Xavier's desire for attention manifested in some crazy fashion statements. "This was, like, in 1984, I remember these leopard-skin cowboy boots, man, and I'd wear like these orange corduroys, I remember them, and these captain's jackets, and I'd dye one leg of the pants, like I'd bleach them and I'd have the other one. I was just a sight. People would stop and [be] like, 'Motherfucker, what is wrong with you? You worship the devil?' I remember that. They'd ask me that. 'You worship the devil?' Yeah, so it was fun. So I'd be dressed like that and just walking around. I remember I used to carry a guitar. I couldn't play it, but I just carried it. It was just cool. I loved carrying that guitar, you know?"

It wasn't all posture, though: his songwriting and dedication to learning music led to something remarkable. At age twenty, Xavier moved to Los Angeles. He wanted to be in a band but couldn't find anyone who wanted to play original music. He recorded tapes of his own music for other artists, and was living in a broken-down Datsun, when one of those tapes made it to Joe Ruffalo—Prince's longtime manager. "I went from starting as a teenager to six years later getting a million-dollar record deal. I could just write songs. I'd think of songs all the time. I'm just a song person." It seemed like a dream. He went from living in cars to a contract with Interscope Records, signed by famed producer Jimmy Iovine. Xavier released his debut, *X Factor,* in 1996. One reviewer in *Vibe* magazine called it "a sophisticated mix of poetry and elaborate musical arrangements with an acid-jazz twist," and the headline for a March story by Jon Matsumoto in the *Los Angeles Times* read: NOT BAD FOR A LATE BLOOMER: XAVIER, SOUL–FUNK–RAP ARTIST OF 'THE X FACTOR,' WRITES, SINGS, PLAYS AND PRO-DUCES. The article spoke about Xavier's determination, how he learned to use a studio and play the instruments, and the six months, sometimes fifteen hours a day, he spent writing over forty new songs. It ended with an almost prophetic quote from the artist: "I just take things one day at a time," he said. "I'm just thankful that I have my legs, my arms, my eyes. . . . I don't have any physical problems. I try to be as positive a person as possible. People forget about simple things. If you're fully functional, you can do anything."

As it turned out, the album was a financial flop. Chalk it up to poor marketing, the hit-making machine, the musical tastes of the time, but whatever the reason, Xavier's bright future became a nightmare. He felt he'd lost his identity and that the business tried to make him into something he wasn't.

Then, on Thanksgiving eve, 1999, Xavier's life changed forever. He was not into drugs or alcohol, but he was into picking up strange women for an evening of "fun," as he calls it. And, not wanting to be alone on Thanksgiving, he recalls, "I spotted a tall girl with braids around the intersection of Highland Avenue and Hollywood Boulevard in Los Angeles. If my memory serves me she was nineteen, from Utah and waiting on a bus." He picked her up. "We walked a block to my car, drove down Highland Avenue; all the while I celebrated quietly in my head, my massive overblown ego fed again. She was mine for the evening, we both knew. Then I woke up and three weeks had passed. While we were driving down Highland Avenue a drunk driver ran a stoplight, striking my vehicle, causing the car to fishtail out of control, flip over three lanes of traffic, [and land] upside down, pinning me underneath." The girl survived, though to this day he's never seen or heard from her. After he emerged from his coma, his body was damaged, his hands destroyed. He couldn't play music anymore. The label dropped him. Then he gave up on music.

Xavier's recovery is an astonishing one. His dear friend David Gilbert told me, "After waking from a three-week coma and eventually leaving the hospital, he worked diligently for over a year to get some use of his right arm. The arm had been crushed by the weight of his car when his seat belt failed and he was ejected out of the vehicle, which landed on top of him after the collision. With the help of a customized rehabilitation device that covered his entire forearm, he eventually recovered some use of his right hand that his doctors had originally wanted to amputate. He didn't play music again, not for a long time."

The first time Xavier picked up an instrument was one night when his year-and-a-half-old son couldn't sleep. The only instrument he hadn't sold was a cheap acoustic guitar. He picked it up and played an open G chord for his son, a simple chord requiring only one finger on the thinnest string of the guitar. The expression on his son's face made a huge impression, and afterward he slowly made his way back to music. "Yeah, I had to relearn everything after the accident because, I mean, my hand doesn't work. It's kinda this thing and it doesn't have tendons so I can't do anything, so I had to learn to play the guitar [with], as I call it, 'the famous claw.' I had this thing and it worked for me. Now, on the piano, I can only do a few chords, so I better do them right, and it works. I think it made me better." Fifteen years after his accident, he was now playing on the streets, sometimes five or six hours a day at the BART stations around the Bay Area. "I wanted to play Fantastic Negrito on the street. . . . I think I got pretty good in the last year, to be honest with you. . . . I learned a few chords and I'd write songs on them. You just learn."

His name, Fantastic Negrito, celebrates blackness; it's meant to be playful and international. In December 2014, NPR put out a call to unknown artists for a chance to play a Tiny Desk Concert. Our intent was not only to discover new talent but to form community around an event, for people to get together and be creative with a sense of purpose. I'm sure most people that entered didn't expect to win, but the creative spirit in the nearly seven thousand entries was deeply heartfelt. What struck me about Fantastic Negrito, out of the twenty-three hundred or so videos I watched, was the conviction in the yearning hum of his voice. I believed his song from the very opening. He was quite the sharp sight, in his skinny gray suit, framed in a gray freight elevator, with his talented band all crouched behind a makeshift desk formed from a steel plate laid between two sawhorses. Fantastic Negrito was muscular and commanding, even though something about him was frail. I didn't understand it at the time. I passed his video and many other top choices to our musical judges—Reggie Watts, Valerie June, Thao Nguyen, and John Congleton. They all felt it, too.

His selection of Prince as the artist who changed his life seems undeniable, perfect really, though he didn't pick a particular song. Prince is a self-contained performer, at times playing dozens of instruments on his records, in fact playing all the instruments on "When Doves Cry." Prince is also an exhibitionist, in his own way, and those artistic characteristics became a source of identity for a young Xavier. Prince has gone through many self-imposed rebirths and new identities. Xavier has done the same, only his were not all by choice. In the past, Xavier's high points turned out to be low points (I'm thinking of his record deal), while his low point turned out to be a high point (I'm thinking of the horrible car crash and how it placed him on his current path). Fame in popular music generally happens when you're young. To achieve fame at forty-eight seems impossible—but all of Fantastic Negrito's life seems impossible. He's a man who has beaten the odds too many times to count. I'm betting on him now.

ACKNOWLEDGMENTS

My thanks to: the thirty-five musicians who took the time to tell me their tales of discovery and passion, and to all the music makers who altered the path of up-and-coming players.

Jessica Williams of HarperCollins, who reached out to me and gave me the opportunity to explore authorship and storytelling.

Greg Villepique, whose sharp eye and extraordinary care for detail brought clarity and accuracy to these pages.

Jessica Mowery, for encouraging me to pick up a camera and tell a story with my photographs, and for her continuing inspiration.

Robin Hilton, for friendship and generally putting up with my ways.

Anya Grundmann, for encouraging an attitude of accomplishment, warding off obstacles, and clearing the path.

Daniel Greenberg, for holding my hand through this, my newest medium, and to Jessica Goldstein, for the pathway to his guidance.

Ashley Messenger, Caitlin Sanders, and the rest of the NPR Team, for their thoughts and support.

Thank you also to those tireless people in the music world who promote and encourage the music they love and who helped me corral the artists in this book.

Ashley Larkin, Ron Gaskill, Eric Molk, Nils Bernstein, Melissa Cusick, Ambrosia Healy, Chloe Walsh, Grace Jones, Steve Martin, Krista Williams, Carla Sacks, Lisa Sonkin, Meghan Helsel, Trina Tombrink, Deb Bernardini, Luke Burland, Elizabeth Freund, Jen Appel, Asha Goodman, Hannah Carlen, Jessica Weber, Jim Flammia, Bertis Downs, Peter Miller, Emilee Warner, Jim Walsh, Michael Krumper, Erin Cooney, Joel Amsterdam.

ABOUT THE AUTHOR

Bob Boilen is the creator and host of NPR Music's *All Songs Considered*, and of their *Tiny Desk Concert* series, in which he hosts well-known and emerging artists for intimate performances filmed at his desk. He was the director of NPR's *All Things Considered* from 1989–2007 and chose the music that played between the news stories. As a composer and musician himself, Boilen has always been passionate about music. Prior to joining NPR, he was a longtime record store clerk and performed with his band, Tiny Desk Unit. Constantly on the lookout for new music, Boilen sees more than five hundred live bands each year. He lives in Washington, D.C.